Understanding and Fighting Corruption in Europe

Enrico Carloni • Michela Gnaldi
Editors

Understanding and Fighting Corruption in Europe

From Repression to Prevention

 Springer

Editors
Enrico Carloni
Department of Political Sciences
University of Perugia
Perugia, Italy

Michela Gnaldi
Department of Political Sciences
University of Perugia
Perugia, Italy

ISBN 978-3-030-82494-5   ISBN 978-3-030-82495-2   (eBook)
https://doi.org/10.1007/978-3-030-82495-2

This Springer imprint is published by the registered company Springer Nature Switzerland AG.
The registered company address is: Gewerbestrasse 11, 6330 Cham, Switzerland

Contents

Chapter 1
Preventing Corruption in Europe: An Interdisciplinary Perspective

Enrico Carloni and Michela Gnaldi

Corruption is still rampant in many countries around the globe, from fragile and conflict afflicted countries to middle-income countries and advanced countries. Although there are very large variations in how corruption functions, it exists in every society, in every sector, and at all levels, from local to transnational. Corruption imposes significant costs on governments, citizens, and businesses (Heywood, 2018). The World Economic Forum estimates the cost of corruption to be more than 5 per cent of global GDP. Yet, corruption impacts negatively not only the global economy. It is detrimental to social and political development. It decreases the quality, effectiveness and efficiency of public services (Rose-Ackerman, 1999; Rose & Peiffer, 2015). It damages government legitimacy (Holmberg & Rothstein, 2012) and weakens the social fabric of democratic society (Melgar et al., 2010; Anderson & Tverdova, 2003; Johnston, 2005).

Containing corruption, by preventing fraud, malfeasance and misconduct is crucial for governments who need to allocate resources across competing priorities. Corruption containment seeks to reduce the scope and likelihood of corruption and, as such, has both a repressive and preventive dimension. While repression intervenes after the commitment of a corrupt event to punish it, corruption prevention aims at detecting and removing the opportunities for corruption. Beyond the central core of criminally relevant conducts, therefore, the monitoring of anti-corruption activities is essential with the view to prevent corrupt events, and represents the chief focus of this book.

The preventive perspective has been at the centre of the worldwide debate on corruption for almost two decades (Graycar & Prenzler, 2013; Cerrillo Martinez & Ponce, 2017). The UN Convention of Merida in 2003 invites each country to develop specific corruption prevention policies that favour the participation of

E. Carloni (✉) · M. Gnaldi
Department of Political Science, University of Perugia, Perugia, Italy
e-mail: enrico.carloni@unipg.it; michela.gnaldi@unipg.it

E. Carloni, M. Gnaldi (eds.), *Understanding and Fighting Corruption in Europe*,
https://doi.org/10.1007/978-3-030-82495-2_1

1

society and reflect the principles of rule of law, good management of public affairs and public assets, transparency and responsibility (Rose et al., 2019). In the last twenty years, thanks to the stimulus from the UN Convention and other international and European pressures (Hoxhaj, 2020), we have witnessed the development of numerous and interesting anti-corruption strategies, above all in the prevention of corruption and the containment of corruption risk (Merloni, 2019; Carloni, 2019).

The pillars of these strategies can be found in the Merida Convention and consist in a greater understanding and analysis of the phenomenon, in the organic policies for containment, in the actions of specialized authorities, in the reinforcement of integrity among officials (in particular through code of conduct), in transparency and the participation of society and citizens, in the protection of whistle-blowers, in the definition of specific rules in the area of public procurement.

In the new Millennium, there has been an acceleration in anti-corruption policies, especially in the European reality, which has led to the maturing of experience and development of solutions that now need to be framed in overall terms, in order to give greater definition to the characteristics and fully understand the potential (but also the limits) of the new approach. An approach, distant from the traditional repressive model, but with which it must necessarily be integrated, with the view to containing an extremely dangerous and pernicious pathology for the economy and above all for the fundamental values of our countries and democratic society. An approach that demands a wide perspective of analysis but also diverse tools of interpretation and methodologies of analysis.

The present book, "Understanding and fighting corruption in Europe: from repression to prevention", aims at providing a comparative and comprehensive forum of discussion of the institutional reactions of governments and anti-corruption agencies across Europe towards the current call for corruption prevention, and to host contributions addressing the issue of corruption prevention from a global, systemic, interdisciplinary and level-specific perspective. In so doing, the book is especially concerned with the interweaves between good administration, integrity, ethical behavior and corruption; the role of transparency and digitalization to prevent corruption and ensure rights, efficiency and impartiality in public administration; the measurement of corruption, with specific reference to preventative measures, indicators of administrative anti-corruption efforts, big data and artificial intelligence; public management codes of ethics, performance targets and skills, and their role in tackling and preventing corruption; public procurement, transparency and anti-bribery measures in the European public procurement system.

Specifically, the book is organized in six chapters.

Chapter 2—by Mazzoni, Marchetti and Mincigrucci—deals with corruption, mass media and public opinion. It provides an overview of the concept of corruption, focusing on the conditions that favour and that limit its spread, by paying special attention to the role of public opinion in preventing corruption and the ways corruption is presented to public opinion by the media. The chapter highlights some distortions in the mediated narration of corruption that make the political system resistant to sanction mechanisms and that hinder anti-corruption measures.

Chapter 3—by Carloni and Cantone—is devoted to an analysis, in general terms, of the characteristics and objectives of the new policies of corruption prevention and the overall strategy outlined in the main European experience in response to calls at a supranational level. The chapter identifies the fundamental traits of the new preventive approach, with particular focus on the logic of containing the risk of corruption and therefore on the "pillars" of a prevention strategy. Having examined the central topics, such as the importance of an anti-corruption "strategy" and dedicated authorities, and having analyzed some specific tools, the chapter reflects upon the impact of the new preventive approach on the notion itself of corruption.

Chapter 4—by Gnaldi, Del Sarto, Falcone and Toìa—deals with corruption measurement. It starts with the revision of current measures of corruption and corruption risk, and stresses potentials, limits and degrees of validity of existing measures. It dedicates a section to preventative measures taken by administrations in the fight against corruption, including a case study based on an Italian administrative anti-corruption survey, and devotes a section to a new generation of corruption indicators empowered by data availability and the development of new data analytics technologies. The authors conclude by highlighting future prospects and developments in the field of corruption measurement, which should enhance the general capability to measure corruption, so that bias is minimized and support for policy making is exploited.

Chapter 5—by Pioggia, Pacilli and Mannella—is devoted to good administration, integrity and corruption. The chapter starts with acknowledging the centrality of good administration—and of the right to good administration—as a general guiding principle within the European Union. The authors underline that working towards the development of good and ethical organizations is key not only because processes at macro level change over time, but also because, employees tend to show increased levels of job satisfaction, productivity, efficiency and well-being when organizations cultivate an ethical culture. In this framework, a key role is played by codes of ethics as worthwhile tools to build ethical organizations and prevent corruption. The chapter devotes also a whole section to the issue of preventing corruption among leaders, and to the ways European countries guarantee managers' independence through anti-corruption measures, recruitment, career and performance.

Chapter 6—by Ponti, Agustí Cerrillo-i-Martínez and di Mascio—deals with transparency, digitalization and corruption. The authors discuss the role of administrative transparency in preventing corruption. Purposely, they explore the several opportunities provided by current processes of digitalization involving public administrations in preventing corruption, notably in terms of cognitive capacity empowered by such processes (big data analytics, open data approach, AI, etc.). The chapter also presents a parallel examination of the key factors that influence the effectiveness of specific mechanisms (such as legislative hurdles/ inconsistencies), organizational structures and stakeholders' roles. The chapter concludes with the view that current transparency processes do not appear to be directly and linearly connected with digitalization processes, but rather be the result of coherent policies, attentive to specific contextual dimensions.

Chapter 7—by Enrico Carloni, Paolo Polinori and Daniele David—examines a strategic sector for the proper functioning of administrations, that of public procurement which is highly vulnerable to the risk of corruption. The analysis, conducted from an economic and legal perspective, reflects upon the need for a "good" regulation of the sector, thus framing the responses developed on the European scenario, addressing the disciplines for tendering procedures and contractor awards, and in more complex terms, through a broader "holistic" approach focused on containing the risk of corruption during the phases leading up to and successive to the tenders. The chapter develops an analysis of specific innovative instruments of corruption prevention, evolved with the Italian experience, and analyzes a case study in which the use of the instruments delivered a positive outcome in a highly problamatic context—that of post-earthquake reconstruction in central Italy.

References

Anderson, C. J., & Tverdova, Y. V. (2003). Corruption, political allegiances, and attitudes toward government in contemporary democracies. *American Journal of Political Science, 47*(1), 91–109.

Carloni, E. (Ed.). (2019). *Preventing corruption through administrative measures*. Morlacchi.

Graycar, A., & Prenzler, T. (2013). *Understanding and preventing corruption*. Palgrave Macmillan.

Heywood, P. (2018). Combating corruption in the twenty-first century: New approaches. *Daedalus, 147*(3), 83–97.

Holmberg, C., & Rothstein, B. (2012). *Good government: The relevance of political science*. Edward Elgar Publishing.

Hoxhaj, A. (2020). *The EU anti-corruption report. A reflexive governance approach*. Routledge.

Johnston, M. (2005). *Syndromes of corruption: Wealth, power, and democracy*. Cambridge University Press.

Martinez, C., & Ponce (Eds.). (2017). *Preventing corruption and promoting good government and public integrity*. Bruylant.

Melgar, N., Rossi, M., & Smith, T. W. (2010). The perception of corruption. *International Journal of Public Opinion Research, 22*(1), 120–131.

Merloni, F. (2019). *Corruption and Public administration*. Routledge.

Rose, R., & Peiffer, C. (2015). *Paying bribes for public services: A global guide to grass-roots corruption*. Palgrave Macmillan.

Rose, C., Kubiciel, M., & Landwehr, O. (Eds.). (2019). *The United Nations convention against corruption: A commentary*. Oxford University Press.

Rose-Ackerman, S. (1999). *Corruption and government: Causes, consequences, and reform*. Cambridge University.

Chapter 2
Limits of Corruption Repression and New Prevention Policies

Enrico Carloni and Raffaele Cantone

2.1 Basic Trends and International Influences

The increasingly mature awareness of the risks and dangers arising from the presence of widespread forms of corruption has led, in the European framework, but more generally in the international context, to the development of a structured approach to the phenomenon, alongside the more traditional repressive-criminal response (Klitgaard, 1988; Rose-Ackerman 1999; OECD, 1999; Huther & Shah, 2000; Graycar & Prenzler, 2013; Cerrillo & Ponce, 2017; Cantone & Carloni, 2018; Carloni, 2019).

This need to prevent the occurrence of episodes of corruption, with *ad hoc* solutions that run parallel to the "general preventive" effect of criminal measures (which, while punishing an act that has taken place, at the same time discourage the carrying out of similar offences) ("police patrol" approach: Rose-Ackerman & Søreide, 2001), is a feature of recent developments in institutional systems, not least in the European context (Hough, 2013; Auby et al., 2014; European Commission, 2014; Betancor, 2017; Mungiu-Pippidi, 2015; Hoxhaj, 2020).

In order to define the new approach with reference to anti-corruption strategies, one cannot, however, disregard the examination of important international conventions, which have contributed significantly, at regional-European and global level, not only to the spread of a greater awareness of the issue and to a broadening of the ways of containing the phenomenon, but above all to a standardisation of response

E. Carloni (✉)
Department of Political Science, University of Perugia, Perugia, Italy
e-mail: enrico.carloni@unipg.it

R. Cantone
Ministry of Justice, Prosecutor of Perugia, Perugia, Italy
e-mail: raffaele.cantone@giustizia.it

measures and to the definition of mechanisms for monitoring and stimulating anti-corruption policies in different countries (Cantone, 2020).

The European Union Convention of May 1997 succeeds a slightly earlier Council of the European Union Protocol (27 September 1996): the aim is, however, still limited, namely, to facilitate the criminalisation of acts of corruption committed by EU officials. Nevertheless, the document provides a definition of corruption and recommends Member States to punish the same conduct, even if carried out by officials of individual countries.

The Convention promoted by the OECD (Organisation for Economic Co-operation and Development) followed after and was approved on 17th December in Paris, with the subject matter of corruption in international transactions: this convention, subsequently implemented by 44 countries, contains an interesting analysis, in the preamble, of the effects of corruption, which "represents a major obstacle to sustainable development and the affirmation of democracy". The preamble continues stating that it "undermines good governance and economic development, and distorts international competitive conditions", concluding that "the fight against corruption is a major challenge for global growth". To ensure the effective implementation of the obligations undertaken, the OECD has provided—with a *modus operandi* that we will also find in other international acts—a mechanism to monitor the activities of the signatory States, by way of a special working group: the Working Group on Bribery—WGB.

These first documents are still characterised by a limited subject matter: it is with the two 1999 Conventions of the Council of Europe—the international organisation in charge of promoting cooperation and human rights in Europe, to which 47 countries currently belong—that a broader and more comprehensive strategy to fight the criminal phenomenon of corruption begins to develop. The Criminal Law Convention on Corruption of 27th January, stating that corruption 'threatens the rule of law, democracy and human rights, undermines good governance, fairness and social justice, distorts competition, hinders economic development and endangers the stability of democratic institutions', sets out a number of measures in order to curb it. These include a list of a series of conducts that require repression through the provision of specific offences (so-called 'criminalisation'), not only for corruption in its strict sense, but also for related offences such as money laundering, fraud in company accounts, embezzlement. Also important is the provision for forms of liability of legal persons, as well as the request to Member States to organise specialised structures to fight corruption, reward mechanisms for possible cooperation, measures to facilitate the collection of evidence and the seizure of profits. The Civil Law Convention on Corruption of fourth November has a more limited aim, namely to provide victims of corruption with redress for the damage suffered, while also providing for a form of state liability for corrupt acts committed by its agents. The most important legacy of these two conventions, under article 24 and article 14 respectively, is, however, the establishment of a special body, GRECO (an acronym for Group d'Etats contre la corruption), which is responsible for ensuring that the parties "implement the Convention". GRECO has been very active over the years and its reports have been a formidable stimulus for Member States to implement the necessary reforms.

Despite the above, the most significant document is most certaintly another one, strongly supported by the UN and launched on 31st October 2003 in Merida, Mexico: the United Nation Convention Against Corruption—UNCAC. This Convention stems from a shared concern about "the gravity of the problems posed by corruption" and the "threat it poses to the stability and security of societies, undermining democratic institutions and values, ethical values and justice and compromising sustainable development and the rule of law".

The UN Convention consists of 71 articles and covers a wide range of topics: the offences that must be provided for at state level (with an extensive list including, in addition to corruption, embezzlement, misappropriation, abuse of office, influence peddling and others), measures to fight these offences and foster cooperation between nations, and measures to enable the seizure and recovery of assets.

For the first time in an international act there is a reference not only to repressive measures, but also to 'preventive measures', to which an entire and very intense chapter is devoted (Rose et al. 2019). The latter opens with a provision (Article 5) which, while not explicitly defining what prevention is, clearly suggests what it should consist of (i.e. avoiding or making the occurrence of corruption acts much more difficult). Furthermore, while not indicating a binding model but leaving it up to the individual states, 'in accordance with the fundamental principles of their legal systems', to determine the practical arrangements, it outlines certain aspects of the preventive strategy: in particular, the objectives to be pursued ('rule of law', 'integrity', 'accountability') and certain means to be used (starting with 'transparency' and 'participation of society'). The following articles (from 6 to 14) set out specific actions to be taken, which together form an essential core for corruption prevention policies (and we will discuss these in the following paragraphs). Also here, a monitoring mechanism based on peer review criteria is envisaged, entrusted to the International Working Group (IWG) at the United Nations Office on Drugs and Crime (UNODC). The Convention has been ratified by many nations, 187 as of February 2021 (out of 193 UN members), including all European countries and the European Union itself. In the case of the European Union, the European institutions have operated with a dual understanding of the European Union's role: on one hand, as a direct subscriber and addressee of the Convention; on the other, as a promoter of the implementation of the Convention by its Member States.

2.2   The Traditional Criminal Approach and Its Limits

Corruption has traditionally been dealt and fought with by criminal law means of repression. Corruption is seen by criminal codes and criminal laws first and foremost as a specific offence: its core, consisting of punishing the action of a person who, receiving an unfair advantage, gives a public official an undue benefit for carrying out his functions, is then extended to include further contiguous behaviours (Davigo

& Mannozzi, 2007; Mendelsohn, 2015). The conduct of corruption, in its nature, has been sanctioned since antiquity (Noonan, 1987; Buchan & Hill, 2014): Cicero's denunciation in his oration *'In Verrem'*, against the corruption perpetrated by Gaius Licinius Verres, is famous. Dante Alighieri himself, in the Divine Comedy, refers to *'barettieri'*, as those who use their public offices to enrich themselves, and lays them in boiling tar within the eighth circle of 'Hell' (Cantone & Carloni, 2018).

It would, however, be wrong to think of corruption as a phenomenon that has recurred identically and constantly throughout history with an always equal penal response. Criminal policy to curb corruption, which, as we have seen, finds solid references in international conventions, has developed over time around a series of "knots" that deserve to be briefly mentioned.

1. The definition of "act of corruption", with a tendency to expand the punishable behaviours. Consider the notion of "public official", of "advantage" (which may be any "utility" even if not strictly patrimonial), of the fact that the exchange may involve third persons (recipients, for example, of the "undue advantage" resulting from the action of the public official), of the act carried out by the corrupt official (which may be a condition for the offence, but may, on the contrary, not be seen as necessary). A standard concept of corruption, in the strict sense of 'bribery', can be found in the aforementioned United Nations Convention, which provides (Article 15) for the necessary criminalisation of both the briber and the corrupted in the presence of the following behaviours: "(a) The promise, offering or giving, to a public official, directly or indirectly, of an undue advantage, for the official himself or herself or another person or entity, in order that the official act or refrain from acting in the exercise of his or her official duties; (b) The solicitation or acceptance by a public official, directly or indirectly, of an undue advantage, for the official himself or herself or another person or entity, in order that the official act or refrain from acting in the exercise of his or her official duties.".

2. The identification of 'extenuating' or 'aggravating' circumstances. The latter including especially the case of activities in open contrast with the public interest, the 'active' role of the public official (who solicits or even 'imposes' the 'bribe').

3. The provision for a series of hypotheses in addition to the 'exchange' between the briber and the bribee, aimed at containing behaviour which in any event produces the effect of an undue advantage for private parties to the detriment of the public interest. In this sense, for example, the UNCAC Convention, which identifies a series of offences relevant to the repression of corruption, is again significant: "Embezzlement, misappropriation or other diversion of property by a public official" (art. 17), "Trading in influence" (art. 18), "Abuse of functions" (art. 19). In each national legal system, we can, therefore, find a list of different offences which, taken as a whole, can be included within a criminal, but broad, concept of corruption without being limited to 'bribery'.

4. Criminalisation of "preliminary" or "precursor" offences, namely, the conduct that does not in itself constitute corruption, but lays the groundwork for it: this is the case, for instance, of offences relating to the management of private companies' budgets.

5. The increasing recognition that corruption is not just an individual affair, but a tool used by both legally organised groups and centres (such as associations and political parties, businesses) and illegal ones (such as criminal associations, especially mafia-type), to take over public resources. This requires an approach that considers aspects other than just criminalising the individuals involved in the corrupt exchange: for example, the attention that the UNCAC Convention already pays to the liability of companies involved in acts of corruption.

6. The definition of the typical features of corruption, as a high "dark number" crime in terms of being immediately recognisable only by its perpetrators (who have an interest in keeping the corrupt exchange secret), draws specific attention to the means of investigation and evidence collection (including the possibility of telephone and "environmental" wiretapping, by means of dedicated devices and software, the use of undercover agents and even agents provocateurs), as well as to the mechanisms for "breaking" the silence agreement (with penalty discounts, or even mitigating factors for whistleblowers).

7. Strengthening the criminalisation approach by increasing the penalties for the various offences, as well as by providing for accessory sanctions such as a ban for holding a public office or, for companies and their representatives, on contracting with public authorities.

Even with these changes and progressive adjustments, the criminalisation strategy alone is perceived, with significant evidence over the last two decades, as insufficient to contain corruption.

There are a variety of reasons for this inadequacy.

Firstly, the criminal law instrument is heavy and costly and cannot therefore be used lightly, especially in the case of particularly widespread conducts.

Secondly, 'outed' corruption (by investigations) is only a part, often a very small part, of the corruption episodes that have taken place: the emergence of a corruption episode is the result of the investigative capacity of the structures in charge of repression (judicial authorities, police forces, etc.), of the corresponding inability to conceal the exchange by the corrupted and the corruptor. In practice, corruption is often discovered by chance, by agents investigating other matters. There is, essentially, a part of the 'iceberg' that does not emerge but that is noticeable, also thanks to the use of other detection tools, and requires to be managed and resized with different solutions and tools than those applicable to "emerged" cases.

Last but not least, repression presupposes a fact, an event (of corruption) that has taken place: resulting in its negative effects (as afore-mentioned, undermining trust in democratic institutions, damaging rights, threatening competition, etc.).

The progressive establishment of corruption prevention strategies capable of intervening not so much on the facts of corruption, but on the factors that favour the development of episodes of corruption, is experiencing a formidable acceleration in the comparative scenario, due to the impetus of the Merida Convention.

2.3   The Architecture of Corruption Prevention

It is within this frameowork that the "common core" of a corruption prevention strategy is outlined, stemming precisely from the aforementioned international conventions and in particular from the indications provided by the UNCAC.

Specifically, on the basis of Chap. 2 of the Convention, an essential structure of a preventive approach to corruption can be developed. Taken together, these elements embody the fundamental "building blocks" in the strategy of rebuilding the "ethics infrastructure" (the set of institutions, mechanisms and systems to promote integrity and prevent corruption in public administrations), the importance of which has long been recognised both in the international and comparative scenario.

2.3.1   The National Anti-corruption Strategy (NAS)

The first, central instruction is to develop specific "corruption prevention policies and practices" (Art. 5, UNCAC): in accordance with the principles of its legal system, each State is obliged to develop "effective, coordinated anti-corruption policies that promote the participation of society and reflect the principles of the rule of law, proper management of public affairs and public property, integrity, transparency and accountability". Furthermore, it is the responsibility of States to "establish and promote effective practices aimed at the prevention of corruption" and "to periodically evaluate relevant legal instruments and administrative measures with a view to determining their adequacy to prevent and fight corruption".

The Convention essentially requires that at national level (and at EU level, given the EU's above-mentioned subscription to the Convention) specific policies to prevent and combat corruption are defined, implemented (and monitored by assessing their effectiveness) in an approach aimed at encouraging the involvement of citizens and society as a whole.

The United Nations have drafted a "Practical Guide" for the development and implementation of this provision, by means of a "national anti-corruption strategy" (UNODC, 2015), suggesting that it should be expressed starting with a careful assessment of the context, the detailed analysis, also with special studies, of the specific features of the phenomenon in its country, the comparative observation, the analysis of experiences already in the field with respect to corruption, the collection of available information, the scrutiny of the system's "vulnerability" .

Such an approach must not ignore the "forces" at work, both in terms of actors who might support an anti-corruption policy and in terms of actors (social forces, political actors, economic operators, etc.) who might oppose it.

The "strategy" must therefore be adapted to the context, with the recommendation to "be ambitious but realistic": concrete and specific measures must be identified, the main objectives of each part of the reform must be established, costs and benefits must be identified, and priorities and sequences must be planned.

According to UN operational guidelines, the function of coordinating the anti-corruption strategy should be entrusted "to a single, high-level entity", in strong liaison with the structures responsible for the application, implementation and monitoring of these policies. All actors involved in coordination and implementation should be adequately empowered.

The same UN guidelines suggest that great attention should be paid to the stages of monitoring and evaluating the effectiveness of the policies in place, breaking down the overall reform into successive steps, selecting progress indicators, setting realistic targets for each indicator, and cautiously using internal evaluations by the administrations involved. Monitoring and evaluation must be functional to a progressive improvement: "utilise evaluations to adjust implementation targets and strategy goals". The warning (rather than the indication) that concludes the operational instructions on this point is important: the process requires time and adequate resources ("allocate sufficient time and adequate resources for evaluation").

The United Nations pays great attention to, and therefore attaches great importance to, the overall issue of "measuring" and "evaluating" corruption, but no less to the effectiveness of anti-corruption policies. The issue is in fact very complex and, although it is the object of great scrutiny also by the scientific community, it continues to raise important issues linked to the intrinsic characteristics of the phenomenon of corruption as a "hidden crime" (with a high "dark number"), which is also reflected in the difficulty of assessing the effectiveness of containment actions.

In shorter terms, the United Nations recommends using multiple indicators, triangulations and proxies in any case, also to try to understand the effect of the individual measures and actions put in place by national strategies (NAS), without referring exclusively to perception indicators such as the Corruption Perception index to assess the effectiveness of the strategy as a whole (on these issues, extensively, see Chap. 3).

From this common ground, differentiated solutions are developed, these depend on internal factors, first and foremost of organisational nature (ultimately linked to the characteristics of administrative systems, more or less centralised, and to the form of government) (Hussmann, 2007; Transparency Int., 2013; UNDP, 2014; United Kingdom, 2015).

The comparative experience suggests a variety of national strategies, adopted with strong emphasis and often on the basis of solicitation and support from supranational bodies, as well as being an attempt to respond to a critical situation on the corruption front (especially as 'perceived' by the Transparency International's corruption index).

In the European scenario, the translation of policies to contain and fight corruption into a specific "policy" document is not always immediate, also due to the strong variability of the "corruption problem", as perceived at institutional and public opinion level. Without generalising, it can reasonably be argued that planning for a specific and formalised "national strategy" tends to depend on the centrality of the matter in terms of political issues and the "need" to provide a response (to the public opinion and stakeholders, including international ones) that is recognisable, at least in terms of intentions, in view of the gravity of the phenomenon.

In the framework of EU joining processes, the definition of a specific anti-corruption strategy, linked both to the phase of repression of criminal conduct and to the definition of prevention plans and strategies, is required by the joining protocols.

2.3.2 Anti-corruption Authorities

A specific aspect that strongly characterises (in terms of recognition) anti-corruption policies, is given by the identification, in each legal system, of a public structure entrusted with the mandate of "anti-corruption", meaning (variably) the task of fighting and/or preventing corruption, the latter being the most interesting aspect for the current work. The growing international awareness of this issue, already in the decade before the Merida Convention and then with a clear acceleration after it (De Jaegere, 2012), has led to the diffusion in many countries of "Anti-Corruption Authorities".

The appeal contained in Article 6 of the UNCAC Convention especially, urges to organise anti-corruption structures with preventive functions, on the basis of a provision that complements the one regarding repression contained in Article 36 (which requires the "existence of a body or bodies or persons specialized in combating corruption through law enforcement").

On this basis, three main models of anti-corruption authorities can be distinguished in the comparative scenario: authorities that concentrate both preventive and investigative powers ("multi purpose agencies"), specialised authorities with investigative and repressive powers ("law enforcement agencies") and, finally, authorities in charge of prevention, with a role in knowledge of the phenomenon and in the definition of anti-corruption policies (OECD, 2013). It should be noted, however, that these models are very different from one another, especially with regards to the powers entrusted to the various agencies and, in particular, their independence (in fact, they are often departments and not separate authorities or agencies). In either case, however, the UNCAC Convention does not require a single agency to have overall responsibility for corruption prevention policies (UNODC 2015), and there is no single model in the development of an anti-corruption system, but there seems to be a prevailing trend towards a single anti-corruption authority at central level.

The supranational framework further reinforces this trend with "regional" instruments, which call for the identification of specialised anti-corruption institutions at national level, for example: in Europe, with the Criminal Law Convention against Corruption of the Council of Europe, in America (with the Inter-American Convention against Corruption) and, especially, in Africa (which even more explicitly pays specific attention to providing for and strengthening of, independent anti-corruption

authorities, in the "African Union Convention on Preventing and Combating Corruption"; similarly to the Arab Convention against Corruption).

Having been included in various conventions, the establishment of national anti-
corruption authorities has been called for and promoted by various international
organisations, international financial institutions, donor agencies and
non-governmental organisations (De Sousa, 2009).

However, the changing forms of corruption, in increasingly sophisticated and
complex ways, and the aforementioned perception of the often non-episodic and
'individual' nature of corruption both also justify the identification of organisational
solutions for its control and contrast, that are different from, and add to, the
traditional ones implemented by widespread judicial and police control over the
corruption crime (Recanatini, 2011; Sekkat, 2018). Hence, the evidence of a "pro-
liferation" of ACAs as part of the overall anti-corruption-oriented reform policies
that are spreading throughout the new millennium (UNDP, 2011; AFA, 2020).

In general terms, albeit with varying solutions and powers, ACAs are often
identified as authorities responsible for the development and implementation of
anti-corruption policies at national level, their enforcement, and overall verification
of the compliance of the actions of public institutions with the law. Despite the
expectations attached to the introduction of anti-corruption authorities, criticism is
nevertheless widespread (Schütte, 2017), especially in relation to the perception of
their limited impact (bordering on irrelevance, in the most problematic cases: De
Sousa, 2009).

From the variety of solutions adopted at European level, one cannot fail to notice
the "gap" that runs across Europe longitudinally, following a ridge that divides the
experience of the north-western countries from the south-eastern ones. On one hand,
in the Anglo-Saxon and Scandinavian countries, but also for instance in The
Netherlands and Germany, the fight and prevention continue to be essentially in
the hands of the traditional repressive and administrative organizations (with responsibility for anti-corruption policies in the hands of the competent Ministries, essentially those in charge of the Home Office, Justice and Public Administration, and law
enforcement and repression tasks in the hands of the judicial and police authorities).
On the other hand, the particularly extensive spread of 'dedicated' anti-corruption
authorities in southern and eastern European countries is clearly noticeable, with
'specialised' solutions tending to focus, with significant exceptions, on prevention.

This is the case in Portugal, with the Council for the Prevention of Corruption; in
Spain, with the Office for Conflicts of Interest and the Council of Transparency and
Good Governance, flanked by regional anti-corruption authorities in Catalonia, the
Balearic Islands and the Valencian Community; in France, with the *Agence
française anti-corruption*, flanked by the *Haute Autorité pour la transparence de
la vie publique*; in Italy, with the National Anti-Corruption Authority (ANAC),
which has prevention roles and a specific competence in public contracts. In Greece,
the General Secretariat against Corruption has been active since 2015, and reinforced
in 2017 as part of a specific OECD initiative.

In many countries of the Balkan region and in particular in the former Yugoslavia
(Bosnia Herzegovina, Serbia, Montenegro, Kosovo, Slovenia, North Macedonia),

the establishment of anti-corruption authorities is not only frequent, but also a well-known practice, since it is often the result of reforms stemming from the beginning of the millennium. We can find the significant cases of, for instance, the Anti-Corruption Agency (ACA) in Serbia, the State Commission for Prevention of Corruption in North Macedonia, the Agency for Prevention of Corruption (ACP) in Montenegro, the Commission for the Prevention of Corruption in Slovenia, the Agency for the Prevention of Corruption and Coordination of the Fight against Corruption in Bosnia Herzegovina; in Kossovo, the Anti-corruption Agency (ACA).

Bulgaria has the Commission for Anti-Corruption and Illegal Assets Forfeiture of the Republic of Bulgaria, which was established in 2018.

The presence of specialised institutions is also particularly widespread in Eastern Europe and Central Europe. The Republic of Moldova has the National Anticorruption Centre. In Ukraine, there is the National Agency on Corruption Prevention and also a specialised enforcement body (the National Anti-Corruption Bureau); in Latvia, the work of the Corruption Prevention and Combating Bureau (KNAB) ranges from prevention to investigation.

Organizations are also set up as specialized branches of ministries: as in Austria, with the Federal Bureau of Anti-Corruption, part of the Home Office; in the Czech Republic, with the Anti-Corruption Unit, Conflict of Interests and Anti-Corruption Department, at the Ministry of Justice; in Poland, with the Central Anti-Corruption Bureau (though it has characteristics similar to an intelligence body). In Romania, the Anti-corruption General Directorate operates within the Ministry of Interior, the National Anti-corruption Directorate, with mainly investigative functions, but also supported by the National Integrity Agency (ANI). The latter agency is responsible especially for the control of assets acquired during the exercise of mandates or performance of public dignities positions, and verification of conflicts of interest and incompatibilities.

In broad terms, the diffusion of the phenomenon in neighouring geographical areas appears evident, with imitation and circulation of model-types (favoured, in some contexts, by specialised umbrella organisations, as in the case of the Regional Anticorruption Initiative—RAI which operates in the Balkan area). In this context, the European influence (primarily that of the Commission, especially through the definition of the conditions of entry in the Union for the countries that joined most recently or those that have applied to join) and that of supranational organisations, both within the framework of the aforementioned international conventions and within the framework of specific intervention projects (in particular, but not only, of the OECD and the World Bank), appears clearly relevant.

2.4   Administrative Corruption Prevention Measures

Following with the guidelines of the UN Convention, and often prompted by GRECO reports as well as supranational *stimuli*, there is a strengthening of a number of mechanisms that constitute 'pillars' of a corruption prevention system.

These pillars may be summarised as follows:

(a) measures to strengthen the integrity of public officials (both bureaucratic and political), in an approach that focuses in particular on the regulation of codes of conduct and the prevention of conflicts of interest. If integrity is posited "at the opposite of corruption" (Heywood, 2018), then the perspective is clear. In operational terms, this matter is linked in more general terms to issues such as staff recruitment, the training of civil servants, the definition of clear rules on incompatibility with the pursuit of other activities, the possibility of switching between public and private positions (issues that call into question limitations on the so-called 'revolving doors' and 'pantouflage'), and the duties of declaration and abstention aimed at avoiding situations of conflict of interest. Nevertheless, it is worth also recalling how the Mérida Convention already contains a number of aspects relating to the challenge to integrity: both when it provides for "adequate procedures for the selection and training of individuals for public positions considered especially vulnerable" (Art. 7(1)(b)), and when (Art. 8) it calls for the adoption of "codes or standards of conduct for the correct, honourable and proper performance of public functions" and the introduction of "systems requiring public officials to make declarations to appropriate authorities regarding, inter alia, their outside activities, employment, investments, assets and substantial gifts or benefits from which a conflict of interest may result". These cases are dealt with in Chap. 4: in this field the action of the OECD was very important, which paid great attention to the issue of the integrity of public officials (OECD, 2011; OECD, 2020).

(b) measures aimed at regulating transparency and the right to knowledge, as a condition of citizens' control over the work of public authorities and therefore, at the same time, an instrument of accountability and responsibility, according to the maxim that "sunlight is the best disinfectant"; among the instruments capable of ensuring transparency, the importance of "freedom of information" legislation is evident, but so is the growing relevance of proactive transparency mechanisms (especially by making information available through public portals or open data solutions). It is worth recalling that the UN Convention provides, in this respect, for the adoption of "the measures necessary to increase the transparency of its public administration, including, where appropriate, its organisation, functioning and decision-making processes" (Article 10, which refers foremost to making information open to the public). However, it is also (as stated in Article 13) a matter of "increasing the transparency of decision-making processes", "ensuring effective public access to information", and "respecting, promoting and protecting the freedom to seek, receive, publish and disseminate information concerning corruption". These issues are dealt with in Chap. 5.

(c) As a corollary of the 'transparency pillar', an important institution such as the protection of whistleblowers can also be considered (whistleblowing creates a mechanism for 'internal' transparency) by offering guarantees and protection to whistleblowers who report wrongdoings discovered during their work. Article 13 of the UNCAC Convention itself, which does not expressly regulate the figure of the "whistleblower", provides that "facts liable to be considered as constituting an offence established in accordance with this Convention may be reported to them, even anonymously". However, it is primarily Article 33, in the part relating to the "suppression of corruption", which claims for "appropriate measures to provide protection against any unjustified treatment for any person who reports in good faith and on reasonable grounds to the competent authorities any facts concerning offences established in accordance with this Convention". The growth of adequate whistleblower protection legislation was most recently brought about by European Directive No. 1937 of 2019, which provided for the introduction by all EU Member States of "common minimum standards providing for a high level of protection of persons reporting breaches of Union law" (Article 1).

In addition to these main areas of action of preventive measures, there are other more specific ones, whose presence in the various legal systems is less recurrent and whose discipline cannot be traced directly to the aforementioned international conventions.

2.5   Regulation of Lobbies and Prevention of Corruption

A specific issue, which recurs in national prevention policies, but whose presence is less constant, can be identified, within the macro-theme of transparency of decision-making processes, in the definition of measures aimed at favouring the participation of stakeholders. The question of regulating the relationship between public decision-makers and lobbyists is closely intertwined with the issues of transparency and conflicts of interest, and it also concerns the issue of the integrity of public officials.

The link between overall anti-corruption reform policies and the increasing focus on lobby regulation is therefore evident (Transparency International, 2015; Carloni, 2017).

This is due both to the introduction of a regulation for public officials' conduct which intersects with the lobbying phenomenon (think of the duties of declaration, the rules of post-employment and revolving doors), and to the growing attention to the transparency of the decision-making processes (which allows the contribution of the bearers of particular interests to be better highlighted), and, finally, due to specific disciplines of direct regulation of the lobbying activity and the lobbying profession.

The call for a regulation of lobbies is the result of different approaches, which are not limited to the need to fight and curb corruption: suffice it to think of the attention to the phenomenon that derives from the need to maintain, first and foremost for participatory purposes and democratic legitimacy, "an open, transparent and regular dialogue with representative associations and civil society" (as required by Article 11.2 of the TFEU for the functioning of the European Union).

This is the context in which some European countries have felt the need to regulate lobbying in the overall frame of reference of anti-corruption reforms which have characterised different realities throughout the new millennium (Laboutková et al., 2020).

Moreover, in this context, the regulatory model developed some time ago, and later adjusted, by the United States (and then Canada) constitutes an obligatory reference. For example, Slovenia, Austria and Ireland, within their framework of a comprehensive anti-corruption regulation, have adopted a regulation of lobbies which, with respect to specific characteristics relating to the regulation of the phenomenon, can be placed in the wake of the North American experience (Ponce, 2015; Carloni & Mazzoni, 2020).

The Slovenian law of 2011 (which also establishes the Special Commission for the Prevention of Corruption) aims to "strengthen integrity and transparency as well as prevention of corruption and avoid and combat conflicts of interest". Lobbyist registration is mandatory for all individuals working to influence legislation in their private capacity, by publishing of a set of data (on lobbyists, lobbying contacts and interests represented) on a Register that is made public on the Commission's website. In the Slovenian experience, specific emphasis is placed on the need for officials to declare their contacts with interest representatives (Transparency int., 2015).

This model has also been followed by Austria, with the Transparency of Lobbying and Advocacy Activities Act, approved in 2012. According to this law, lobbyists who receive remuneration for influencing public policy, as well as interest groups that employ lobbyists, are required to register in the Register for Interest Representatives, again with a set of mandatory data (most of it made public). Registration also entails the obligation to comply with a code of conduct, the rules of which are protected by sanctions (Petrillo, 2019).

The Irish norm is even more recent, introduced in March 2015 with the Regulation of Lobbying Act, aiming to inform the public about who lobbyists are, how they relate to public decision-makers and expected goals, who, among the decision-makers, does the lobbying contact develop with. The law, therefore, regulates a special register, the obligations to register and update information on lobbying activities, a code of conduct for lobbyists, and defines the tasks of the authority responsible for regulating it, the Standards in Public Office Commission (Carloni & Mazzoni, 2020).

In the public debate, not least in relation to the scandals that emerged during the management of the Covid-19 emergency, the need for a more careful regulation of the relationship between decision makers and bearers of interests is felt. Recently, Germany's choice to adopt a more robust regulation of lobbying (2021) is a sign of this.

2.6 Plans and Procedures for the Management of "Corruption Risk"

Among the most modern and interesting approaches that characterise some of the leading experiences in administrative corruption prevention is the development of plans and procedures for corruption risk management in public administrations.

This approach, tailored to individual organisations, is to be distinguished from the aforementioned "strategies" (which reflect an overall view of the phenomenon and also define the reforms to be introduced to prevent and fight corruption in the various States), although in some experiences the boundary is not so clear-cut. One such example is Italy, which is also the most interesting model-type in the European scenario in terms of risk management plans in the public sector, where the 'national anti-corruption plan' (PNA) is a general guideline for individual administrations to draw up their own risk management plan (three-year corruption prevention plan). This document, adopted by the National Anti-Corruption Authority, in the absence of a strategy defined at government level, ends up being regarded as the general tool for defining corruption prevention policy. However, it is an act of guidance that lacks the overall vision of a national strategy and, above all, it cannot outline systemic reforms, but only direct individual administrations to draft their own risk management plans.

This viewpoint is rooted in the corruption risk management measures developed within the framework of ISO standardisation rules, and in particular ISO 370001. From this "risk" approach and related standards, an anti-corruption path can be inferred, that develops within organisations: this is done by analysing activities and functions, identifying the corruption risks affecting them, determining the tolerable risk level (taking into account the probability of the corruption event and/or its impact), comparing the tolerable corruption threshold with the existing one, deciding on "risk mitigation" where necessary, and selecting the most suitable measures in the light of a "cost-benefit" assessment.

It is on the basis of the application of ISO modelling that the Australian example has developed (and in particular the one expressed by the federal anti-corruption authority of New South Wales, the ICAC), which has established itself as the best practice with respect to the application in the public sector of organisational risk management principles with regards to anti-corruption. ICAC, in particular, has developed guidelines for the adoption of a corruption prevention plan, rich in methodological indications. Specifically, some keypoints can be highlighted: administrations must develop and disseminate a comprehensive and integrated policy on corruption prevention; responsibilities for the adoption and implementation of the measures contained in the corruption prevention plan must be clearly defined; all functions and activities should be analysed, by assessing the level of risk in each area; on this basis, administrations should develop integrated corruption prevention strategies, defining a clear timetable for their development. Moreover, it is the responsibility of the administrations to develop awareness-raising actions addressed to citizens (on values, strategies, ways to report offences) and to involve and train staff (to disseminate the culture of integrity and prevention of corruption); an effective system of internal reporting (whistleblowing) and management of complaints (also with the involvement of the Anti-Corruption Authority and the judicial authority) and incentives to report must be developed.

It is mainly thanks to the OECD that this approach model has been promoted in the context of public institutions (OECD, 2009, 2010). In the 2009 document aimed at strengthening the integrity of public systems, a "risk analysis process" is advocated, which "consists in identifying the processes (e.g. procurement, personnel management, controls, etc.) and the subjects (persons with roles of responsibility in the aforementioned processes or in the decision-making process in general) most exposed to integrity violations" and also in "identifying the critical points in terms of vulnerability of the organisation (e.g. selection of the award method or identification of variants to the contract)". From this perspective, "risk analysis is the foundation for identifying measures within the organisation to increase resilience to such vulnerabilities" (OECD, 2009, 31).

GRECO itself, in its "lessons learned from the three evaluation rounds" (2000–2010), highlighted that "the first requirement for adequate corruption prevention action is the implementation of an objective risk analysis and assessment"; this statement is first and foremost aimed at the overall anti-corruption strategy, which must be supported by adequate knowledge of the elusive phenomenon, but it also ties in well with the action to be taken within the various administrations (GRECO, 2012).

The Italian case is an interesting and original reference in the European scenario, since it is the context in which the risk-based approach has been most developed. In the Italian system, each public administration (both national and territorial entities, even private entities controlled by public administrations) is required to adopt a corruption prevention plan every three years, drawn up on the basis of the indications provided by the National Anti-Corruption Authority with its National Anti-Corruption Plan (Cantone & Carloni, 2018; Merloni, 2019). The ANAC document is an act of guidance, containing instructions on the methodologies of risk analysis and management, on general measures (which all public administrations are required to adopt, adapting them to their context), on specific problems and responses that characterise different types of administrations (thus, for example, specific indications have been formulated for administrations operating in the health sector, for universities, for small municipalities, for tax agencies, etc.). It is up to each administration, with its own prevention plan, to make ANAC guidelines binding, by adopting specific measures tailored to the characteristics of the organisation, its overall risk (defined through an analysis of the external and internal context), and the specific risk of each operation or procedure (Cantone & Carloni, 2017).

This adaptation operation, which is central to the success of the intervention, is entrusted to a central figure in the design of the Italian anti-corruption strategy as outlined by the Anti-corruption Law (Law 190 of 2012), the so-called "head of corruption prevention". The latter is a senior official, who must be entrusted with an appropriate and adequate office, with whom the "political" and bureaucratic top management of the administration collaborate, and who is called upon to prepare and then supervise the corruption prevention plan. It is his or her specific responsibility to take the necessary measures to avoid the occurrence of episodes of corruption (in the criminal meaning of the term: bribery and other related offences), upon the occurrence of which he or she must in any case be able to prove the adequacy of the measures and/or the unforeseeability of the event (under penalty of disciplinary sanctions and liability for the consequences, to which an ancillary part of remuneration is added) (Cantone, 2020).

2.7   The Concept of Corruption in Light of Prevention Policies

The development of comprehensive corruption prevention strategies affects the very notion of corruption, redefining the scope of relevant activities and conduct.

There is a recurring idea that the new draft also outlines a notion of administrative corruption, which is broader than the "criminal" one and can basically be traced back to maladministration.

The idea of maladministration finds an indirect basis in documents of both the World Bank (where corruption is understood as "the use of public office for private gain" (World Bank, 1997) and the OECD (OECD, 2013), as well as the European Commission (European Commission, 2014) in which the need to adopt measures aimed at curbing unlawful conduct linked to an abuse of public functions for the benefit of private interests is, in fact, emphasised, regardless of whether such conduct is considered a criminal offence.

Thus, for example, in the documents accompanying the development of the new system of prevention of corruption in Italy, it is argued that it is possible to speak of corruption in the face of "relevant situations broader than criminal offences", which include "not only the entire range of offences against the public administration", but also situations in which "regardless of the criminal relevance, a malfunctioning of the administration due to the use of the functions assigned for private purposes becomes evident".

On closer inspection, however, it seems more appropriate to ackowledge that through the prevention system, a new notion of corruption is not introduced at all, since it remains a concept whose meaning is firmly anchored to the criminal law definition of exchange of acts and/or function with a utility, but the approach is modified, because the field of intervention is broadened, having previously been limited to sanctioning specific individual conduct, it now addresses preliminary questions, organizational aspects, regulation and proceduralisation of specific activities, and so on.

This "broadening" is therefore merely the result of the different logic of prevention compared to repression: a change of perspective whereby situations become relevant where the risk is merely potential, when a conflict of interests has not yet materialised, but it is necessary to activate measures to "distance" the risk, with choices that sometimes completely disregard individual conduct.

The new system, precisely because it is concerned with prevention and not with sanctions, aims to intervene on what 'may happen' and does not look (only) at what has happened, it addresses the organisation and not only the action: the focus shifts from the pathology of the offence to the presence of a risk and the contrast strategy addresses conflicts of interest, to be avoided, known, controlled and made transparent (Cantone & Carloni, 2017).

Consequently, the scope of anti-corruption measures is very wide, which does not (any longer) correspond to the confines of the phenomenon of corruption in the above-mentioned criminal definition of the term.

However, it can be argued that there is only "one" concept of bribery, the criminal one (with the *caveat*, however, that here, too, reference must be made to a plurality of offences in addition to bribery only, and thus the more precise term is perhaps that of "corruptive acts").

This line of interpretation is consistent with the evolution of comparative experiences of prevention, and, above all, with the same indications that can be derived from the UNCAC Convention, where, although in the absence of an explicit definition, it is clear that the preventive measures are aimed at avoiding the occurrence of episodes of corruption which are otherwise pursued, according to the indications of Chap. 3, by "incrimination, detection and repression".

References

AFA – Anti-Corruption Agency. (2020). Global mapping of anti-corruption authorities. *Analysis Report*. Paris: AFA.

Auby, J. B., Breen, S., & Perroud, T. (Eds.). (2014). *Corruption and conflict of interests: A comparative law approach*. Edward Elgar.

Betancor, A. (Ed.). (2017). *Corrupcion, corrosion del estado de derecho*. Thomson Reuters.

Buchan, B., & Hill, L. (2014). *An intellectual history of political corruption*. Palgrave Macmillan.

Cantone, R. (2020). *Il sistema della prevenzione della corruzione*. Giappichelli.

Cantone, R., & Carloni, E. (2017). La prevenzione della corruzione e la sua autorità. *Diritto pubblico, 3*, 903–944.

Cantone R., & Carloni E. (2018). *Corruzione e anticorruzione*. Dieci lezioni. Milano, Feltrinelli.

Carloni, E. (2017). Lobby regulation to prevent corruption. In M. A. Cerrillo & J. Ponce (Eds.), *Preventing corruption and promoting good government and public integrity*. Bruxelles.

Carloni, E., & Mazzoni, M. (2020). Il cantiere delle lobby. *Processi decisionali, consenso, regole*. Roma: Carocci.

Carloni, E. (Ed.). (2019). *Preventing corruption through administrative measures*. Morlacchi.

Cerrillo, M. A., & Ponce, J. (Eds.). (2017). *Preventing corruption and promoting good government and public integrity*. Bruylant.

Davigo, P., & Mannozzi, G. (2007). *La corruzione in Italia. Percezione sociale e controllo penale*. Laterza.

De Jaegere, S. (2012). Principles for anti-corruption agencies: A game changer. *Journal for Public Policy, 1*(1), 79–120.

De Sousa, L. (2009). *Anti-corruption agencies: Between empowerment and irrelevance*. EUI Working Papers, RSCAS.

European Commission. (2014). *Report from the Commission to the Council and the European Parliament: EU anti-corruption report*, document COM(2014)38. Bruxelles: European Commission.

Graycar, A., & Prenzler, T. (2013). *Understanding and preventing corruption*. Palgrave Macmillan.

GRECO. (2012). *Lessons learnt from the three Evaluation Rounds (2000–2010)*. Thematic articles. : Council of Europe.

Heywood, P. (2018). Combating corruption in the twenty-first century: New approaches. *Daedalus, 147*(3), 83–97.

Hough, D. (2013). *Corruption, anti-corruption and governance*. Palgrave Macmillan.

Hoxhaj, A. (2020). *The EU anti-corruption report. A reflexive governance approach*. Routledge.

Hussmann, K. (Ed.). (2007). *Anti-corruption policy making in practice: What can be learned for implementing article 5 of UNCAC? Report of Six Country Case Studies*. U4 Anti-Corruption Resource Centre.

Huther J., & Shah A. (2000). Anti-corruption policies and programs: A framework for evaluation. *Policy Research Working Paper*; No. 2501. Washington, DC: World Bank.

Klitgaard, R. E. (1988). *Controlling corruption*. University Of California Press.

Laboutková, S., Šimral, V., & Vymětal, P. (2020). *Transparent Lobbying and Democracy*. Palgrave Macmillan.

Mendelsohn, M. F. (Ed.). (2015). *The anti-bribery and anti-corruption review*. Law Business Research Ltd..

Merloni, F. (2019). *Corruption and Public administration*. Routledge.

Mungiu-Pippidi, A. (2015). *The quest for good governance: How societies develop control of corruption*. Cambridge University Press.

Noonan, J. T., Jr. (1987). *Bribes: The intellectual history of a moral idea*. University of California Press.

OECD. (1999). *Public sector corruption: An international survey of prevention measures*. OECD Publishing.

OECD. (2009). *Toward a sound integrity framework: Instruments, processes, structures and conditions for implementation*. OECD.

OECD. (2010). *Risk and Regulatory Policy*. OECD Publishing.

OECD. (2011). *Asset declarations for public officials: A tool to prevent corruption*. OECD Publishing.

OECD. (2013). *Specialised anti-corruption institutions: Review of models*. OECD Publishing.

OECD. (2020). *Public integrity handbook*. OECD Publishing.

Petrillo, P. L. (2019). *Teorie e tecniche del lobbying*. Il Mulino.

Ponce, J. (2015). *Negociacion de normas y lobbies*. Thomspn Reurers Aranzadi.

Recanatini, F. (2011). Anti-corruption authorities: An effective tool to curb corruption? In S. Rose-Ackerman & T. Søreide (Eds.), *The international handbook on the economics of corruption*.

Rose, C., Kubiciel, M., & Landwehr, O. (Eds.). (2019). *The United Nations convention against corruption: A commentary*. Oxford University Press.

Rose-Ackerman, S. (1999). *Corruption and government: Causes, consequences, and reforms*. Cambridge University Press.

Rose-Ackerman, S., & Søreide, T. (Eds.). (2001). *The international handbook on the economics of corruption*. Edward Elgar Publishing.

Schütte, S. A. (2017). *Bespoke monitoring and evaluation of anti-corruption agencies*. U4 Anti-Corruption Resource Centre.

Sekkat, K. (2018). *Is corruption curable?* Palgrave Macmillan.

Transparency International. (2013). *Examples of national anti-corruption strategies*. Transparency International.

Transparency international. (2015). *Lobbying in Europe: Hiding influence, privileged access*. Transparency International.

UNDP. (2011). *Practioner's guide to capacity assessment of anti-corruption agencies*. UNDP.

UNDP – United Nations Development Programme. (2014). *Anti-corruption strategies: Understanding what works, what doesn't and why? Lessons learned from the Asia-Pacific region*. UNDP.

United Kingdom – Department for International Development. (2015). Why corruption matters: Understanding causes, effects and how to address them. In *Evidence Paper on Corruption*. Department for International Development.

UNODC. (2015). *The global programme against corruption: UN AntiCorruption Toolkit*. United Nations Office on Drugs and Crime.

UNODC. (2015). *National anti-corruption strategies: A practical guide for development and implementation*. United Nations.

World Bank. (1997). *World Development Report 1997*. World Bank.

Chapter 3
Corruption, Mass Media and Public Opinion

Marco Mazzoni, Rita Marchetti, and Roberto Mincigrucci

3.1 Introduction

Corruption is one of the most serious challenges facing contemporary democracies. It is a problem that affects various aspects of democratic life, from the economy to the rule of law, from the stability of institutions to the observance of human rights (van Schoor, 2017). A wide-ranging and multi-disciplinary literature has associated the issue with that of economic development (Mauro, 1995; Shleifer & Vishny, 1993) or greater income inequality (Gupta et al., 2002). Another much-treated argument is that of the consequences of corruption on the political system. It is quite clear that corruption destabilizes the democratic rules by favoring some groups over others, thereby generating mistrust between citizens and their political leaders. Corruption also exacerbates social inequality which in turn reduces people's social trust (Rothstein & Uslaner, 2005). In addition, corruption lowers trust not only in the government and public administration but also in parliament and political parties in general (Kostadinova, 2012). Corruption also depresses electoral turnout, because high levels of perceived corruption lead to more negative evaluations of political authorities and the political system in general (Fieschi & Heywood, 2004).

For these reasons, the phenomenon has attracted the interest of the academia: indeed, we have found numerous efforts in the literature to establish an unequivocal definition of the phenomenon (Mungiu-Pippidi & Heywood, 2020; Rothstein & Varraich, 2014), to establish its diffusion (Heywood, 2015; Charron, 2016) and its impact on the economies of various countries (Treisman, 2000; Mauro, 2002). In recent years, efforts to study possible remedies to the phenomenon have also increased, with the theme of anti-corruption becoming strategic, especially for legal and socio-political studies. However, several limitations to this approach

M. Mazzoni (✉) · R. Marchetti · R. Mincigrucci
Department of Political Science, University of Perugia, Perugia, Italy
e-mail: marco.mazzoni@unipg.it; rita.marchetti@unipg.it; roberto.mincigrucci@unipg.it

© The Author(s), under exclusive license to Springer Nature Switzerland AG 2021   25
E. Carloni, M. Gnaldi (eds.), *Understanding and Fighting Corruption in Europe*,
https://doi.org/10.1007/978-3-030-82495-2_3

have emerged. Policy analysts and scholars have often privileged the analysis of anti-corruption strategies evaluating the "cure"—i.e. the expected change in the incentive structures that agents face—rather than the adaptive response of the "patient", either at individual or organizational level. The standard approach to anticorruption studies has mainly been looking at external remedies (i.e. anticorruption reforms) and spill-overs (such as mechanisms of electoral punishment), not at internal governance mechanisms of corruption, nor at the organizational failure or adaptive change of political actors (della Porta & Vannucci, 2012). Political systems have shown to be remarkably resilient against anticorruption reforms, while the collapse of political corruption networks is more often due to or facilitated by endogenous pressures rather than the result of exogenous shocks (della Porta & Vannucci, 1999).

In this chapter, we will provide an overview of the concept of corruption, focusing not so much on legislative efforts to fight it but on the "environment" that favors or limits its spread. Indeed, as we will try to highlight here, anti-corruption policies can only be effective if they find a fertile ground capable of receiving and implementing them. Our chapter will largely turn around the concept of public opinion, in particular on the role it plays in relation to corruption, because has been generally demonstrated that an aware and receptive public opinion is the best tool to "fertilize" the ground to grow civic sense and respect for rules.

As we will see, public opinion plays a decisive role in determining the phenomenon, both because, through perception indices, it offers useful indicators to establish its diffusion, but also because through a constant redefinition of moral codes, it is possible to define what is fair and what is wrong for a given social context (Ettema & Glasser, 1998). In order to be receptive to corruption, public opinion needs a valuable ally, namely the media system. We have had an excellent opportunity to assess the mass media role to hinder corruption thanks to our involvement to "Anticorruption Policies Revisited. Global Trends and European Responses to the Challenge of Corruption", a large-scale research project funded by the European Commission's Seventh Framework Programme.[1] The starting point is that the media play a fundamental role in determining a climate of observance of social rules that may be more effective than a written law: in contemporary societies, the media are considered socialisation agencies. They are the main tools through which most people get information about corruption, what it is, who practices it, how it is practised and how widespread it is, and this also determines the quality of perception of the phenomenon (Rose, 2015). However, in some situations, the media can go from being an ally to an obstacle. When public opinion is not adequately informed and it does not have the instruments to properly recognise corrupt phenomena, efficient sanction mechanisms against corruption, such as electoral accountability, are not effectively achieved and anti-corruption efforts are weakened. This phenomenon has been defined as "perceptive and representational asynchrony" (Mazzoni et al., 2017) and has a lot to do with the kind of coverage the press gives to the issue

---

[1] All findings of this European project were published on https://anticorrp.eu/

of corruption. On account of this, we will reflect under what conditions public opinion manages to build an unfavourable environment towards corruption, but also under what conditions degeneration occurs and public opinion becomes impervious to sanction mechanisms and inhibits anti-corruption measures. In particular, we will deal with the phenomenon of "politicisation of corruption" (Sberna & Vannucci, 2013; Vannucci, 2020), namely an increase in the polarization of opinions, interests, or values about judicial investigation and the extent to which this polarization is strategically advanced towards the political debate by parties, political leaders and media.

3.2 The Complexity of Corruption

Corruption is a complex phenomenon. It has been tackled from different perspectives, within different academic disciplines (Rothstein & Varraich, 2014), and one of the few assumptions on which most scholars seem to agree is precisely the difficulty in correctly determining it (Kurer, 2015; Gardiner, 2001; Mungiu-Pippidi & Fazekas, 2020). This means that scholars consider corruption as an "umbrella concept" (Varriaich, 2014), an intentionally very broad concept within which different cases correspond. This conceptual disorder reflects in the difficulty of establishing a clear-cut definition. One of the most commonly used definitions, adopted also by Transparency International (2009), states that corruption can be considered as "*abuse of power for private gain*". This definition is well diffused because it is simple to recognize and is inclusive (van Schoor, 2017), but it has a number of limitations, mainly due to the difficulty of drawing clear and marked boundaries as to which conduct falls within the category of corruption and which does not. One of the major difficulties in defining the phenomenon lies in the wide variety of actions that are considered as abuse, which differ in many countries.

Scholars often tend to choose a definition that fits their purpose (Kurer, 2015), based on their field of expertize. Such as, the "economic" definitions of corruption are based on the "principal-agent theory" that thinks in terms of costs and benefits for the actors involved. According to this criterion, corruption can be considered as "*divergence between the principal's or the public's interest and those of the agent or civil servant: corruption occurs when an agent betrays the principal's interests in pursuit of her own*" (Klitgaard, 1988: 24). Another widely used definition is the "legalistic" one (Gardiner, 2001). A "legal" definition is proposed by Nye, which says corruption is "*behaviour which deviates from the normal duties of a public role because of private-regarding (family, close private clique), pecuniary or status gains; or violates rules against the exercise of certain types of private-regarding influence*" (Nye, 1967: 419). This latter criterion has the great advantage of clarity: it gives univocal definition to the phenomenon, considering as corruption everything that the law defines as such. Under legal rules, it would be possible to establish precisely which conducts can be regarded as corrupt and which cannot. However, this criterion does not capture all aspects of this multi-faceted phenomenon

(Rothstein & Varraich, 2014; van Schoor, 2017). It makes it difficult to compare different countries (or a single country at two points in time) when their formal norms of office are quite divergent and corruption may be labelled differently because of differences in laws (Scott, 1972). Moreover, the legislator is not always able to contemplate all types of misuse in advance. Assuming this criterion, we would exclude the "grey area", i.e. those behaviors that are not illegal but nevertheless unethical.

The solution to this problem is to leave behind the idea of corruption as a univocal phenomenon and to accept that, in order to recognise it, it needs to be placed in a specific context using socio-political criteria as well as legal ones. Several researchers (Vannucci, 2012; Lambsdorff, 2007; Gardiner, 2001) combine the "legalistic" principle with other two dimensions in order to define the phenomenon of corruption more exhaustively: the "public interest" dimension and the "public opinion" dimension. Regarding the former, conducts that disregard the collective interest in favour of private interests are regarded as corruptive. Similarly, in the latter, any behaviors that violate social values are considered forms of corruption. In other words, corrupt activities are those that the public considers to be such (Vannucci, 2012). Both theories show that corruption has a lot to do with a specific sociocultural context. Both what can be recognised as public interest and social value are not ontological realities but are social constructions generated in a given context. It is not a matter of prescribed rules, but of dynamics articulated within a value system that is constantly redefined. It is a "labelling" process in public opinion: behavior that violates the public interest or a value system through an abuse of power is implicitly "labelled" as corrupt.

This sets cultural implications to the common definition of what can be considered abuse. Corruption is an abuse of power according to what is commonly understood as violation in a given historical period and social context. Such labelling process has a lot to do with political culture, citizens' attitude toward norms and political accountability. Cultural dimensions may influence the individual's perception of ethical situations (Vitell et al., 2013); therefore, cultural differences are expected to influence citizens' ability in recognizing (and blaming) corrupt behaviours. This means that there may be discrepancies between different contexts in recognizing the phenomenon, affecting its perception and making it difficult to establish in a univocal way its actual diffusion.

3.3   Perception of Corruption and Populism

If it is not easy to find a definition for the phenomenon of corruption, it is equally difficult to establish its diffusion. While for most phenomena of deviancy judicial data is a valuable source of information, for corruption this cannot be the case. As Davigo and Mannozzi (2007) state, corruption is a crime with "silent victims", namely nobody has an interest in publicizing the illegal behaviour. Thus, the data on judicial statistics represent only a "tip of the iceberg" (Vannucci, 2012) while the majority of offenses tend to remain hidden and invisible to the public. Judicial data does not consider corrupt those events that have not been uncovered by prosecutors, events that represent an important percentage of the total amount of corruptive behaviors.

For this reason, scholars and stakeholders often rely on perception indices to evaluate the level of corruption as substitute of "hard measures" (Charron, 2016). The most common index is the Corruption Perception Index, provided by "Transparency International", which is based on "experts assessments" (Transparency 2019). Other indices, such as the Eurobarometer (2013), are based on surveys conducted on the general public. Perception of corruption, essentially, does not represent an absolute situation, but it is a social phenomenon depending on the social rules and culture of each citizen. Perception is affected by various types of external variables that can end up distorting its value. For example, research by Olken (2009) on corruption focused on road construction in Indonesia showed that young people, the most educated people, and the men were most likely to perceive corruption. By contrast, those who had a personal connection with the construction project, whether through social or personal circles, tended to have a perception of significantly less corruption (Olken, 2009). Other factors that influences the perception of corruption may be inequality (Jong-sung & Khagram, 2005), where a greater level of inequality contributes to the determination of a higher level of perceived corruption. Political bias (Rose, 2015) may also be a factor in determining the degree of perceived corruption.

Noelle-Neumann (1984) notes that citizens generally use two sources to generate their opinions: their direct experiences and media content. The role of the media in corruption perception is probably more important than in other areas. In many situations, especially in Western countries, common citizens have very little or no firsthand experience of the problem in their daily lives. What they know about corruption comes from media reports. The degree of exposure towards news of corruption can have a significant influence on the perception of the spread of the phenomenon. An increase in news about misuse, therefore, does not necessarily reflect an increase in the levels of corruption, but might influence the level of perception and above all the degree of attention of public opinion towards the theme (Rizzica & Tonello, 2015).

This means that the type of coverage paid to the phenomenon is able to strongly influence its perception, no matter how widespread it actually is. For this reason, it is important to consider how the media deal with the phenomenon, the cases they report and those they do not cover. In the selection of news, the media follow criteria of newsworthiness that do not always respond to ethical/moral principles. Some episodes of wrongdoing that are not considered newsworthy enough by the media tend not to be covered, while particularly dramatized scandals tend to be overcovered. As noted by Rizzica and Tonello (2015), if the media reports excessively on scandals, sometimes even in the absence of real corruption events, this might lead to a bias in the formation of individuals' perceptions about the extent of corruption in a society. Mazzoni, Stanziano and Recchi call it (2017) "a perceptual and representational asynchrony", i.e. a perception of corruption that does not correspond to the real extent of the crimes but tends to overestimate some aspects (for example political corruption) and underestimate others (petty corruption, private corruption, etc.).

Even if the media have a societal function, namely to bear public responsibility for promoting the public awareness, they are at the same time businesses that produce commodities (information and entertainment) for a market (Allern, 2002). The media market competition induces journalists to adapt their news to "commercial logics" (Landerer, 2013). The news media usually select specific aspects of corruption and emphasize them, producing a suitable distortion to market needs. To attract a wider range of audience, journalists tend to report the simplest aspects of corruption, by focusing their attention on single cases: data on the systemic implication of corruption are less accessible than the reporting of a story. In other words, commercialization pushes the journalistic coverage of corruption towards ready marketable product, through the use of strong headlines or emotional high-impact pictures, assigning numerous pages, or using a particular tone or language to describe the story. This trend has intensified with the increasingly pervasive spread of digital media. In this context, the need to gain clicks has introduced new criteria for newsworthiness alongside traditional ones. In particular, along with using the concept of newsworthiness, is increasingly used that of "shareworthiness", related to the potential of a news content to be shared and disseminated by different users (Trilling et al., 2017). Yet, corruption is narrativized into a scandal which inspires widespread interest and discussion, in fact, as Lull and Hinnerman (1997: 13) highlighted, "*in a scandal the story triumphs over the facts at some point and in doing so takes on a life of its own*". Storytelling techniques, such as "*simplification, polarization, intensification, personalization, visualization, stereotyping, and particular ways of framing the news*" (Strömbäck & Esser, 2009:213), are used to turn raw information into compelling news stories. According to the interests of the public, corruption reporting usually focuses on something worse than normal, something a little bit different, bizarre or unusual (Pratt, 2007).

Commercial needs do not inspire coverage of the common aspects of corruption but look for its most trivial or spectacular aspects that may create sensationalism and capture public attention. Due to the importance that media coverage assumes in the perception of corruption, the scandalization of particular events may produce a bias in the general perception of the phenomenon. Such bias can sometimes culminate in mistrust and even populist sentiments (Fieschi & Heywood, 2004). The relationship between corruption and populism is an issue that has recently been attracting increasing attention from scholars (Kubbe & Loli, 2020). The media, especially through scandals, strengthen this link (Mincigrucci & Stanziano, 2017, 2018). Indeed, as Mazzoleni noted, there is a "media complicity" in the rise of a populist rhetoric: "*public cynicism of particular media outlets and certain campaigns against political corruption, government misdeeds and controversial policies, may be held responsible for the diffusion of political discontent and even anti-political attitudes among the citizenry*" (Mazzoleni, 2008, p. 51). In this regard, the impact of social media on these issues cannot be ignored as shown by recent research projects that have emphasized the role of the social media for populist propaganda (Kriesi, 2014; Engesser et al., 2017; Postill, 2018; Ernst et al., 2019).

The core narrative of populist movements is that society is separated into two homogeneous and antagonistic groups, *"the pure people"* versus *"the corrupt elite"* (Mudde, 2004; Albertazzi & McDonnell, 2016). In other words, corruption could be considered the discriminating factor that distinguishes élite's members from the common people (Gidron & Bonikowski, 2013). When the journalistic coverage of corruption is based on political corruption scandals, it creates a breeding ground for populism. With this kind of coverage, news media produce a social emergency that increases distrust toward institutions and favors populist politicians, fostering the populist ideology. A study conducted on the Italian context (Aassve et al., 2018) has investigated the long term—not only in short run—impact of corruption on trust toward institutions. The study revealed that young citizens who voted for the first time between 1992 and 1998 against a backdrop of a huge judicial investigation and the revealing of widespread political corruption (Tangentopoli) today, 25 years later, present low levels of confidence in the institutions. Further research has shown that the exposure to the news in that period on corruption reaped repercussion even in the 2018 general elections when the populist parties enjoyed mass voting gains. Thus, perception bias on the widespread of corruption may have serious effect on citizens' attitudes toward institutions and on voting behaviors. This encourages an instrumental use of corruption, especially in its scandalizing form. This assumption has also been demonstrated by Bågenholm and Charron (2014) who have shown in a study that new political parties which talk about corruption are more successful than new parties that do not. As we shall see below, corruption often becomes an instrument for achieving private interests, mostly of a political nature.

3.4 The Media's Role in Curbing Corruption

There is no doubt that the media perform a "social function" toward corruption. Such social function results in particular in the anti-corruption role played by the media: by denouncing malfeasance, the latter contribute in a decisive way to the "criminalisation of corruption" (Sberna & Vannucci, 2013), namely effective activism against corrupt practices that can create formal and informal constraints toward it. Journalists play, at least in the ideal dimension, a function of social watchdogs, investigate episodes of malfeasance, stimulate public awareness of the phenomenon by increasing the threshold of accountability that is required of political figures and public officials.

Several studies have shown that the control exercised by the press could reduce corruptive behaviors bringing them to light, diffusing and reinforcing sentiments of shame and indignation (Berti et al., 2020; Chowdhury, 2004). One of the most representative researches in this field is that of Brunetti and Weder (2003) *"A free press is bad news for corruption"*. Using as an independent variable the indices of press freedom provided by Freedom House and as a dependent variable some indices measuring corruption, the two scholars show that there is a statistically significant negative correlation between the two variables, and therefore that press freedom is an effective deterrent against corrupt practices. Several researches developed the concept assessed by Brunetti and Weder: according to Lindstedt and Naurin (2010), higher levels of newspaper circulation increase conditions of publicity that reduce corruption, while a developed media industry discourage bureaucrats from engaging in corruption given their risk of being caught (Suphachalasai, 2005). Camaj (2013) argues that media freedom might have a stronger indirect effect on corruption when coupled with powerful institutions of horizontal accountability, such as parliamentary systems instead of presidential systems. According to Stapenhurst (2000), journalists can produce two types of effects in instances of misconduct, such as corruption: tangible and intangible. The formers are those which produce direct and visible results, for example, when a journalistic investigation leads to a concrete act, such as a charge or a judicial inquiry, or they can even lead to impeachments and force political figures or public officials to resign. Intangible effects, on the other hand, are those that affect public opinion, creating a hostile environment for corruptive behaviors. By denouncing episodes of wrongdoing, the media affirm moral codes in public opinion. They implicitly outline what is tolerable and what is not for public opinion and foster public indignation among the latter. Redefining the canons of public morality is one of the functions historically attributed to the mass media: the two pivotal scholars for media studies, Paul Lazarsfeld and Robert Merton (1948) argued that by selecting and denouncing certain wrong behaviors they implicitly suggest what is in conformity with prevailing morality and what is not, also stimulating public reaction. Therefore, we can assume that the media play the social function of defining and condemning episodes of corruption, allowing public opinion to recognize them.

Those assumptions recall the so-called "normative theories" of journalism (Benson, 2008), namely the ideal function of the press, i.e. what the press should do for society. In fact, research has taken into account journalism as the "watchdog" of democracy: a type of journalism that is assigned a specific institutional function which consists in monitoring the holders of power and exposing the imperfections of democracy. With their stories/narrations, journalists can channel the public debate towards certain topics, thereby making the public opinion more aware of certain issues, raising the threshold of accountability that is asked of political representatives and/or public officials. This type of journalism can spread the sense of a common good, promoting a culture of legality and a sentiment of disapproval of the corruption among the readership (Ettema & Glasser, 1998).

However, the watchdog role of the media cannot be taken for granted (Vaidya, 2005). The efficiency and virtue of journalistic watchdog practices need to be examined in light of the socio-cultural and economic conditions that they occur in. In many countries, watchdog journalism did not establish itself because it did not find the same fertile ground that it did, for instance, in Anglo-American model of journalism (Gerli et al., 2018). In many journalistic contexts such as the Eastern European countries (Stetka, 2012) or Mediterranean countries (Cornia, 2016), the news market is not particularly remunerative (see Wan-Ifra report, 2019), as the newspaper circulation is not so high, and profit margin is low. In these countries, those people who invest in newspapers do so not for any economic income, but to pursue external interests, whether economic or political. Jan Zielonka (2015) claims how the media in the emerging democracies of Eastern Europe are not without political and economic interference, especially because ownership is often in the hands of national powerful business actors (mainly oligarchs) with political ambitions. In this case, this phenomenon is referred as "media colonization". A similar situation can also be observed in Mediterranean countries such Italy (Marchetti et al., 2017), although a different concept is used: it is, in fact, referred to as the "impure publisher" (Seghetti, 2010), meaning that the media owners earn their main profits from economic sectors outside of publishing and use the media for their own and political purposes. Furthermore, the Mediterranean model is a media system that has always been considered as having a "high level of political/ideological parallelism" (Hallin & Mancini, 2004). However, following the secularization process of society, which led to the declining influence of political parties, the links between media outlets and political ideologies gradually gave way to forms of partisanship that are less ideological and more connected to contingent interests (political but also, and increasingly, economic) (Mancini, 2012), making it very similar to the new democracies. In light of the above considerations, the strongly interconnected relationship between political, economic and media interests is what characterizes the examined countries: Colin Sparks (2000) refers to this as "political capital". To reach their own goals, each player acting in any one of these spheres is extremely dependent on the support and resources of the other two, thereby favoring the spread of those informal practices which subsequently encourage patronage-like behavior. Many scholars refer to "media capture" (Mungiu-Pippidi, 2008) or "partisan polyvalence" (McCargo, 2012) to describe practices of instrumentalization of corruption news, namely a coverage of corruption cases as a weapon to damage enemies (both political and economic).

The aforementioned research focuses mainly on the relationship between corruption and legacy media. In recent years, however, the media ecosystem has become profoundly more complex. Digital media, and especially social media, have become fundamental agencies of socialization, as well as newspapers and television, and consequently their role toward corruption cannot be underestimated, especially regarding its social perception (Goel et al., 2012). However, this branch of study is still scarcely congested (Berti et al., 2020). Most research has focused on the positive role of digital media, grass roots initiatives or citizen journalism. The main assumption on this field states that in being less conditioned by political/economic influences, digital journalists are more capable of controlling power. On the other hand, there are several underestimated aspects of digital media, and in particular of social media, such as affordances of platforms, disintermediation, in-group vs out-group bias, incivility or echo-chambers that may even reinforce the polarization and dramatization mentioned earlier and, as a result, yield new, unexplored forms of external influence and instrumentalization.

When this instrumentalization becomes systemic, both for digital and legacy media, it sets off a mechanism of politicization of corruption (Sberna & Vannucci,

2013), where corruption is no longer an issue that is unanimously condemned but it becomes an object of partisan dispute, effectively inhibiting the watchdog role of the media in curbing it.

3.5 The Politicization of Corruption

In the previous paragraphs we have argued that, given its complexity and variety, corruption very often appears as a "labelling process" that occurs within a given social context. Corruption implies a process of attribution of meaning toward certain events within public opinion. This attribution of meaning is the result of a competition among several opinions, namely a conflict is triggered between those who want to label a behavior as corrupt and those who instead try to avoid this (Lang & Lang, 1983).

In the mass media literature, this process fits into the strand of agenda building studies, according to which different actors compete in the public arena to affirm the issues and frames most favourable to them, and thus set priority issues on the public agenda (McCombs, 2004; Nisbet, 2008). However, it is important to keep in mind that corruption is not an issue like any other, and the way it is framed can have disruptive effects on the value system of a given society. First, as mentioned above, this is a highly newsworthy topic (Mancini et al., 2017). It is a negative issue, easily dramatized and spectacular, therefore it inherently assumes a level of newsworthiness that easily attracts the attention of the media. The most effective messages are negative ones and a corruption scandal is the clearest form of negativity (Castells, 2011). Secondly, it is an issue that can have disruptive effects in the political system, which is why it is very much engaged by political actors in the agenda-building process. This second point has to do with the so-called "politics of trust" (Thompson, 2000), that sets reputation as a key factor in achieving political success. With the disappearance of the great ideologies of the twentieth century that have affected Western democracies, the figure of the leader is becoming increasingly important for gaining consensus and, without a clear distinction between right and left, citizens address their vote on the basis of the trustworthiness, or above all of the honesty, that a candidate manages to transmit. In the "politics of trust", reputation is an element of fundamental importance for the construction of the consensus necessary to exercise any form of political activity, and it is also easy to imagine how much a corruption scandal can be detrimental to the exercise of such activity (Mancini, 2018). Corruption thus becomes a highly salient issue, i.e. a topic that is strongly discussed in the public debate, but also a highly polarized one, because it can bring concrete benefits to a given political group, can be used as a "picklock" to unhinge a government majority or, more generally, to weaken an adversary.

Issue salience (namely the intensity with which a issue is covered), actor expansion (the range of actors dealing with the topic) and polarisation (the distance of position of different actors on the same issue) are the three key elements adopted by Hutter and other authors (2016) to analyse the politicization of an issue, and it has been documented that they characterize corruption's public discussion in many countries (Mancini et al., 2017). We can talk about the politicization of corruption whenever there is not a unanimous condemnation by political actors of corruption, but corruption becomes a real social cleavage (Vannucci, 2020; Sberna & Vannucci, 2013), a theme exploited to conduct political battles. This does not mean that there is no consensus on the need to fight corruption. Everyone claims that corruption is a problem to be fought, while no one argues that it can somehow be functional. Curini (2019) proposes a distinction of electoral issues based on the degree of division it generates between parties and political actors: (a) "valence issues", namely issues where there is a broad amount of consensus among voters (Stokes, 1963); (b) "positional issues" which involve a clear conflict among different groups. According to Curini, corruption (and anti-corruption) represents a typical example of valence issue, because it does not create divisions or clashes between the parties and between the voters, all agree with the idea that corruption is an important problem and that it is necessary to stem it. In the presence of a valence issue, voters will not tend to evaluate candidates on the basis of their position on the problem but they will evaluate them on the basis of their performance regarding the problem. In this specific case, voters will evaluate the candidates on the basis of their involvement in corruption cases, trying to identify the candidate who could actually start concrete actions to fight corruption.

Through politicization, a strong polarization on the issue is created, with political actors trying to show themselves as honest and different from their "corrupt" competitors. It is an "affective polarization" and not "ideological one" (Iyengar et al., 2019). It means that it is not based on different ideological views on the topic, but it consists in the attribution of negative traits to parties other than the one they belong to in the *in-group/out-group logic*. Aversion to others, according to Iyengar et al. (2019), has nothing to do with the specific nature of the issue with respect to which the difference of opinion is manifested. In other words, in our case, it is not disagreement about how to deal with corruption that triggers these forms of rejection for those who think differently. It certainly is possible that there are also differences about the measures to be taken, but these seem to take a back seat to the distance that is felt from the members of the out-group. For example, when the subject under discussion is a case of corruption involving politicians from opposing sides, the classic dynamic of attack towards the other (out-group) is activated. This type of public discussion is not a debate between peers proposing different and legitimate positions on an issue, but it is a real process of delegitimization, in which they challenge the legitimacy of their opponents to fulfil a political role. This process is implemented by both political actors and the media who, due to the political and economic influences mentioned earlier, are inclined to side with one or the other faction.

Politicization has detrimental effect on the institutional system. The fight against corruption fails to produce effects, because any attempt to combat it, whether by prosecutors or by watchdog journalists, is absorbed into the political debate and subjected to partisan judgments (Vannucci, 2020). Politicization increases the salience of the topic, but paradoxically it decreases the indignation of public opinion because episodes of malfeasance are not unanimously condemned but are subject to partisan judgments. This makes the political system resilient to any attempt to fight corruption, because political actors are not subject to those mechanisms of accountability and social control that prevent the perpetuation of malfeasance.

3.6   Conclusions

To address corruption, we used an archipelago of overlapping concepts, quoting studies related to different disciplinary sectors. This is because corruption is a highly multifaceted phenomenon which affects various aspects of the democratic, economic and social life of a specific country. Since it is impossible to formulate a comprehensive "general theory" of corruption (Belligni, 1987), to the same extent it is impossible to find "universal cures" for the problem. These "cures" in fact must take into account a wide variety of factors: from the nature of the judicial system to that of the economic system, but in particular to the responsiveness of public opinion towards these issues. As we have explained in the course of the chapter, public opinion has a fundamental role in enabling action against corrupt phenomena, without which no legislative measure could be successful. At the same time, however, if not adequately informed, public opinion can be highly resilient and impervious to corruption (Fieschi & Heywood, 2004), rendering ineffective efforts to combat it. This emerges clearly with what Sberna and Vannucci (2013) call "politicization", namely the polarization of opinions, interests, or values about anticorruption activities. Politicization is a subject that deserves future academic exploration, because it represents one of the major, yet barely explored, obstacles to the creation of a proactive climate capable of fighting corruption. It inhibits any accountability mechanism aimed at removing corrupt individuals from the political scene, because it turns corruption into a partisan issue instead of a universal problem that afflicts society as a whole. In many situations therefore, above all in the countries of Eastern Europe (Zielonka, 2015); or of the Mediterranean (Hallin & Mancini, 2004), to fight corruption, besides formulating efficient laws, it is important to tackle polarization, both in public opinion and in the media. The media play a fundamental role in shaping public opinion, especially on obscure issues such as corruption. They fulfil a series of "functions" of intangible nature strengthening social norms (Ettema & Glasser, 1998) and reinforcing respect for the "common good" (Mancini et al., 2017). However, alongside these "positive functions", they also develop a series of dysfunctions, which not only do not create a hostile environment against corrupt phenomena, but sometimes even favor them, fostering distrust in institutions and the political system. It is important that research delves into these dysfunctions that are still little explored. In recent years, in fact, these dysfunctions have increased their impact, especially in the light of the rising of digital media and the increased polarization in news coverage around the world (Iyengar et al., 2019), which is radicalizing society's opinions. Corruption is not spared from this polarization, and is increasingly exploited by populist movements and parties, which use it as a picklock to demolish the political system, but at the same time transform it into a partisan battle.

Acknowledgment This work was supported by MIUR PRIN 2017 – 2017CRLZ3F: PolitiCanti. The Politicisation of Corruption and Anticorruption strategies in Italy.

References

Aassve, A., Daniele, G., & Moglie, M. L. (2018). Never forget the first time: The persistent effect of corruption and the rise of populism in Italy. *BAFFI CAREFIN Centre Research Paper* 2018 (96). https://papers.ssrn.com/sol3/papers.cfm?abstract_id=3280498. Accessed 30 March 2021.

Albertazzi, D., & McDonnell, D. (2016). *Populists in power*. Routledge, Taylor & Francis Group.

Allern, S. (2002). Journalistic and commercial news values news organizations as patrons of an institution and market actors. *Nordicom Review, 23*, 137–152.

Bågenholm, A., & Charron, N. (2014). Do politics in Europe benefit from politicising corruption? *West European Politics, 37*(5), 903–931. https://doi.org/10.1080/01402382.2014.909164

Belligni, S. (1987). Corruzione e scienza politica: Una riflessione agli inizi. *Teoria Politica, 3*(1), 61–88.

Benson, R. (2008). Normative theories of journalism. In W. Donsbach (Ed.), *The Blackwell international encyclopedia of communication* (pp. 2591–2597).

Berti, C., Bratu, R., & Wickberg, S. (2020). Corruption and the media. In A. Mungiu-Pippidi & P. M. Heywood (Eds.), *A research agenda for studies of corruption* (pp. 107–117). Edward Elgar Publishing. https://doi.org/10.4337/9781789905007.00015

Brunetti, A., & Weder, B. (2003). A free press is bad news for corruption. *Journal of Public Economics, 87*(7–8), 1801–1824. https://doi.org/10.1016/S0047-2727(01)00186-4

Camaj, L. (2013). The media's role in fighting corruption: Media effects on governmental accountability. *The International Journal of Press/Politics, 18*(1), 21–42. https://doi.org/10.1177/1940161212462741

Castells, M. (2011). *Communication and power*. Oxford University Press.

Charron, N. (2016). Do corruption measures have a perception problem? Assessing the relationship between experiences and perceptions of corruption among citizens and experts. *European Political Science Review, 8*(1), 147–171. https://doi.org/10.1017/S1755773914000447

Chowdhury, S. (2004). The effect of democracy and press freedom on corruption: An empirical test. *Economics Letters, 85*(1), 93–101.

Cornia, A. (2016). TV-centrism and politicisation in Italy: Obstacles to new media development and pluralism. *Media, Culture & Society, 38*(2), 175–195. https://doi.org/10.1177/0163443715594035

Curini, L. (2019). *Corruption, ideology, and populism: The rise of valence political campaigning*. Palgrave Macmillan.

Davigo, P., & Mannozzi, G. (2007). *La corruzione in Italia: Percezione sociale e controllo penale*. Laterza.

della Porta, D., & Vannucci, A. (1999). *Corrupt exchanges*. Aldine De Gruyter.

della Porta, D., & Vannucci, A. (2012). *The hidden order of corruption: An institutional approach*. Ashgate Pub.

Engesser, S., Ernst, N., Esser, F., & Büchel, F. (2017). Populism and social media: How politicians spread a fragmented ideology. *Information, Communication & Society, 20*(8), 1109–1126. https://doi.org/10.1080/1369118X.2016.1207697

Ernst, N., Blassnig, S., Engesser, S., Büchel, F., & Esser, F. (2019). Populists prefer social media over talk shows: An analysis of populist messages and stylistic elements across six countries. *Social Media Society, 5*(1), 205630511882335. https://doi.org/10.1177/2056305118823358.

Ettema, J. S., & Glasser, T. L. (1998). *Custodians of conscience: Investigative journalism and public virtue*. Columbia University Press.

Eurobarometer. (2013). *Special Eurobarometer 397*. European Commission, Directorate-General for Home Affairs and co-ordinated by the Directorate-General for Communication. https://data. europa.eu/euodp/it/data/dataset/S1076_79_1_397. Accessed 30 March 2021.

Fieschi, C., & Heywood, P. (2004). Trust, cynicism and populist anti-politics. *Journal of Political Ideologies, 9*(3), 289–309. https://doi.org/10.1080/1356931042000263537

Gardiner, J. A. (2001). Defining corruption. In A. J. Hedenheimer & M. Johnston (Eds.), *Political corruption. Concepts and contexts* (pp. 25–40). Transaction Publisher.

Gerli, M., Mazzoni, M., & Mincigrucci, R. (2018). Constraints and limitations of investigative journalism in Hungary, Italy, Latvia and Romania. *European Journal of Communication, 33*(1), 22–36. https://doi.org/10.1177/0267323117750672

Gidron, N., & Bonikowski, B. (2013). *Varieties of populism: Literature review and research agenda*. Weatherhead Working Paper Series, No. 13-0004.

Goel, R. K., Nelson, M. A., & Naretta, M. A. (2012). The internet as an indicator of corruption awareness. *European Journal of Political Economy, 28*(1), 64–75. https://doi.org/10.1016/j. ejpoleco.2011.08.003

Gupta, S., Davoodi, H., & Alonso-Terme, R. (2002). Does corruption affect income inequality and poverty? *Economics of Governance, 3*(1), 23–45.

Hallin, D. C., & Mancini, P. (2004). *Comparing media systems: Three models of media and politics* (1st ed.). Cambridge University Press. https://doi.org/10.1017/CBO9780511790867

Heywood, P. (Ed.). (2015). *Routledge handbook of political corruption*. London, New York.

Hutter, S., Grande, E., & Kriesi, H. (2016). *Politicising Europe: Integration and mass politics*. Cambridge University Press. https://doi.org/10.1017/CBO9781316422991

Iyengar, S., Lelkes, Y., Levendusky, M., Malhotra, N., & Westwood, S. J. (2019). The origins and consequences of affective polarization in the United States. *Annual Review of Political Science, 22*(1), 129–146. https://doi.org/10.1146/annurev-polisci-051117-073034

Jong-sung, Y., & Khagram, S. (2005). A comparative study of inequality and corruption. *American Sociological Review, 70*(1), 136–157. https://doi.org/10.1177/000312240507000107

Klitgaard, R. (1988). *Controlling corruption*. University of California Press.

Kostadinova, T. (2012). *Political corruption in Eastern Europe: Politics after communism*. Lynne Rienner Publishers.

Kriesi, H. (2014). The populist challenge. *West European Politics, 37*(2), 361–378. https://doi.org/ 10.1080/01402382.2014.887879

Kubbe, I., & Loli, M. (2020). Corruption and populism: The linkage. In A. Mungiu-Pippidi & P. M. Heywood (Eds.), *A research agenda for studies of corruption* (pp. 118–130). Edward Elgar Publishing. https://doi.org/10.4337/9781789905007.00016

Kurer, O. (2015). Definitions of corruption. In P. M. Heywood (Ed.), *Routledge handbook of political corruption* (pp. 30–41). Routledge.

Lambsdorff, J. G. (2007). *The institutional economics of corruption and reform: Theory, evidence, and policy*. Cambridge University Press. https://doi.org/10.1017/CBO9780511492617

Landerer, N. (2013). Rethinking the logics: A conceptual framework for the mediatization of politics: Rethinking the logics. *Communication Theory, 23*(3), 239–258. https://doi.org/10. 1111/comt.12013

Lang, G. E., & Lang, K. (1983). *The battle for public opinion*. Columbia University Press.

Lazarsfeld, P. F., & Merton, R. K. (1948). Mass communication, popular taste and organized social action. In L. Bryson (Ed.), *Communication of ideas* (pp. 95–118). Harper e Brothers.

Lindstedt, C., & Naurin, D. (2010). Transparency is not enough: Making transparency effective in reducing corruption. *International Political Science Review, 31*(3), 301–322. https://doi.org/10. 1177/0192512110377602

Lull, J., & Hinerman, S. (Eds.). (1997). *Media scandals: Morality and desire in the popular culture marketplace*. Columbia University Press.

Mancini, P. (2012). Instrumentalization of the media vs. political parallelism. *Chinese Journal of Communication, 5*(3), 262–280. https://doi.org/10.1080/17544750.2012.701415

Mancini, P. (2018). "Assassination Campaigns": Corruption Scandals and News Media Instrumentalization. *International Journal of Communication*, 12.

Mancini, P., Mazzoni, M., Cornia, A., & Marchetti, R. (2017). Representations of corruption in the British, French, and Italian Press: Audience segmentation and the lack of unanimously shared indignation. *The International Journal of Press/Politics, 22*(1), 67–91. https://doi.org/10.1177/1940161216674652

Marchetti, R., Mazzoni, M., & Pagiotti, S. (2017). La copertura della corruzione in Italia e nei paesi dell'Europa Centro Orientale: (Molte) somiglianze e (poche) differenze. *Problemi dell'informazione, 2*, 229–256. https://doi.org/10.1445/87066

Mauro, P. (1995). Corruption and growth. *The Quarterly Journal of Economics, 110*(3), 681–712. https://doi.org/10.2307/2946696

Mauro, P. (2002). The effects of corruption on growth and public expenditure. In A. J. Hedenheimer & M. Johnston (Eds.), *Political corruption. Concepts and contexts* (pp. 339–352). Transaction Publisher.

Mazzoleni, G. (2008). Populism and the media. In D. Albertazzi & D. McDonnell (Eds.), *Twenty-first century populism* (pp. 49–64). Palgrave Macmillan. https://doi.org/10.1057/9780230592100_4

Mazzoni, M., Stanziano, A. & Recchi, L. (2017). Rappresentazione e percezione della corruzione in Italia. Verso una strumentalizzazione del fenomeno. *Comunicazione politica, 1*, 99–118. https://doi.org/10.3270/86131.

McCargo, D. (2012). Partisan polyvalence: Characterizing the political role of Asian media. In D. C. Hallin & P. Mancini (Eds.), *Comparing media systems beyond the western world* (pp. 201–223). Cambridge University Press.

McCombs, M. E. (2004). *Setting the agenda: The mass media and public opinion*. Polity, Blackwell.

Mincigrucci, R., & Stanziano, A. (2017). Il coverage della corruzione tra il 2004 e il 2015 in Italia: Controllo di virtù; o populismo penale? *Problemi dell'informazione, 2*, 201–228. https://doi.org/10.1445/87065

Mincigrucci, R. & Stanziano, A. (2018). How corruption coverage harms Italy's society. *European Journalism Observatory*. https://en.ejo.ch/research/the-journalistic-coverage-ofcorruption-in-italy-an-example-of-penal-populism. Accessed March 30.

Mudde, C. (2004). The Populist Zeitgeist. *Government and Opposition, 39*(4), 541–563. https://doi.org/10.1111/j.1477-7053.2004.00135.x

Mungiu-Pippidi, A. (2008). How media and politics shape each other in the New Europe. In C. Jakubowicz & M. Sükösd (Eds.), *Finding the right place on the map: Central and Eastern European media change in a global perspective* (pp. 87–100). Intellect Ltd.

Mungiu-Pippidi, A., & Fazekas, M. (2020). How to define and measure corruption. In A. Mungiu-Pippidi & P. M. Heywood (Eds.), *A research agenda for studies of corruption* (pp. 7–26). Edward Elgar Publishing. https://doi.org/10.4337/9781789905007.00008

Mungiu-Pippidi, A., & Heywood, P. (2020). *A research agenda for studies of corruption*. Edward Elgar Publishing. https://doi.org/10.4337/9781789905007

Nisbet, M. C. (2008). Agenda building. In W. Donsbach (Ed.), *The international encyclopedia of communication*. Wiley. https://doi.org/10.1002/9781405186407.wbieca035

Noelle-Neumann, E. (1984). *The spiral of silence: Public opinion—our social skin*. The University of Chicago Press.

Nye, J. S. (1967). Corruption and political development: A cost-benefit analysis. *American Political Science Review, 61*(2), 417–427. https://doi.org/10.2307/1953254

Olken, B. A. (2009). Corruption perceptions vs. corruption reality. *Journal of Public Economics, 93* (7–8), 950–964.

Postill, J. (2018). Populism and social media: A global perspective. *Media, Culture & Society, 40* (5), 754–765. https://doi.org/10.1177/0163443718772186

Pratt, J. (2007). Penal populism: key ideas in criminology. , Taylor & Francis Group.
Rizzica, L. & Tonello, M. (2015). *Exposure to media and corruption perceptions*. Working Paper Banca d'Italia n.1043.
Rose, J. (2015). Corruption and the problem of perception. In P. M. Heywood (Ed.), *Routledge handbook of political corruption* (pp. 172–182). Routledge.
Rothstein, B., & Uslaner, E. M. (2005). All for all: Equality, corruption, and social trust. *World Politics, 58*(1), 41–72.
Rothstein, B., & Varraich, A. (2014). Corruption and the opposite to corruption. A map of the conceptual landscape. *State-of-the-art report on theories and harmonised concepts of corruption. Deliverable. Work Package: WP1. Social, legal, anthropological and political approaches to theory of corruption. Project title: Anti-Corruption Policies Revisited, Gothenburg: The Quality of Government Institute*, 1–111.
Sberna, S., & Vannucci, A. (2013). "It's the politics, stupid!". The politicization of anti-corruption in Italy. *Crime, Law and Social Change, 60*(5), 565–593. https://doi.org/10.1007/s10611-013-9480-8
Scott, J. C. (1972). *Comparative political corruption*. Prentice-Hall.
Seghetti, R. (2010). Comunicazione e informazione in Italia: Gli assetti proprietari ed economici. *Problemi dell'Informazione, 35*(1–2), 29–62.
Shleifer, A., & Vishny, R. W. (1993). Corruption. *Quarterly Journal of Economics, 108*(3), 599–617.
Sparks, C. (2000). Media theory after the fall of European communism: Why the old models from east and west won't do anymore. In J. Curran & M. J. Park (Eds.), *De-westernizing media studies* (pp. 35–50). Routledge.
Stapenhurst, R. (2000). *The media's role in curbing corruption*. Washington, DC.
Stetka, V. (2012). From multinationals to business tycoons: Media ownership and journalistic autonomy in central and Eastern Europe. *The International Journal of Press/Politics, 17*(4), 433–456. https://doi.org/10.1177/1940161212452449
Stokes, D. E. (1963). Spatial models of party competition. *American Political Science Review, 57*(2), 368–377. https://doi.org/10.2307/1952828
Strömbäck, J., & Esser, F. (2009). *Shaping politics: Mediatization and media interventionism.* https://doi.org/10.5167/UZH-29325.
Suphachalasai, S. (2005). Bureaucratic Corruption and Mass Media. *SSRN Electronic Journal.* https://doi.org/10.2139/ssrn.722403.
Thompson, J. B. (2000). *Political scandal: Power and visibility in the media age*. Polity Press; Blackwell.
Transparency International. (2009). *Plain Language Guide*. https://www.transparency.org/en/publications/the-anti-corruption-plain-language-guide. Accessed March 30.
Transparency International. (2019). *Corruption perception index*. https://images.transparencycdn.org/images/2019_CPI_Report_EN.pdf. Accessed March 30.
Treisman, D. (2000). The causes of corruption: A cross-national study. *Journal of Public Economics, 76*(3), 399–457.
Trilling, D., Tolochko, P., & Burscher, B. (2017). From Newsworthiness to Shareworthiness: How to predict news sharing based on article characteristics. *Journalism & Mass Communication Quarterly, 94*(1), 38–60. https://doi.org/10.1177/1077699016654682
Vaidya, S. (2005). Corruption in the media's gaze. *European Journal of Political Economy, 21*(3), 667–687. https://doi.org/10.1016/j.ejpoleco.2005.03.001
van Schoor, B. (2017). *Fighting corruption collectively: How successful are sector-specific coordinated governance initiatives in curbing corruption?* Wiesbaden: Springer Fachmedien Wiesbaden: Imprint: Springer VS. https://doi.org/10.1007/978-3-658-17838-3.
Vannucci, A. (2012). *Atlante della Corruzione*. Gruppo Abele.
Vannucci, A. (2020). Systemic corruption and disorganized anticorruption in Italy: Governance, politicization, and electoral accountability. *Civitas – Revista de Ciências Sociais, 20*(3), 408–424. https://doi.org/10.15448/1984-7289.2020.3.37877

Varriaich, A. (2014). *"Corruption. An Umbrella Concept"*. Working paper 04. The quality of government institute. University of Gothenburg.

Vitell, S. J., Nwachukwu, S. L., & Barnes, J. H. (2013). The effects of culture on ethical decision-making: An application of Hofstede's typology. In A. C. Michalos & D. C. Poff (Eds.), *Citation classics from the journal of business ethics* (pp. 119–129). Springer Netherlands. https://doi.org/10.1007/978-94-007-4126-3_6

Wan Ifra. (2019). *Report: World Press Trends 2019*. https://wan-ifra.org/insight/report-world-press-trends-2019/. Accessed March 30.

Zielonka, J. (Ed.). (2015). *Media and politics in new democracies: Europe in a comparative perspective* (1st ed.). Oxford University Press.

Chapter 4
Measuring Corruption

Michela Gnaldi, Simone Del Sarto, Matteo Falcone, and Matteo Troìa

4.1 Knowing and Measuring Corruption

Corruption is one of the most challenging threats facing contemporary societies globally and yet there is still a rather weak consensus on how best to measure it. Questions such as 'What do we measure exactly when measuring corruption?', 'Do we measure the frequency of corrupt events or the risk that corrupt events will occur?', 'What kind of corrupt events are we accounting for?' must be at the core of any measurement effort and need to be carefully addressed if we want to understand whether we are progressing in tackling corruption and in developing effective policies to fight it.

Widespread approaches such as the Transparency International's Corruption Perception Index (CPI) or the Control of Corruption Index in the World Bank Governance Indicators provide some insights, but also suffer from several methodological limitations. There have been various attempts to find more 'objective' measurements, including conviction rates (Galli et al., 2012), experience-based surveys such as Transparency International's Global Corruption Barometer (GCB); context analyses (e.g. newspapers); press reports; experimental approaches and proxy approaches, e.g. Golden and Picci (2005) and Olken (2007), which look at

M. Gnaldi (✉) · M. Falcone
Department of Political Science, University of Perugia, Perugia, Italy
e-mail: michela.gnaldi@unipg.it; matteo.falcone@unipg.it

S. Del Sarto
Department of Statistics, Computer Science, Applications "G. Parenti", University of Florence, Florence, Italy
e-mail: simone.delsarto@unifi.it

M. Troìa
Capgemini – Insights & Data, Bologna, Italy
e-mail: matteo.troia@capgemini.com

the difference between physical quantities of public infrastructure delivered and the price paid by the government. In addition, there are private sector surveys, focusing mainly on corporate corruption behavior; mixed-method designs, combining indicators and statistical measures with qualitative and local measures; risk and preventive measures of corruption, focused on an *ex-ante* strategy to prevent corruption beyond the central core of punishable criminal conducts (Carloni, 2017a).

Overall, the international literature has proposed a wide range of measurement instruments, particularly over the last two decades. Latest developments, together with past efforts to measure corruption, highlight that the field of corruption measurement is highly diverse, with some measurement instruments best suited to measure specific objects and address particular research and policy issues.

Following the key general issues in the measurement of corruption highlighted above, this chapter aims at a closer examination of the following aspects: Which indicators are in place to assess corruption and anti-corruption policy success? What are the potentials, limits and degrees of validity of existing measures? Which new generation of corruption indicators is empowered by data availability in a machine readable format and the development of new data analytics technologies? Which future prospects and developments would enhance our capability to measure corruption?

4.2   An Overview of 'Classical' Measures and Indicators of Corruption

Traditionally, corruption is measured through (i) perception-based—or subjective—indicators of corruption, (ii) 'objective' indicators of corruption, and (iii) judiciary measures of corruption. Perception-based measures are founded on the subjective perception of corruption provided by experts and are generally expressed at a country-level. The two most widely known perception-based measures are the World Bank's Control of Corruption (Kaufmann et al., 2010) and the Transparency International's Corruption Perceptions Index—CPI (Transparency International, 2020). The latest is a composite index of corruption perception expressed by experts and managers of the private sector. The CPI uses 13 external databases produced by the World Bank, the World Economic Forum, private companies, and Think Tanks. These data, originally expressed in different measurement scales, are subsequently standardized and expressed on a percentage scale from 0 to 100. The averaged values of the transformed indicators are then taken to represent each country average corruption level and for interactional comparisons, through rankings, show the relative position occupied by a country with respect to the others.

Despite their widespread use in comparative studies, corruption measures based on perceptions are questioned. Critics point out that perception-based measures are prone to bias and serve as imperfect proxies for actual levels of corruption, because perceptions may not be related to actual experiences of corruption (Rose & Peiffer, 2012), and can be driven by the general sentiment reflecting prior economic growth

(Kurtz & Schrank, 2007) or media coverage of important cases of corruption (Golden & Picci, 2005; Mancini et al., 2017). What is more, rankings of countries based on corruption perception are obtained through composite indicators and are liable to their typical limits, that is: (i) the judgments made during the process of construction of a composite measure are sources of uncertainty in the measurement process, so that, for instance, choosing to adopt a certain criterion for aggregating simple indices (summative or multiplicative) or a certain weighting system (subjective or objective) will impact the final ranking position of individual units (Saisana et al., 2005; Munda et al., 2009); (ii) through the aggregation of many simple indices, each reflecting the perceived corruption in a specific aspect/context, the final synthetic indicator appears limiting in the range of questions that can be asked, providing limited support for policy actions.

In an attempt to overcome the limitations of perception-based indicators of corruption, surveys or questionnaires that include questions assessing the direct involvement of individuals and firms in corrupt practices in well-defined instances (i.e., when obtaining a water contract or an electricity connection) have been proposed. The World Bank Enterprise Surveys (WBES) and the Business Enterprise Economic Surveys (BEES) are examples of such latest measures collecting the most widely used firm-level survey data on corruption. These measures provide information on the distribution of corruption across various activity sectors. They allow us to identify the distributional costs of corruption, in this way overcoming some limitations of perception-based indicators. Despite important steps forward, such measures show drawbacks as well. A major challenge is the extent to which a respondent may purposefully misreport corruption events. Fear or shame of exposure can lead respondents to under-report corruption, while a strategic concern with influencing action on a particular corrupt practice can lead to over-report instances of corruption.

Judiciary measures are further measures gauging corruption through judicial deeds, such as judgments, sentences and convictions for corrupt crimes. Despite showing fewer statistical criticalities compared to the previous measures, judiciary measures show a number of drawbacks linked primarily to their (i) limited usability in cross-country studies, because different countries adopt different judicial systems; (ii) partial utility for preventing corruption, as a conviction for corruption crimes may occur many years after the corrupt event took place; (iii) misleading information potential as, for instance, an increase in the number of convictions for corruption might depend on an increased level of efficacy of the underlying judicial system, rather than on an increased level of corruption.

Statistical inference and market measures are further methods estimating corruption through *proxies,* that is, variables considered expressions of behaviors or situations close to corruption, and then approximating corruption. Some of these measures rely on a comparison between real data and a theoretical statistical (or economic/econometric) model hypothesizing the non-corrupted behavior. Purposely, they estimate the incidence of corruption in specific contexts or sectors, by verifying to what extent the real observed data deviate from the hypothesis of absence of corruption (i.e., what should be observed in the absence of corruption, under a specific theoretical model). Proxy measures allow users to estimate the incidence of corrupt practices in specific contexts or sectors, to understand the micro-dynamics of corruption, and to study the economic impact of corruption. On the other hand, they are indirect measures of corruption. Their main limitation lies in where they might not express corruption itself but other forms of inefficiency (Sequeira, 2012). In this sense, a high deviation of observed data from the hypothesized condition of absence of corruption might be a signal of inefficiency, rather than corruption.

Further contiguous measures use 'red flag' indicators as proxy measures for corruption. They originate from a common ground, which acknowledges that corruption control has both a repressive and a preventative dimension. While repression intervenes after the commitment of a corrupt event to punish it, prevention aims at detecting and removing the opportunities for corruption. In other terms, corruption prevention seeks to identify potential weaknesses—i.e., in a public organization, its structure, processes and staff—in order to alert red flags capable of uncovering vulnerabilities and opportunities for malpractices, and advise recommendations for their reduction and minimization (Carloni, 2017a; Gallego et al., 2021). The key target of such measures is, then, no longer quantifying ex-post the "amount of corruption" but rather identifying, in advance, situations at risk of corruption.

Indeed, corruption prevention can be addressed by implementing a wide range of instruments, from administrative anti-corruption national programmes—and their subsequent assessment through surveys and indicators of administrative steps to oppose corruption—to corruption risk analysis. In Sect. 4.3 and 4.4, we will deal, in particular, with these last two groups of measurement instruments focused on preventing corruption, in line with the key theme of the present volume.

4.3 Administrative Anti-corruption Assessment Through Surveys

Administrative anti-corruption national programs aim at developing and implementing deterrence systems of *ex ante* controls of public officials from the commission of corruption crimes (Li, 2014; Carloni, 2017b). In the Italian context, the national legislation adopted a preventive perspective to tackle corruption with law n. 190 of 2012, which introduced two main tools to reduce the risk of corruption in public administrations: (i) a three-year plan for corruption prevention (PTPC), by which each administration is required to assess its own exposure levels to the risk of corruption and indicate the organizational changes to reduce such a risk; (ii) the introduction of a new figure, the supervisor for corruption prevention (RPC) who, among other duties, takes part in a national survey by filling in a report on the degree of accomplishment of national anti-corruption measures by the public administration they represent.

Indicators of administrative fight against corruption are obtained from such latest surveys, and provide information on the capability of administrative offices to effectively oppose the spread of deviant behaviors and corrupted practices in the administration offices they represent, by adopting and executing the preventative measures entrusted by the national legislation (i.e., in terms of staff turnover, transparency requirements, etc.). In Sects. 4.3.1, 4.3.2, 4.3.3, we provide details of these indicators developed in the Italian anti-corruption legislation.

As anticipated earlier in this chapter, the rationale for the development of this group of measures is a broader approach to corruption, where not only repression comes into play but also prevention targets, and for which the monitoring of anti-corruption activities adopted by administrations becomes a condition for assessing the effective adoption of national measures and their effectiveness in preventing corruption.

Despite potentials, indicators of administrative fight against corruption do show some weaknesses. A main limitation, common to all measures based on official government-led corruption audits, is that once officials understand the workings of a system that attempts to consistently detect and measure corruption through systematic audits, they may adapt their behavior and find ways to elude it. Further, the capability to identify situations at risk of corruption largely depends on the truthfulness of claims and, eventually, on the control system of the correspondence between such claims and real circumstances. Besides, as the indicators of administrative fight against corruption are summary indicators based on auto-declarations by officials, they provide information on the capability of the administrative system to effectively adopt preventative measures, rather than on the actual effectiveness of preventative measures themselves. Therefore, they are valid indicators of the degree of compliance and adoption of preventative measures, rather than of the actual effectiveness of anti-corruption measures.

4.3.1   An Indicator of Administrative Fight Against Corruption: An Italian Case Study

In this paragraph we illustrate the case study of Italy, where, as outlined above, the attention is paid to the preventative side of corruption after law 190 of 2012 entered into force. By studying the content of the annual survey questionnaire completed by the supervisor for corruption prevention, we analyze the evolution of the accomplishment of corruption prevention measures within Italian municipalities over the first three years of application of law 190.

4.3.1.1   The Italian Survey Questionnaire

According to law 190 of 2012, each Italian public institution must equip itself with a supervisor for corruption prevention (RPC), to be selected within its staff. Among other tasks, the supervisor has to complete an annual report by means of a predetermined survey form. The survey questionnaire assesses the extent to which the preventative measures—planned within the PTPC—have been accomplished by the administration office the supervisor represents.

The questionnaire at issue is divided in several sections, each devoted to a specific measure for preventing corruption. In the following of this paragraph, a brief description of each part is provided.

Risk Management

Risk assessment is the main phase of the risk management process, related to the documentation and analysis of corruption risks, with the aim of pinpointing intervention priorities and potential corrective and preventive measures (Piano Triennale di Prevenzione della Corruzione, 2017, page 20). The magnitude of interventions to undertake is defined according to a risk assessment process (Carloni, 2017a): in case of high risk of corruption, robust measures must be undertaken as regards organization, transparency, control, and preventative regulation. In addition to these latest mandatory measures, a specific part of the RPC form foresees whether further and specific measures are implemented in order to customize prevention strategies.

Transparency

Administrative transparency is another important part of the questionnaire. Among the strategic purposes to be fulfilled to guarantee transparency, ANAC requests public administrations to effectively implement IT platforms for information flows and on-line data publication (Piano Triennale di Prevenzione della Corruzione, 2017, page 47). The national legislation also reinforces monetary and disciplinary penalties against officials who do not meet transparency duties. Each institution is also required to periodically update the publication of relevant information so as to allow public access to updated information. With this aim, the RPC form asks each public administration to indicate if the flow to feed data publication has been digitized, if the administration has received civic requests to access data, and if the administration has periodically monitored and updated the data publication process on the website.

Staff Training

In a logic of accountability and service towards citizens and stakeholders, the Italian legislation pays much attention to staff training specifically devoted to the prevention of corruption, in order to ensure a wider and conscious involvement of the entire administrative structure in the national anticorruption strategy (Carloni, 2017a). The RPC annual report asks administrations to declare whether training, specifically devoted to the prevention of corruption, has been provided, to whom, and if not, to specify the reasons.

Staff Rotation

The rotation of staff is adopted to avoid allowing officials to occupy the same administrative position, role or function for a long duration with the consequent possible consolidation of privileged liaisons and the expectation for illegal responses based on collusion (Carloni, 2017a). The RPC form sets the question whether staff rotation has been carried out as a prevention measure, in addition to requiring the recording of the number of employees engaged in the administration offices.

Unfitness for Public Positions

According to legislative decree 39 of 2013, unfitness implies the permanent or temporary inability to assign public positions to employees with a criminal conviction and to those who have been in charge of positions both in political and private bodies regulated or financed by public law. To this aim, the RPC supervisor has to declare in the annual report whether checks have been carried out to verify the truthfulness of the declarations made by public officials as regards the absence of unfitness causes.

Incompatibility for Specific Administrative Positions

According to legislative decree 39 of 2013, incompatibility refers to the obligation for officials in charge of a public position to opt, under penalty of loss, between their actual public position and further positions both in political bodies and in private bodies regulated or financed by the public administration conferring the position. With the aforementioned obligation, the Italian national legislation aims at preventing public officials from being subject to improper influences in the exercise of their public duties. A declaration must be completed on the RPC form as to whether adequate measures to verify the existence of the above conditions have been undertaken.

Appointments and Authorization of Assignments

According to legislative decree 165 of 2001, public employees can be appointed to hold positions in public or private bodies only if they are authorized by the administration they belong to. Authorization criteria are established by the administration, to prevent employees from carrying out illegal activities or any other activity determining a conflict of interest while questions devoted to the subject on the RPC form ask (i) whether a procedure has been adopted for assignment authorizations, (ii) if not, clarification of the reasons for not adopting an authorization procedure, (iii) whether the administration has received alerts reporting non-authorized appointments among public employees.

Whistleblowing

Whistleblowing is the legal instrument that offers legal protection for workers who report any form of irregularities, including cases of corruption or bribery. Within the RPC form, questions in the section devoted to whistleblowing ask (i) whether a formal procedure has been adopted for the collection of reports by whistleblowers, (ii) if not, clarification of the reasons for not adopting a whistleblowing procedure, (iii) the means of adoption of the related procedure (i.e., paper or electronic form).

4.3.1.2 Data and Methods

The data analyzed in the present work refer to the RPC responses to specific items of the survey questionnaire, whose sections have been previously introduced. In particular, ten questions are considered, which ask the institution at issue to declare whether specific activities for corruption prevention have been accomplished in the reference year. Table 4.1 summarizes the item content and the questionnaire section they belong to.

Table 4.1 Summary of the ten questions selected for the analyses. For each one, the content is reported (in terms of measures for corruption prevention), along with the section it belongs to

Question content	Section
1. Monitoring of the sustainability of all measures (mandatory and specific) identified in the PTPC	Risk management
2. Fulfilment of specific measures (in addition to mandatory ones)	Risk management
3. "Transparent administration" website section: digitalizing the flaw to fuel data publication	Transparency
4. Monitoring of data publication processes	Transparency
5. Arrangement of staff training, specifically dedicated to prevention of corruption	Staff training
6. Fulfilment of staff rotation procedures	Staff rotation
7. Checking the truthfulness of statements made by parties concerned with unfitness for office causes	Unfitness for public positions
8. Accomplishment of measures to verify the existence of incompatibility conditions	Incompatibility for specific administrative positions
9. Accomplishment of prearranged procedures for issuing permits for assignments fulfilments	Appointments and authorization of assignments
10. Reporting the collection of misconduct by public administration employees	Whistleblowing

Three different responses can be given to the ten selected questions. The affirmative answer labelled as "a" means that the administration accomplished the specific activity in the reference year; response "b" indicates that the administration did not accomplish the activity, even if it was expected by the national PTPC; response "c" indicates that the administration did not accomplish the activity, whose adoption was neither compulsory nor expected by the PTPC.

We use data collected for 111 Italian municipalities over years 2014, 2015 and 2016, that is, the first three years of application of law 190/2012. Municipalities included in the sample are all Italian province municipalities and particular "flagged" municipalities (as stated by ANAC act n.71 of 2013). Survey data for each municipality are collected by downloading them from the municipality institutional website, where data must be made available in the "Transparent administration" section.

Considering the response pattern of the sampled municipalities in the three-year period (2014–2016), we study the evolution over time of the accomplishment of corruption prevention measures by means of a Composite Indicator for Corruption Prevention (CICP; Gnaldi & Del Sarto, 2019), obtained as follows:

$$CICP_{it} = \sum_{j=1}^{10} w_{ijt},$$

where $CICP_{it}$ is the Composite Indicator for Corruption Prevention of municipality i in year t, $i = 1,\ldots,111$ and $t = 2014, 2015, 2016$. As can be noticed, this composite indicator is the sum of weights w_{ijt}, defined as follows:

- $w_{ijt} = 1$ if the response of municipality i to question j ($j = 1,\ldots,10$) in year t is equal to "a" (affirmative answer);
- $w_{ijt} = 0$ if the response of municipality i to question j in year t is equal to "c" (negative answer but the activity was not envisaged by the PTPC), or missing;
- $w_{ijt} = -1$ if the response of municipality i to question j in year t is equal to "b" (negative answer but the adoption of the activity was required by the PTPC).

As such, this composite indicator ranges from -10 to 10: the higher the indicator, the greater the level of accomplishment of corruption prevention measures. A CICP equal to 10 implies that the administration at issue has accomplished all the ten selected measures for corruption prevention. On the other hand, if the administration has fulfilled none of the activities, even if they were envisaged by the PTPC, it gets a CICP score equal to -10.

4.3.1.3 Evolution Over Time of Corruption Prevention Accomplishment

Response patterns are summarized in Table 4.2, where the frequencies of each response category are reported for each year. In 2014 (when law 190 entered into force), a small proportion of municipalities fulfilled controls on unfitness and incompatibility for specific positions (questions 7 and 8 of the questionnaire,

Table 4.2 Response patterns (%) in the considered period for each item of the questionnaire

	2014				2015				2016			
Question	a	b	c	NA	a	b	c	NA	a	b	c	NA
1	77.5	6.3	14.4	1.8	75.7	2.7	20.7	0.9	83.8	3.6	11.7	0.9
2	58.6	0.9	38.7	1.8	68.5	4.5	27.0	0.0	69.4	5.4	23.4	1.8
3	60.4	1.8	36.0	1.8	65.8	8.1	23.4	2.7	70.3	5.4	18.9	5.4
4	83.8	1.8	10.8	3.6	87.4	4.5	6.3	1.8	90.1	0.9	6.3	2.7
5	88.3	9.9	0.9	0.9	91.0	5.4	3.6	0.0	89.2	7.2	2.7	0.9
6	42.3	13.5	40.5	3.6	42.3	16.2	38.7	2.7	48.6	9.0	37.8	4.5
7	19.8	6.3	65.8	8.1	39.6	17.1	42.3	0.9	52.3	9.0	35.1	3.6
8	23.4	8.1	62.2	6.3	39.6	15.3	39.6	5.4	52.3	6.3	35.1	6.3
9	82.9	2.7	12.6	1.8	87.4	2.7	9.9	0.0	86.5	2.7	10.8	0.0
10	55.9	10.8	32.4	0.9	75.7	10.8	12.6	0.9	78.4	12.6	7.2	1.8

Response categories: "a" = affirmative answer; "b" = negative answer, but activity envisaged by the PTPC; "c" — negative answer, as activity not envisaged by the PTPC; NA = missing

showing affirmative response proportions equal to 19.8% and 23.4%, respectively). Furthermore, in this year, most of the municipalities (more than three out of four) accomplished corruption prevention measures envisaged by questions 1, 4, 5 and 9—related to the monitoring of measure sustainability and data publication processes, to employees' training and to procedures for issuing permits for performance assignments. Moreover, by looking at the affirmative response patterns over the years, a clear increasing trend can be noticed for all the questions, meaning that the degree of accomplishment of corruption prevention measures has increased over the considered time period.

Finally, it can be observed that the response proportions in category "c" are higher than those in "b". This implies that fulfilment of corruption prevention measures slackens when the national legislation (the PTPC) does not impose the adoption of such measures. A unique exception can be noticed as regards the training of employees (question 5), for which observed proportions of response in "b" are higher than those in "c", over the three years. Moreover, responses in category "c" are the lowest over the entire questionnaire (0.9% in 2014, 3.6% in 2015 and 2.7% in 2016). This has a two-fold meaning: on the one hand, training courses focused on corruption prevention is a measure largely met by most sampled municipalities; on the other hand, when this measure is not compulsory envisaged by the PTPC, clear non-virtuous behavior arises, as only a very small proportion of administrations did not accomplish the measure.

The CICP is computed for each year and for each administration, by considering the weighting system introduced in Sect. 4.3.1.2. The CICP distribution in each year is summarized in Table 4.3 and Fig. 4.1. A clear shift of the indicator distribution towards higher values may be noticed, as the CICP mean and the distribution quartile constantly increase over the three years. As high values of the indicator imply high implementation of corruption prevention measures, this shift may be considered as a summary evidence of the tendency, within Italian municipalities, to intensify their

Table 4.3 Descriptive statistics of CICP for each year

Year	Min	1Q	Median	Mean	3Q	Max	Std. dev.	CV[b]
2014	−1.0	3.0	5.0	5.3	7.0	10.0	2.5	29.6
2015	−7.0	4.5	6.0	5.9	8.0	10.0	2.9	36.7
2016	−3.0	5.0	7.0	6.6	9.0	10.0	2.9	39.1

1Q: first quartile; 3Q: third quartile; Std. dev.: standard deviation; CV[b]: coefficient of variation for bounded scale, computed as the standard deviation divided by the square root of (mean—min)(max—mean)

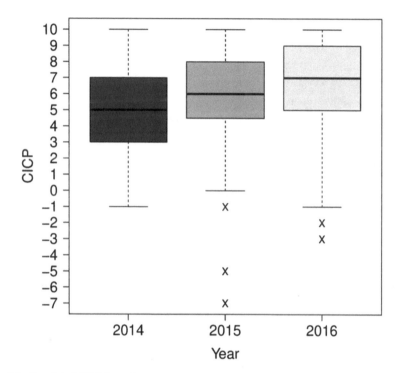

Fig. 4.1 Boxplot of CICP in each year

level of accomplishment of corruption prevention activities (noticed also earlier by looking at the response patterns in Table 4.2).

This trend is also evident in Fig. 4.1, where the shift of the boxes towards greater CICP values over the three years can be clearly observed. However, while no "extreme" behavior can be noticed in 2014, some "atypical" conducts occurred in 2015 and 2016 (i.e., outliers), as indicated by the "X" symbols in the related boxplots of Fig. 4.1. Specifically, CICP extreme values can be found in the bottom of the distribution (negative values), hence they consist in extremely non-virtuous behaviors. Therefore, despite a general improvement over time, in terms of accomplishment of corruption prevention measures, a number of non-virtuous conducts can be spotted. The presence of outliers in the distribution leads to an increase of the

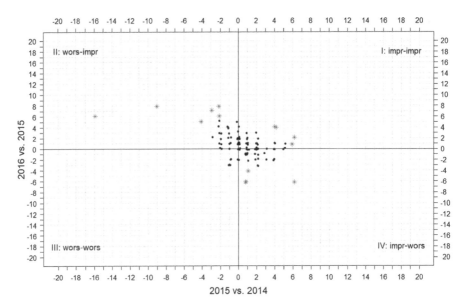

Fig. 4.2 Scatterplot of CICP absolute differences: each point represents a municipality, characterized by a CICP variation occurred in 2015 with respect to 2014 (x-coordinate) and in 2016 with respect to 2015 (y-coordinate). Asterisks represent administrations with extreme behaviors

indicator variability (see CV^b in Table 4.3) in 2015 and 2016. In this regard, since the possible values of CICP are bounded from -10 to 10, in order to properly measure its variability, a modified version of the well-known coefficient of variation (CV) is considered. Unlike dividing the indicator standard deviation by its mean (as usually performed), a different denominator is used, as follows (Burdon, 2008):

$$CV^b = \frac{std.dev.}{\sqrt{(mean - min)(max - min)}}.$$

In order to further evaluate the evolution over time in the fulfilment of anti-corruption measures, municipalities' behavior is inspected by considering the CICP absolute variations over time, that is, in the 2015 with respect to 2014 and in the 2016 with respect to 2015. The sign of the variation reveals a worsening or an improvement, with respect to the previous year, in terms of fulfilment of corruption prevention measures. As an example, let us imagine that a municipality reports a CICP equal to 6, 4 and 8 in 2014, 2015 and 2016, respectively. The changes in the indicator are therefore equal to -2 (in 2015 with respect to 2014) and $+4$ (in 2016 vs. 2015). As a consequence, each municipality can then be represented by a pair of absolute variations. By drawing these pairs of absolute variations in a Cartesian plan, we obtain the scatterplot depicted in Fig. 4.2, where each point represents a municipality, characterized by an absolute variation in the CICP in 2015 with respect to 2014 (on the x-axis) and in 2016 with respect to 2015 (y-axis).

In so doing, the plan is split into four quadrants, identified with different labels. Quadrant I (top-right) is characterized by points (i.e., municipalities) with positive value coordinates: these are municipalities showing constant increases in their CICP over years. Besides, the greater the distance from the origin of axes, the greater the absolute variation in the CICP, and the greater the improvement in the fulfilment of corruption prevention measures. On the other hand, quadrant III (bottom-left) includes municipalities with negative value coordinates, hence exhibiting constant decreases in the CICP over the two periods within the three years. Finally, quadrants II and IV collect municipalities with varied behaviors (CICP increase in 2015 vs. 2014 and decrease in 2016 vs. 2015, or vice versa).

Figure 4.2 is very useful for catching extreme behaviors, which can be identified in terms of wide distance (horizontal, vertical and/or both) from the origin of the axes. For example, grey points depicted with an asterisk in quadrant I (top-right) identify those municipalities that have achieved a constant and particularly large increase in the CICP in the triennium, whereas grey asterisks in quadrant IV (bottom-right) represent administrations with a consistent increase in the CICP in the first period (2015 vs. 2014) and a consistent decrease in the second period (2016 vs. 2015). The same also applies for the other quadrants. Finally, this representation sheds light on two highly extreme situations, that is, those located far from the origin in quadrant II. In fact, these two municipalities exhibited the highest negative differences in the CICP in the first period (hence large decreases in terms of accomplishment of corruption prevention measures in 2015 vs. 2014), while the opposite occurred in the second period (2016 vs. 2015), in which these two administrations achieved a significant improvement in the CICP.

Overall, the study above provides detailed information on the capability of the administrative system to effectively adopt the preventative measures, the trend over time, and the existence of extreme cases, in terms of both best practices on one side and worst behaviors on the other. However, given the type and nature of the survey at issue, the study does not provide insights on the actual effectiveness of the preventative measures themselves. A more comprehensive objective would involve the study of the effectiveness, or quality, of preventative measures, which in turn would imply the cross-referencing of a large amount of data from different sources. The precondition for the development of effectiveness indicators in the field of preventing administrative corruption is, then, being able to rely on data held by different administrations, primarily with respect to the adopted decisions and the occurrence of administrative, financial, and disciplinary events experimented by the administration offices themselves. Regrettably, this need crashes against the lack of an overall data-driven culture targeted at having datasets from different administrative sources matched together in a coherent system of communicating national databases.

4.4   Corruption Risk Assessment Through Red Flags

The greatest and most direct potential for use and development for the purposes of constructing corruption red flag indicators is provided by public procurement databases, where a number of practical occurrences—i.e., delay or failure to award a contract, excessive use of emergency procedures or contract extensions, recurrence of small assignments with the same object etc.—can signal potentially risky circumstances to monitor.

To systematize the literature on corruption risk in public procurement, and related proposed indicators, Fazekas and colleagues (Fazekas et al., 2017) have recently proposed a classification of red flag indicators into four blocks:

- *Tendering Risk Indicators* (TRI), reporting risks of corrupt manipulation in the process of publication of a tender for the purpose of generating profits by distributing them among related companies.
- *Political Connections Indicators* (PCI), providing an indication of the direct/indirect political connections between the contracting authority and the private companies, which can influence the public procurement process through corrupt agreements.
- *Supplier Risk Indicators* (SRI), signaling the instrumental use of tender winning companies, as means to ensure the illegal distribution of profits and advantages necessary to reward all the actors involved in the illegal agreement.
- *Contracting Body Risk Indicators* (CBRI), measuring the weaknesses of the formal contracting bodies, that is, those public structures conceived to defend and preserve companies from undue pressures aimed at favoring particular bidders.

Papers proposing indicators belonging to the *Tendering Risk Indicators* group largely focus on the proposal of one or two indices. For instance, Olken (2007) calculates the amount and value of missing inputs to indicate corruption during contract implementation. Golden and Picci (2005) use the difference between the stock of infrastructure and cumulative public spending on it to assess the amount of missing procurement outputs in infrastructure. Auriol et al. (2011) propose using exceptional procedure types as red flags, while Coviello and Gagliarducci (2010) employ the recurrence of awarding contracts to the same firms. In the study of Fazekas and colleagues (Fazekas et al., 2016), the Authors build a composite indicator of corruption risk in public procurement using as single red flag indicators (i) single bidding, (ii) same firm awarded contracts recurrently, and (iii) short advertisement period for the contract.

The literature on *Political Connections Indicators* concentrates mostly on personal political connections and political influence established through political party donations. Most studies in this group look at individual countries with only partially comparable research questions (Fazekas et al., 2017). For example, Amore and Bennedsen (2013) show that in Denmark, one of the least corrupt countries of the world, direct family ties between companies and politicians increase company profitability, particularly in sectors dependent on public demand, such as public procurement. In general, evidence of direct ties is hard to obtain, and studies classified in this second group provide indirect evidence for the corrupt use of particularistic relationships, by showing the varieties of political connections and the effects they can have on public procurement award.

Supplier risk indicators can be described by referring to four groups, following main data types and corruption techniques (Fazekas et al., 2016), that is, company registry attributes, company financial information, company ownership and management data, and company governance information.

Company registry information captures characteristics of suppliers—such as headquarters location, incorporation date, or size—which do not signal direct involvement in corrupt exchanges, but rather may suggest anomalous features compared to known clean businesses. Location can raise red flags mainly because it can be used to increase the cost of possible investigations. Both close proximity and unusual distance between the procuring body and the winning firm can signal corruption. Distant companies located in corrupt areas and winning small scale contracts are indicated as possible signals of corruption in the work of Caneppele et al. (2009). Differently, Coviello and Gagliarducci (2010) finds that, where there is long term political stability, local companies tend to win public contracts with a high probability. Caneppele et al. (2009) also show that multiple companies registered at the same address can point to corruption as they often hide suspicious connections between the companies themselves. Incorporation date can also indicate corruption, especially when it is combined with additional information. Fazekas et al. (2015) show that companies established around a government change, or right before, and winning large contracts are likely to be used as vehicles for rent extraction, rather than genuine business activities, especially if they are unusually successful. Furthermore, Zindex (2016) consider a company abrupt dissolution right after contract completion as a corruption red flag, because this circumstance may mirror an instrumental use of companies, used primarily for winning contracts and extracting rents from them. In general, the use of these last indicators to signal corruption must be cautious, given that there are many cases of non-corrupt companies having an address in corrupt regions or having a common address (when they have a common ownership). Purposely, to reliably estimate corruption, the most recent literature (Fazekas et al., 2015) suggests making a combined use of such indicators with other corruption risk indicators, especially those related to political cycles.

Papers dealing with company financial information show (Cheung et al., 2012; Dávid-Barrett & Fazekas, 2016; Cingano & Pinotti, 2013), in a rather consolidated way, that the indicators based on the growth of revenues/profits of companies awarded public contracts are widely associated with corruption risks, especially when this growth takes on exceptional connotations. At the same time, the literature also suggests validating these indicators through the joint use with other proxies, to minimize false positives, that is, the case of companies for which an exceptional increase in profits due to genuine high levels of efficiency and growth are observed.

The literature focused on company ownership and management structures show that missing or hidden ownership can point at corruption. Van der Does de Willebois et al. (2011), for example, shows that grand corruption is often associated with unknown owners, who are kept hidden in at least two ways: either through the use of "opaque" jurisdictions to register the company (such as tax havens) or simply by failing to correctly register the company owners. A further way to keep proprietary information hidden is by using complex proprietary structures, such as "Chinese box" structures (Riccardi & Savona, 2013). In addition to missing data on company ownership structures, other elements considered as red flags in the literature are the changes in the corporate structure of the company, especially when these changes are associated with increases in the company profits, as claimed by Caneppele et al. (2009). A further risk factor is the socio-economic profile of company owners. Studies in the literature (Caneppele et al., 2009; Riccardi et al., 2016) show that the owners of companies in the same sector tend to share similar socio-economic profiles, in terms of age, gender and educational level. Therefore, any deviation from the "typical" profile of a company owner in a specific sector can be used as a red flag.

The corporate governance literature focuses on the way responsibility and discretion are allocated within a company and their connections with company performances. Regrettably, only very few studies focus on the relationships between corporate governance and corruption, but the works of Wu (2005). Starting from the intuition that external supervision and monitoring can decrease corruption risks, the latest paper finds that bribing propensity is higher in companies governed by individual owners or families, with respect to companies governed by boards.

The literature on *Contracting Body Risk Indicators* (CBRI) aims at capturing corruption risks at the organizational or agency-level and focuses on some organizational features relating to corruption risks, such as organizational capacity, influence, integrity, transparency and accountability. In this direction, the survey of the Public Expenditure Financial Accountability programme PEFA (2016) proposes an indicator on the independence of the Supreme Audit Institution (SAI). The Sustainable Governance Indicators (SGI) measure the quality of accountability of the Auditor General through an expert survey. The Tax Administration Diagnostic Assessment Tool measures corruption risk assessment, as a combination of some sub-dimensions, like internal audit mechanisms, staff integrity, external oversight. The Global Integrity Report survey captures corruption-related aspects of various unique agency types in the format of expert assessments.

4.5   Toward Latest Corruption Measures: The Big Data and Computational Data Revolution

Over recent years, corruption risk assessment has been increasingly empowered by both data availability in a machine-readable format and the development of new technologies based on the collection and cross-processing of public procurement data with other data sources of public administrations. The potentials of new technologies in the fight against corruption is demonstrated by the 2018 Pannonia

Declaration adopted by the European Partners against Corruption (EPAC)—a discussion forum composed of the Anti-Corruption Authorities and police monitoring bodies of the Council of Europe member countries—and the European Contact-point Network against Corruption (EACN), made up of the Anti-Corruption Authorities of the EU Member States. With this declaration, involved bodies decided to make structural the mutual comparison on the use and implementation of big data analytics and artificial intelligence in European and national anti-corruption policies, confirming the continuation of the work of the working group on Analysis of Big Data, Related Legal Aspects, Use of Databases, coordinated by the Lithuanian Special Investigation Service (STT) and the Romanian National Anti-Corruption Directorate (DNA), created in 2017.

With 'new technologies', we refer to all those technologies, which in recent years have characterized the computational data revolution, i.e., the set of changes that the exponential growth of data availability and the increase in the computational capacity of information and communication technologies are bringing to the economy and society. Consider the case of technologies such as the internet of things, big data analytics, or artificial intelligence systems.

IT tools have revolutionized the management of data, their collection, storage and processing. They allow users to collect a great deal of data in real time, much more than in the past (such as the internet of things); to process data in a massive way, even by crossing different databases, with unprecedented computing power (such as big data analytics tools). These technologies, in particular artificial intelligence systems, also facilitate choice options during a decision-making process—which would traditionally require excessive data processing effort for humans—and, in conclusion, delegate complex decisions, which are taken directly and autonomously by algorithms contained in computer programmes (as in machine learning and deep learning systems) (Council of Europe, 2020; Algorithm Watch, 2020).

In addition to these features, which alone have changed the technological landscape in recent years, the cognitive results that some of these technologies produce are particularly innovative. Big data analytics, for example, is capable of correlating very different variables with each other, bringing to light original links and correlations, which had hitherto remained hidden and undiscovered. Big data analytics can predict probabilistically the future evolution of the phenomena under analysis, thanks to the huge amount of data it can process. These characteristics allowed scholars, institutions and policymakers to build a solid knowledge base on corruption, to measure and quantify it better, to provide new interpretations of the corruptive phenomenon, and to concretely improve control activities directing administrative corruption prevention policies in a more conscious manner.

4.6   The Latest Generation of Corruption Measures

Thanks to the use of far more data than in the past, the increased computational capacity of algorithms and the emergence of new data mining tools in recent years, a new generation of indicators has been developed, which is considered more accurate and effective than previous ones (Mungiu-Pippidi, 2016).

One of such measures is the Corruption Risk Index (CRI), constructed by scholars of the Corruption Research Center in Budapest. The CRI is a composite index based on the collection and cross-processing of public procurement data with other data of public administrations, or in any case made public by law, concerning the economic operators involved in tendering procedures. The elementary risk indices that make up the CRI, by cross-referencing a large amount of data, attempt to signal anomalies in individual tender procedures, political connections between party representatives and economic operators, anomalies in the economic character-istics of the companies involved and, also, regulatory, organizational and procedural weaknesses in public tenders and, in general, in the administrations concerned. In the case of missing data or in the case of difficulty in finding certain categories of data, the Hungarian scholars also used a text mining process to find the missing data. In the construction of this index, therefore, big data analytics was used not only to improve the amount of data used and its processing, but was also decisive in finding data that was not possessed, improving the quality and accuracy of the available data and the risk index (Fazekas et al., 2018).

Another interesting instance is the Opentender.eu platform, launched in January 2018 by Digiwhist, a European Union project bringing together six European research institutes. The platform aims to facilitate a generalized societal scrutiny of public corruption through the systematic collection, structuring, analysis and wide dissemination of information on 17.5 million public procurements executed within the European Union since 2003. The platform contains a filter function to assess the integrity of bids, i.e., it is able to identify the bids with relatively high corruption risks. This filter is actually a composite index, resulting from the average of seven elementary risk indicators. The index is constructed through the computational work of an algorithm that systematically scans websites containing open data on public procurements (such as the European Union's Tenders Electronic Daily, for exam-ple), downloads and stores the data contained therein and, then, combines it with data from other datasets useful for reconstructing the history, economic position, political connections of the top management of the companies that win the contracts (https://opentender.eu/start).

A further example in this field is the Transparency International Ukraine's new public procurements monitoring system called Dozorro, which attempts to improve the risk assessment system of Ukrainian public institutions, called Prozorro. This tool is based on a software using a machine learning algorithm to improve the detection of violations in public tendering procedures. The machine learning system was trained by the developers themselves through a learning process that involved sending about 3500 tender bids to 20 experts, contextually sending a question ("Do you see any risks in these procedures?") and then entering the answers into the AI algorithm. Based on the learning process, the system assesses the probability of corruption risks in tenders and shares the results to civil society organizations in the Dozorro community. To assess the reliability of risk analyses, a continuous learning process is set: if the system risk analyses are supported by experts' positive feedbacks, the software remembers the agreement between system results and experts' positive viewpoints; otherwise, the system ignores the choice made. According to the developers, thanks to the system, mainly among the most expensive bids (and most attractive for corrupt phenomena), 26% more bids without the requirements, 37% more bids unfairly excluded from the tender, 298% more bids with the presence of an agreement between the participants than in the traditional risk analysis Prozorro were identified (https://ti-ukraine.org/en/news/dozorro-artificial-intelli gence-to-find-violations-in-prozorro-how-it-works/).

One of the greatest potentials of big data analytics and artificial intelligence systems lies in their ability to probabilistically predict and estimate the trend of the economic and social phenomena they analyze. This is an aspect recently emerging also with regard to corruption prevention, even if still on an experimental basis. In Spain, for example, a group of researchers developed a warning system based on neural networks, especially on self-organizing maps, with the aim of estimating the probability of cases of public corruption occurring in a given territory, by analyzing the presence or absence of certain economic factors (property taxation, economic growth, property prices, the number of depository institutions and non-financial companies) and political factors (the permanence in power of the same political party for long durations) over a three-year period. For the construction of the model, data from actual cases of corruption reported in the media (or that ended up in court) between 2000 and 2012 in the Spanish provinces were used. The study provided short, medium and long term predictive scenarios of corruption over three years, depending on the variation of the economic or political factors mentioned earlier (López-Iturriaga & Sanz, 2017).

By cross referring to large datasets and integrating them with each other, the Spanish proposal shows how new technologies can contribute to widen the analysis spectrum, which is no longer focused on a quantification of corruption, but also on an estimate of its evolution over time, allowing public institutions to prepare effective counter-strategies in time.

The potentials of big data analytics and artificial intelligence systems are not only exploited at the academic level on an experimental basis, but are starting to be integrated in public institutions as well. Recently, the OECD reported that many national control authorities have started to make concrete use of new technologies to target and make more efficient their control activities in order to combat and prevent corruption. Think of the experience of the Central Procurement Office of the German Federal Ministry of the Interior (Beschaffungsamt des Bundesministeriums des Innern—BMI); the Observatório da Despesa Pública (ODP) of the Ministério da Transparência e Controladoria-Geral da União (CGU) in Brazil; the monitoring activities of the Korea Fair Trade Commission or, even, the experimentation initiated by the OECD with the Grupo Aeroportuario de la Ciudad de México on infrastructure procurements for the construction of the Nuevo Aeropuerto Internacional de México, NAIM (OECD, 2016, 2019).

All such latest experiences demonstrate how big data analytics and artificial intelligence systems can be used to improve corruption risk assessment, particularly in the area of public contracts and public accounting, for both implementing targeted controls of specific interventions and for *ex post* evaluation and predictive estimation of the effectiveness of prevention policies adopted by public institutions (U4 Report 2019).

4.7 Prospects and Future Developments in the Measurement Of Corruption

In this section, we deal with prospects and future developments that would enhance our capability to measure corruption and corruption risk, in such a way that bias in measuring corruption is minimized. Purposely, we stress (i) the need to validate either single red flags (Sect. 4.7.1) and new generation composite indicators of corruption risk (Sect. 4.7.2); (ii) the need to adopt common ontologies to guarantee interoperability of data sources (Sects. 4.7.3 and 4.7.4); (iii) the need to effectively employ and take advantage of measurement tools in control activities and in the planning of administrative corruption prevention policies (Sect. 4.7.5).

4.7.1 Toward Valid Single Indicators of Corruption Risk

Overall, a measure is valid when it measures what it is intended to measure. Since corruption indicators aim at measuring corruption and since corruption cannot be observed and analyzed directly in the data, given its illicitness, corruption indicator validity cannot be straightforwardly 'proved'. As a consequence, the issue of corruption indicator validity is still an open and largely unresolved issue.

In the literature on corruption measurement, the validity of corruption indicators is seldom accounted for, but in very recent studies, most of which deals with corruption risks in public procurement. Among them, Fazekas and colleagues (2018) propose a procedure where single red flag indicators are validated against a criterion chosen on the basis of their definition of institutionalized grand corruption, as "unjustified restriction of access to public contracts to favour a certain bidder to maximise value for money, most importantly through soliciting competing bids". Thus, corruption arises when competition is blocked in order to earn a corruption rent. The most obvious signal of absence of competition for a public contract is when a tender receives only one bid (Amaral et al., 2009). The single bidding (i.e., only one company submitting a bid) is then chosen as the main criterion to assess red flag reliability. Specifically, the validation procedure proposes to consider valid only single red flags which are significant in predicting the single bidding outcome variable. Such a 'significance' is evaluated by relying on the regression coefficients estimated within a logistic regression modeling framework.

While any definition can be questioned and/or extended, the merits of the proposed procedure consist in (i) having anchored it to a reference conceptual framework—that is, to an operational definition of corruption in public procurement, otherwise largely missing in the current international literature—and (ii) being replicable, as the single offer indicator can be easily calculated with data available in most countries.

A further validation procedure is the one proposed by Decarolis and colleagues (Decarolis et al., 2019; Decarolis & Giorgiantonio, 2020). Single red flags are validated with respect to their strength in predicting corruption risk in public procurement as measured by a new variable, derived from police investigations. Specifically, the new variable measures, for each company winning a contract, whether any of its owners or top managers have been subject to a police investigation for corruption-related crimes. The Authors assess the predictive capability of single red flags with respect to this latest corruption risk variable, using common ML Algorithms (i.e., LASSO, ridge regression and random forest).

The strength of this last validation procedure rests on the choice and availability of the variable expressing corruption risk and derived from police investigations. On the other hand, the procedure replicability appears limited, given that the data is non-open and comparable data, outside the present context of study, can be barely obtained.

4.7.2 Toward Robust Composite Indicators of Corruption Risk

Actual international efforts—at both the academic and policy/institutional level—are very valuable and have the great merit of having dealt successfully with (i) the first crucial phase of the procedure of risk measurement and, generally, of a KDD process—i.e., the process of extraction of value from big data through data mining—consisting in the creation and organization of relevant administrative datasets; and (ii) the convergence towards the selection of a set of relevant single red flags of corruption risk. However, few energies have been devoted to developing a robust synthetic/composite indicator of corruption risk in public procurement, as an aggregated measure of single red flags.

Indeed, summarizing information available from a set of single indicators (i.e. red flags) into a single metrics, such as a Composite Indicator (CI) of corruption risk, is a major challenge in the measurement of corruption and corruption risks. Generally, CIs can be useful communication tools for conveying summary information in a relatively simple way. In fact, they are used widely across different sectors in public services as policy analysis and public communication tools. In the context of corruption measurement, CIs of corruption risk would allow us: (i) reliable comparisons of corruption risk at the territorial level (regions, nations, contracting bodies etc.) and per categories (i.e., contracting stations); (ii) consistent appraisals of trends over time, providing insights on the ways past, present and emerging corruption risk schemes relate to current risk drivers.

In the current international literature, a proposal of CI of corruption risk in public procurement is presented in a handful of the studies and reports. Indeed, among them, as previously highlighted within the present chapter, the proposal of Fazekas and colleagues (2016) stands out. In that work, the authors develop a composite score of tendering red flags, called Corruption Risk Index (CRI), as a proxy measure of high-level corruption in public procurement, derived from public procurement data from 28 European countries for 2009–2014. A similar study is carried out by Troìa (2020) with data and red flag indicators developed from the Italian National Dataset of Public Contracts (Banca Dati Nazionale dei Contratti Pubblici). Further, in the Single Market scoreboard Initiative (https://ec.europa.eu/internal_market/scoreboard/performance_per_policy_area/public_procurement/index_en.htm), the single indicators (i.e., red flags) are aggregated by summing them to show how different EU countries are performing on key aspects of public procurement.

From a statistical point of view, the composite indicators of corruption risk developed within the previous works are computed by relying on a rather simple methodological base. In fact, they are obtained as a simple un-weighted arithmetic mean of individual risk indicators. None, at present, advise a validation procedure of the proposed composite indicator of corruption risk in public procurement, reporting a sensitivity analysis of the composite indicator with the aim of verifying its robustness with respect to variations in the choice of individual indicators, systems of normalization, weights and aggregation schemes.

Indeed, in the construction of composite indicators, many methodological issues need to be addressed carefully if the results are not to be misinterpreted and manipulated. It is known (OECD, 2008) that CIs development involves stages where a number of subjective judgements have to be made, from the selection of individual indicators (i.e., red flags) to the choice of normalization methods, weighting schemes, and aggregation models. All the previous are not merely methodological aspects, as they reflect substantial choices. What is more, all these judgements are potential sources of uncertainty of the CI, likely to affect the value of the composite, its robustness and its validity. In other words, it is expected that the choice to include a particular red flag in the CI, or the choice to employ a specific normalization/weighting/aggregation scheme, rather than a different one, have an impact on the value assumed by the composite risk indicator and its robustness. It is envisaged that further research and efforts are needed to strengthen the robustness of CIs of corruption risks, with the aim of validating a replicable and robust statistical procedure within a corruption risk assessment procedure.

4.7.3 The Need for Ontologies

The fight against corruption involves the use of data driven approaches for which ontologies represent necessary and powerful instrumental tools as they allow us to compare data from different sources and to guarantee data interoperability at national and international levels.

In 2001, Tim Berners Lee published a paper that became a milestone for the development of computer science, and especially for the web development in the years to come. In the article "The Semantic Web" (Berners-Lee et al., 2001), Berners Lee together with James Hendler and Ora Lassila envisioned *"a new form of Web content that is meaningful to computers [and that] will unleash a revolution of new possibilities."* Behind the concept of building a "new form of web", there was the idea to make the web able to learn a language for the exclusive use of machines, so that machines themselves could understand the meaning of information: *"most of the Web's content today is designed for humans to read, not for computer programs to manipulate meaningfully. Computers can adeptly parse Web pages for layout and routine processing, here a header, there a link to another page, but in general, computers have no reliable way to process the semantics."*

Giving a semantics to information is nowadays a challenge for those who are involved in knowledge representation. Artificial intelligence (AI), for example, needs formal representations of knowledge. The more this formalization has a semantic nature, the easier it will be for AI to use this semantic nature and to be able to make choices based on the context.

One of the forms of knowledge representation most used in the semantic web is called "ontology". An ontology is a formal and shared representation of a particular domain of interest, closely related to the first-order logic, a set of atomic formulas called predicates, that assert a relationship among certain elements. An ontology can indeed be described as first-order theory, or better, as a set of first-order axioms from which consequences can be inferred. The building of ontologies capable of modeling specific domains feeds the semantic web and helps machines to draw conclusions in the form of new knowledge (an activity usually typical of the human mind).

The issue of ontologies is central also in the field of corruption measurement. An ontology usually divides a portion of knowledge into classes, properties and restrictions, similar to what is done in an entity–relationship model (ER—model) for a database. A subdivision of this type, applied to the world of corruption, helps to organize information, to explain semantic features, and to make the information ready for dialogue with other databases.

The need for a shared ontological standard for public data is guided by two key aims:

- building a common data description language recognized by any public organization;
- guaranteeing the semantic interoperability between different data collections, both national and international.

The importance of semantic interoperability, especially towards databases developed in different linguistic and cultural contexts, is also emphasized by the European Commission (EU). In the *"e-Government Core Vocabularies manual handbook— Using horizontal data standards for promoting interoperability"* (Directorate-General for Informatics European Commission, 2006), the EU highlights how easy it is currently to cross national borders, for personal or business reasons: *"in Europe, citizens and businesses increasingly live, work, and conduct business across borders."* This leads to the consequent need to rely on public services capable to communicate across different countries: *"their increased mobility must be supported by cross-border public services, such as the registration of a foreign branch, obtaining a license to conduct business in another country, or getting a birth certificate."*

It is for these reasons that public administrations across the globe must be able to process information from different sources which share common standards.

4.7.4   OntoPiA: The Collection of Italian Ontologies

OntoPiA is a network of ontologies created by the Digital Italian Agency (AgID), under the stimulus of the work initiated by the Italian Government on the creation of different ontologies for the Italian public administration, with the aim of enhancing its information assets and aligning with European standards.

OntoPiA is a collection of ontologies and controlled vocabularies based on the guidelines indicated in the Three-Year Plan 2017–2019 for ICT in the Public Administration. The document states that *"the first step in the process concerns the identification of key databases to be exploited to meet the needs of the community, making them available in the form of open data (...) through Application Programming Interface (API). These key databases must be described both at the metadata level and at the data level, with clear shared data-models, compliant with others already existing at the European level and on the Web."*

The need to standardize the most important Italian public databases arises from the awareness of the institutions that technological fragmentation, such as the current one, is no longer sustainable. *"Most of the public databases existing today have been designed and built in a distinct way, without the support of a general overview useful to lead actions capable of improving data quality. Over time, the approach described above has produced the fragmentation of the Public Administration information assets into silos: "containers" in which data are often replicated and stored in an inconsistent way."*

OntoPiA aims to reduce this fragmentation by proposing a framework of conceptual models within which it should be possible to describe the most significant databases of the Italian public administration.

OntoPiA is based on four principles:

1. facilitating the development of new information systems, based on an existing basic model;
2. promoting the exchange of data, based on a common language;
3. enabling the integration of data from different sources;
4. standardizing data.

The OntoPiA project is accessible to everyone, as it is uploaded in the GitHub platform, so that anyone can make their contribution, while remaining under the supervision of AgID. The intent is to develop new ontologies capable of accurately describing the Italian information assets in order to take advantage of its full potential.

OntoPiA contains the ontology of public contracts, called "PublicContract". This ontology is made of Resource Description Framework (RDF) triples, which make it compliant with the linked data paradigm (Bizer et al., 2011). RDF triples are formal expressions that codify a statement made of three elements: a subject, a predicate and an object. The data contained in the National Database of Public Contracts (BDNCP) of the Italian Anti-corruption Agency (ANAC) could therefore be modeled by this ontology.

The image below describes a part of the "PublicContract" ontology. The focus is on the "Procedure" class and is represented with its closer nodes. For example, the "Procedure" class (the subject) is related with "Lot" class (the object) through "includesLot" relationship (the predicate) as well as with "ProcurementDocument" class (another object) through "hasProcurementDocument" relationship (another predicate). In this way, each element characterizing a public contract is formalized and becomes meaningful for the machines. The PublicContract Ontology therefore represents a powerful tool to facilitate the understanding and analysis of data on public contracts, because it allows semantic reasoning.

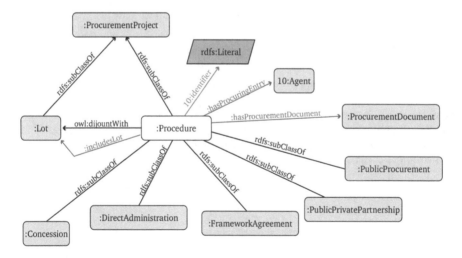

4.7.5 Perspectives and Open Issues of AI Exploitation in European Administrative Systems

The use of big data analytics and artificial intelligence systems as tools for measuring corruption seems to confirm and strengthen two trends that had already emerged with the second-generation indicators. The first trend is to increasingly use administrative data as a source to learn about and try to better quantify the level of corruption in a state. The second trend is to move beyond the measurement of country-specific corruption and try to quantify it with an approach that pays more attention to specific sectors with a higher corruption risk, such as the public procurement sector, or to territorial differences in corruption risk within a state. These two trends pose a number of problems that need to be addressed in order to allow new technologies to express their full potential for the benefit of policy makers and society at large.

Both issues need to be faced mainly within the responsibility of the administrative systems of European countries. The first regards the need to guarantee the availability, obtainability, usability and, in general, the quality of public data. The development of preventative indicators based on big data analytics and artificial intelligence systems, capable of exploiting all the reconstructive and predictive potential of these technologies, is only possible if public databases are open, well organized, complete and up to date. The openness of public data is then the first, basic condition to guarantee a positive cognitive return, useful to the administration system itself.

The second issue concerns the capacity of European administrative systems to effectively employ and take advantage of these tools in control activities and in the planning of administrative corruption prevention policies. Considering that the objective of many European countries, such as Italy, is to move in this direction, the proper organization of public databases is a crucial issue. Equally, it is important to have an administrative organization that is functional to the use of new technologies, i.e., able to understand its own cognitive needs to fight corruption and, consequently, to build new collections of administrative data functional to these needs; able to equip itself with adequate technological tools and professional figures qualified to use them in support of policy-makers' activities.

Lastly, the regulatory issues that are still open at the European level in relation to the use of big data analytics and artificial intelligence systems during administrative activities are not marginal and need to be accounted for. The European General Data Protection Regulation, in particular, does not allow for a full exploitation of these tools, considering the limitation it imposes to massive data processing, especially when involving data of a personal nature, and decisions impacting identifiable subjects.

References

Aarvik, P. (2019). Artificial Intelligence – A promising anti-corruption tool in development settings?. *U4 Report 2019*. Chr. Michelsen Institute. https://www.cmi.no/publications/7146-artificial-intelligence-a-promising-anti-corruption-tool-in-development-settings. Accessed 31 March 2021.

Algorithm Watch. (2020). *Automating Society Report 2020*. https://automatingsociety.algorithmwatch.org/. Accessed 31 March 2021.

Amaral, M., Saussier, S., & Yvrande-Billon, A. (2009). Auction procedures and competition in public services: The case of urban public transport in France and London. *Utilities Policy, 17*, 166–175.

Amore M. D., & Bennedsen M. (2013). The value of local political connections in a low-corruption environment. *Journal of Financial Economics, 110*(2), 387–402.

Auriol, E., Flochel, T., & Straub, S. (2011). Public procurement and rent-seeking: The case of Paraguay. *TSE Working Papers*, 11–224, Toulouse: Toulouse School of Economics (TSE).

Berners-Lee, T., Hendler, J., & Lassila, O. (2001). The semantic web. *Scientific American, 284*(5), 34–43.

Bizer, C., Heath, T., & Berners-Lee, T. (2011). Linked data: The story so far. In T. Heath, M. Hepp, & C. Bizer (Eds.), Semantic services, interoperability and web applications: Emerging concepts (pp. 205–227). IGI global.

Burdon, R. D. (2008). Short note: Coefficients of variation in variables with bounded scales. *Silvae Genetica, 57*(3), 179.

Caneppele, S., Calderoni, F., & Martocchia, S. (2009). Not Only Banks. Criminological models on the infiltration of public contracts by italian organized crime. *Journal of Money Laundering Control, 12*(2), 151–172.

Carloni, E. (2017a). Misurare la corruzione? Indicatori di corruzione e politiche di prevenzione. *Politica del diritto, 3*, 445–466. https://doi.org/10.1437/88492

Carloni, E. (2017b). Italian anti-corruption and transparency policy. In A. Grasse, M. Grimm, & J. Labitzke (Eds.), *Italien zwischen Krise und Aufbruch. Auf dem Weg zur dritten Republik?* Springer Fachmedien.

Cheung, Y.-L., Raghavendra, R., & Stouraitis, A. (2012). *Which firms benefit from bribes, and by how much? Evidence from corruption cases worldwide. 1689–99*. National Bureau of Economic Research Working Paper Series, w17981. https://www.nber.org/system/files/working_papers/w17981/w17981.pdf. Accessed 27 April 2021.

Cingano, F., & Pinotti, P. (2013). Politicians at work: The private returns and social costs of political connections. *Journal of the European Economic Association, 11*(2), 433–465.

Coviello, D., & Gagliarducci, S. (2010). *Building political collusion: Evidence from procurement auctions*. IZA DP No. 4939, Bonn: Institute for the Study of Labor (IZA).

Council of Europe – CAHAI. (2020). *Towards regulation of AI systems*. https://www.coe.int/en/web/artificial-intelligence/-/-toward-regulation-of-ai-systems-. Accessed 31 March 2021.

Dávid-Barrett, E., & Fazekas, M. (2016). *Corrupt contracting: Controlling partisan favouritism in public procurement*. Working Paper series: GTI-WP/2016:02. http://www.govtransparency.eu/wp-content/uploads/2016/06/GTI_WP2016_2_David-Barrett-Fazekas_Elite_Favouritism_in_PP_draft_160801.pdf. Accessed 8 April 2021.

Decarolis, F., & Giorgiantonio, C. (2020). *Corruption red flags in public procurement: New evidence from Italian calls for tenders*. N. 544. Questioni di Economia e Finanza. Banca D'Italia Eurosistema. ISSN 1972–6627 (print); ISSN 1972–6643 (online).

Decarolis, F., Fisman, R., Pinotti, P, & Vannutelli, S. (2019). *Corruption in procurement: New facts from Italian Government Contracting*. NBER Working Paper Series 28209. National Bureau Of Economic Research 1050 Massachusetts Avenue Cambridge, MA. http://www.nber.org/papers/w28209. Accessed 8 April 2021.

Directorate-General for Informatics European Commission. (2006). *E-Government core vocabularies handbook*. https://ec.europa.eu/isa2/library/e-government-core-vocabularies-handbook_en. Accessed 3 April 2021.

Fazekas, M., Cingolani, L., & Tóth, B. (2017). *A comprehensive review of objective corruption proxies in public procurement: Risky actors, transactions, and vehicles of rent extraction.* Government Transparency Institute Working Paper Series No. GTI-WP/2016:03, Budapest.

Fazekas, M., Cingolani, L., & Tóth, B. (2018). Innovations in objectively measuring corruption in public procurement. In H. K. Anheier, M. Haber, & M. A. Kayser (Eds.), *Governance indicators. Approaches, progress, promise* (pp. 154–185). Oxford University Press.

Fazekas, M., Tóth, I. J., & King, L. P. (2016). An objective corruption risk index using public procurement data. *European Journal of Criminal Policy and Research, 22*(3), 369–397.

Fazekas, M., & Kocsis, G. (2015). *Uncovering high-level corruption: Cross-national corruption proxies using government contracting data.* GTI-WP/2015:02, Budapest: Government Transparency Institute.

Fazekas, M., Lukács, P. A., & Tóth, I. J. (2015). The political economy of grand corruption in public procurement in the construction sector of Hungary. In A. Mungiu-Pippidi (Ed.), *Government favouritism in Europe. The Anticorruption Report 3*. Barbara Budrich.

Galli, E., Fiorino, N., & Petrarca, I. (2012). Corruption and growth: Evidence from the Italian regions. *European Journal of Government and Economics, 1*(2), 126–144.

Gallego, J., Rivero, G., & Martínez, J. (2021). Preventing rather than punishing: An early warning model of malfeasance in public procurement. *International Journal of Forecasting, 37*(1), 360–377.

Gnaldi, M., & Del Sarto, S. (2019). Corruption prevention: first evidences from the 2015 RPC survey for Italian municipalities. In A. Bianco, P. Conigliaro, M. Gnaldi (Eds.), *Italian studies on quality of life* (pp. 81–96). Social indicators research series, vol. 77. Cham: Springer.

Golden, M. A., & Picci, L. (2005). Proposal for a New Measure of Corruption, illustrated with data. *Economics and Politics, 17*(1), 37–75.

Kaufmann, D., Mastruzzi, M., Kraay, A., & Mastruzzi, M. (2010). The worldwide governance indicators. Methodology and analytical issues. *Policy Research working paper; no. WPS 5430. World Bank*. Washington, DC.

Li, R. B. L. (2014). *Measures to prevent corruption and to encourage cooperation between all sectors of society*. Work product of the 16th Unafei Uncac training programme. Resource material series n.92, part two. http://www.unafei.or.jp/English/pdf/RS_No92_13VE_Li2.pdf. Accessed April 16, 2021.

López-Iturriaga, F. J., & Sanz, I. P. (2017). Predicting public corruption with neural networks: An analysis of Spanish provinces. *Social Indicators Research*. https://doi.org/10.2139/ssrn.3075828.

Mancini, P., Mazzoni, M., Cornia, A., & Marchetti, R. (2017). Representations of corruption in the British, French, and Italian Press: Audience segmentation and the lack of unanimously shared indignation. *The International Journal of Press/Politics, 22*(1), 67–91. https://doi.org/10.1177/1940161216674652

Munda, G., Nardo, M., Saisana, M., & Srebotnjak, T. (2009). Measuring uncertainties in composite indicators of sustainability. *International Journal of Environmental Technology and Management, 11*, 7–26.

Mungiu-Pippidi, A. (2016). For a new generation of objective indicators in governance and corruption studies. *European Journal on Criminal Policy and Research, 22*, 363–367. https://doi.org/10.1007/s10611-017-9693-3

OECD (2016). *Preventing corruption in public procurement*. http://www.oecd.org/gov/ethics/Corruption-Public-Procurement-Brochure.pdf. Accessed 31 March 2021.

OECD. (2019). *Analytics for integrity. Data-driven approaches for enhancing corruption and fraud risk assessments*. https://www.oecd.org/gov/ethics/analytics-for-integrity.pdf. Accessed 31 March 2021.

OECD. (2008). *Handbook on constructing composite indicators: Methodology and user guide*. Paris: OECD Publishing. https://www.oecd.org/els/soc/handbookonconstructingcompositeindicatorsmethodologyanduserguide.htm Accessed April 16, 2021.

Olken, B. A. (2007). Monitoring corruption: Evidence from a field experiment in Indonesia. *Journal of Political Economy, 115*(2), 200–249.

Public Expenditure Financial Accountability programme PEFA. (2016). https://www.pefa.org. Accessed April 27, 2021.

Piano triennale di prevenzione della corruzione. (2017). http://www.anticorruzione.it/portal/public/classic/AmministrazioneTrasparente/AltriContCorruzione/_anno2017_2019. Accessed 1 March 2021.

Riccardi, M., & Savona, E. U. (2013). *The Identification of Beneficial Owners in the Fight against Money Laundering*. Transcrime, Università degli Studi di Trento, Trento.

Riccardi, M., Soriani, C., & Giampietri, V. (2016). Mafia infiltration in legitimate companies in Italy: From traditional sectors to emerging businesses. In E. U. Savona, M. Riccardi, & G. Berlusconi (Eds.), *Organised crime in European businesses*. Routledge.

Rose, R., & Peiffer, C. (2012*). Paying bribes to get public services: A global guide to concepts and survey measures* (No. SPP 494). : Centre for the Study of Public Policy.

Kurtz, M. J., & Schrank, A. (2007). Growth and governance: models, measures, and mechanisms. *The Journal of Politics, 69*(2), 538–554.

Saisana, M., Saltelli, A., & Tarantola, S. (2005). Uncertainty and sensitivity analysis techniques as tools for the quality assessment of composite indicators. *Journal of the Royal Statistical Society. Series A, 168*, 307–323.

Transparency International. (2020). *Transparency international*. CPI Index. https://www.transparency.org. Accessed April 16, 2021.

Troìa, M. (2020). *Data analysis e costruzione di indicatori di rischio di corruzione per la Banca Dati Nazionale dei Contratti Pubblici*. Autorità Nazionale Anticorruzione, working paper n. 5, Collana scientifica ANAC, Roma.

Sequeira, S. (2012). Advances in measuring corruption in the field. In D. Serra & L. Wantchekon (Eds.), *New Advances in Experimental Research on Corruption (Research in Experimental Economics)*. Emerald Group Publishing.

van der Does de Willebois, E., Halter, E. M., Harrison, R. A., Won Park, J., & Sharman, J. C. (2011). *The puppet masters: How the corrupt use legal structures to hide stolen assets and what to do about it*. The World Bank, Washington DC. https://openknowledge.worldbank.org/handle/10986/2363 License: CC BY 3.0 IGO. Accessed April 27, 2021.

Wu, X. (2005). Corporate governance and corruption: A cross-country analysis. *Governance: An International Journal of Policy, Administration and Institutions, 18*(2), 151–170.

Zindex. (2016). *zIndex – public contracting authorities rating*. http://wiki.zindex.cz/doku.php?id=en:start. Accessed April 27, 2021.

Chapter 5
Good Administration, Integrity and Corruption

Alessandra Pioggia, Maria Giuseppina Pacilli, and Federica Mannella

5.1   The Ethical Infrastructure Between Politics and Bureaucracy

Issues arising in connection with control and prevention of corruption and, more generally, with administrative malpractices, emerge from the necessity to reconcile an objective fact—such as the impact that the administrative misconduct (as well as corruption itself) would have on the functioning of the public organization at different decision-making levels—with a regulatory and prescriptive dimension that provides, as well as well-understood sanctioning tools against corruptive phenomena, the opportunity and the space for a regulatory and ethical intervention. In this perspective, the interdisciplinary analysis we intend to conduct will focus on the phenomena of corruption and administrative deviance in general, as hypothetical components of public action that can condition at least in part the outcome, with consequent need to formulate and implement suitable public policies. These two lines of inquiry—the actual and hypothetical role of illegal or unethical behavior and the policies aimed at minimizing such behavior—are analytically independent but logically related.

The preliminary topic for the analysis that we are going to conduct concerns the concept of "good administration", understood as a pervasive principle that arises in

---

1. The ethical infrastructure between politics and bureaucracy; 2. Corruption and the right to good administration; 3. Preventing corruption through the promotion of the right to good administration; 4. Unethical behavior in organizational settings: a socio-psychological perspective; 5. Codes of ethics as a tool for preventing corruption; 6. The role of public management in fighting corruption and their independence: anti-corruption measures, recruitment, career and performance.

A. Pioggia (✉) · M. G. Pacilli · F. Mannella
Department of Political Science, University of Perugia, Perugia, Italy
e-mail: alessandra.pioggia@unipg.it; maria.pacilli@unipg.it; federica.mannella@unipg.it

the single national contexts before evolving and integrating into an actual right of the community in the defence of public power, expanding, in its necessary measures, at a European and international level. The consequent protection of this right (in its various forms) and the instruments at disposal for its implementation will therefore be interpreted as the first measures for action in preventing administrative corruption.

This contribution will then resort to a socio-psychological analysis with the purpose of identifying the elements that define ethical leadership, understood as an organizational model of public action, with a view to preventing corruption through the promotion of an ethical culture.

Lastly, the contribution will examine, at the level of practical application of what has been stated so far, the models of ethical codes and conduct and their contents, with particular attention to public managers as actors and recipients of anti-corruption measures.

5.2   Corruption and the Right to Good Administration

5.2.1   Evolution of the Concept of "Good Administration"

Administrative prevention of corruption is a method that opens up a new way to counteract the phenomenon alongside repression through exclusively judicial means, in order to contain and thereby repress the set of behaviours that form the so-called "maladministration", currently far more widespread than is criminally punishable. It is therefore possible to define a series of instruments aimed, specifically, at pre-empting, containing and even preventing the emergence of corruptive behaviour or more generally improper administration.

It is in this area of inquiry that the absolute importance of a so-called "right to good administration" emerges, in its many meanings and forms.

Before defining the ways and the terms through which that right is used as a tool to counteract corruption, above all prevention, we need to map out the right itself, taking it out of single national contexts, in its evolution and conformation in Europe and internationally.

The concept of "good administration" has undergone an important evolution in a functional sense: from a principle based on the efficacy of public administration to a principle based on the protection of citizens' rights. If therefore the original definition was to guarantee the efficacy of public power, it has become an instrument of defence against public power.

In this way, the concept of "good administration" has acquired a programmatic value, it represents an aim foreseen by national constitutions and addressed to legislators for its implementation. It therefore provides, initially, a limited value, internal to each single state apparatus, to guarantee, as stated, the effectiveness of public power. It evolves later into an exigency of good administration, with more pervasive and generalized value, that as such starts to receive mention in various international documents from the beginning of the nineties projecting itself outside the single state, into the community and recognizing rights of the individual and corresponding *obligations-duties* (of different kinds) of public administrations (Fortsakis, 2005).

As noted and as we will see shortly, the right to a good administration will be expressly enshrined as a fundamental right of the individual (Kristjànsdòttir, 2013), for the first time, with the adoption of the Charter of Fundamental Rights of the European Union: it will constitute an absolute novelty, appearing for the first time in an international catalogue of fundamental rights.

In consideration of these brief observations, it is possible to state that the "right to a good administration" presents today a variable content, or rather, it must be understood as a "crutch" notion (Cassese, 2009) to which variable content is tied:

- it is made up of certain *core principles* such as the right to access, the right to be heard, the right to receive a justified decision, the right to be defended through justice, (which entails further obligations on the part of the administration: the obligation for publication and transparency of administrative acts, the obligation of justification, etc.): this meaning of good administration overlaps, in a broader sense, *due process of law*, that is expressed mainly in procedural rights, which have external relevance;
- it then includes a series of further principles that must always characterize administrative activity in general, which also become obligations for the administration, such as the principles of impartiality, reasonableness, fairness, objectivity, consistency, proportion, absence of discrimination: again, these have external relevance, but are not usually expressed in procedural forms;
- and lastly, it includes milder rules from a strictly legal viewpoint, that fall within the broader concept of public ethics, guaranteed by the recognition of a series of duties on the part of the administration, such as, for example, the duty of courtesy or the duty to write in reply to the questions posed by citizens which are directive in nature but not generally singularly actionable.

The scope and the strategic value of this right, in terms of what has been said so far, cannot be limited in its working to a strictly juridical sphere, but also involves both economic and social spheres. Good administration, understood as transparency, simplification and efficiency of the action of public apparatuses, subjects the administrative bodies to forms of widespread control, inducing them to engage in legitimate behavior aimed at the good performance and efficient management of resources to hinder corruption phenomena or more generally of bad administration. It follows that, applied in this sense, good administration entails greater reliability of the institutions, reduces administrative burdens and attracts greater investments in the territories in which it is carried out.

5.2.2 The Right to Good Administration in the European and International Context: Art. 41 of the Charter of Fundamental Rights of the European Union

In the catalogue of rights and prerogatives that the European Union recognizes and guarantees to its citizens in their relations with public administration (following the evolution of the European integration process, characterized by the formation of its own administrative legal system and the progressive development of the phenomenon of *co-administration*) we find the so-called *"right to good administration"*, as enshrined by art. 41 of the Charter of Nice under Chap. 5, related to citizenship and strictly connected, in the broader interpretation of the concept of good administration, to successive articles 42 (the right of access to documents), 43 (Ombudsman) and 44 (the right of petition).

The right to good administration is of growing importance in the European Union as a *general principle* to which the organization and functioning of public administrations and their actions towards citizens must conform. In particular, its contents are very broad and flexible, able to summarize the doctrinaire elaborations and the previous jurisprudential milestones related to various claims of private subjects—claims considered deserving of protection, and made against public administrations, just like, in fact, other rights (Wakefield, 2007). The codified formula in art. 41, moreover, thanks to its very broad semantic scope, may easily extend, by way of interpretation, into further situations, not yet specifically identified, but equally deserving of protection.

In truth, the Charter did nothing but transfuse into an *ad hoc* normative text the principle of good administration that, although not expressly stated in the founding Treaty, has been progressively elaborated, with broad outlines, in jurisprudence by important pronouncements by the Court of Justice: recognition of the obligations of diligence and impartiality by the Community institutions, the obligation of an administration to provide a thorough and timely investigation of the questions in hand, and the obligation of neutrality on the part of officials, all undoubtedly are at the heart of the above-stated principle. Other corollaries may be added, through a *non-exhaustive but illustrative* list, such as the duty to open an investigation, the reasonable duration of a procedure, the duty to hear the interested parties, the guarantee of a cross-examination process and the right of defence.

More specifically, art. 41, while essentially regulating a number of procedural features, recognizes crucial importance in the concept of good administration, defining it as a recognized right of every person; it is no longer treated on a par with a mere principle, organizational and functional in nature, but as a subjective legal situation, meaning a legally pursuable claim, recognized to whomever, for whatever reason, finds themselves in contact or relations with European institutions or administrations (and not just European citizens) (Ka'nska, 2004). In such a sense, alongside political rights par excellence, are two newly minted rights (to good administration and the subsequent right of access under art. 42), marking a change of perspective in the relationship that secures the individual to public administration, in a decidedly more democratic sense. It follows that the recognition of a right to good administration in Europe ends up placing the citizen, and not just the citizen, at the centre of the administrative system, be it national or European.

The contents of art. 41 were subsequently taken up, explained and integrated, as is known, by the European Code of Good Administrative Behaviour, together with the Principles of Public Service, defined in 2012 by the European Ombudsman (Mendes, 2009).

Among the fundamental rights of the individual, the codification of the right of administrative nature, with a minimum of guarantee apparatus, subject to expansion through interpretation (the Court of Justice's role is fundamental in this sense), which is added to the classic content of political citizenship and contributes to the creation of a European administrative citizenship, represents an innovation on the Community legal landscape. The very introduction of a Charter of Fundamental Rights, which gathers in a single document a series of civil, political, economic, social and administrative rights, represents, especially after Lisbon, a significant step: it is the first time that the Treaties recognize and guarantee *a catalogue of fundamental rights* with respect to the work of public authorities, strengthening the legal position of individuals and their participation in decision-making.

However, good administration as a fundamental right is also a novelty on the *international* landscape, given that it appears for the first time in a catalogue of rights: it must be noted in fact that it was not codified in the Universal Declaration of Human Rights, nor in the two subsequent United Nations Conventions on civil and political rights and on economic, social and cultural rights, nor by the ECHR, nor by the American Convention on Human Rights (Nehl, 2009).

From a pervasive analysis of the various interpretative declinations of this right, it is possible to list, by way of example but not limited to, applicative features which it covers (already recognized by domestic laws) contributing to the configuration of a European notion of good administration, also according to the application given by the jurisprudence of the Court of Justice (before the Charter of Nice and the relative codifications of this right entered into force), which are:

- the right to impartiality and fairness of administrative decisions;
- the right to reasonableness in procedural deadlines;
- the right to notice of rejection;
- the right to be heard (a specification of the more general principle of cross-examination) and the right of access to the file;
- the obligation of justification in administrative measures;
- the right to compensation for damages incurred on the part of European administrations in the performance of their duties.

The identification of the afore-stated prerogatives shows how the concept of good administration, at European level, is now predominantly understood in the interest and protection of citizens. It sets out a series of general parameters through which it is not only possible to assess the illegitimacy of possible inertia of a single institution, but which also serve to measure the possible further responsibilities of such bodies towards citizens, harmed by guilty behaviors or omissions, which are not always susceptible, per se, to sanction at a strictly criminal level. In concrete terms, it should be noted that the sphere of maladministration appears to be broader and more pervasive than that of illegitimacy, since it includes, but is not limited to the latter, which is why it does not always imply it (in this context, the role of the European Ombudsman becomes decisive).

5.3 Preventing Corruption Through the Promotion of the Right to Good Administration

This last consideration, corroborated by the previous ones, justifies and enhances the approach of the right to good administration within the contexts of the instruments for combating, but above all *preventing*, corruption.

Specifically, as a *crutch notion* that has variable meanings, good administration takes on an important meaning in the area of *actions to combat corruption*.

And in fact, especially the principles of *transparency and publication*, appear to be encouraged and enriched by the rules on the fight against corruption: transparency is regulated not only to guarantee the rights of citizens and promote their participation in the administration, but also to combat corruption and illegality, found, more and more frequently, wherever there is a lack of transparency (Carloni, 2017a, b).

Another aspect to which the fight against administrative corruption is linked is found in the concept of *public ethics*, which pursues the correctness of the administrative work: if it is true that the fundamental objective of the administrative activity is the realization and care of the interests of the community, the need for good performance of the administration as a whole and the correctness of the relationship between the administration and citizens goes far beyond the sanctioning of criminal behaviors implying, moreover, the monitoring and the consequent prohibition of further behaviors that may in some way undermine the final objective of good administration (Cerrillo i Martìnez & Ponce, 2017).

A *broader definition of corruption* follows therefore the one elaborated within criminal law common to the European member states, a notion that includes aspects such as integrity, transparency, responsibility and good management; this, because of the proven limited effectiveness of the only criminal strategy of *repression* of corruption (a 2003 paper by the European Commission—On a comprehensive EU policy against corruption), with the view to preparing an appropriate strategy of *prevention*. This different preventive perspective has been at the centre of worldwide debate on the subject of fighting corruption: The UN Convention of Merida in 2003, as well as other measures aimed at reinforcing repression through judicial means, invites each State to prepare specific policies of corruption prevention that are "co-ordinated and efficient that favour the participation of society and that reflect the principles of rule of law, of good management of public affairs and public assets, of transparency and responsibility".

In order to find a *new definition of "good administration"*, especially in the perspective of the general quality of life of citizens, we firstly need to clarify that the ultimate aim of an administration is the *care of public interests*. From this, other requirements related to the quality of an administration then emerge, such as, for example, the fact that an administration can dialogue with its citizens without adding burden not strictly functional to the service performed, or creation of a transparent administration through the use of a range of tools such as publication of acts, greater digitalization of activities or easier access given to administrative documents. The new definition is closely linked to and corroborates the broader definition of corruption, helping to provide the instruments needed to combat maladministration, in a view to the prevention of possible forms of corruption.

5.4 Ethical Behavior in Organizational Settings: A Socio-psychological Perspective

5.4.1 Groups, Social Norms, and Ethical Behavior

Moral behaviors are often intended as the outcome of individual stable and dispositional convictions overlooking as such the influence of social, cultural, and group values in affecting individuals' ethical decisions (Ellemers & Van der Toorn, 2015). In group contexts, norms and standards of behavior are shared by group members and represent fundamental regulation tools that can guide and constrain social behavior even beyond the force of law (Cialdini & Trost, 1998). When individuals internalize these norms, formal and informal groups become major moral anchors for distinguishing what is right from what is wrong (Ellemers, 2017). Although norms can be defined as formal laws taken by recognized authorities to govern individuals, this is just one side of the coin. When we refer to norms, and more precisely to social norms, we can define them as a grammar of social interactions and like grammar, they identify what is legitimate and acceptable and what is not in a society or a group (Bicchieri, 2005). Social norms often stem from the interaction between people in a given group and turn out to be a behavioral guide for the group itself in a process of mutual influence between single individuals and the whole group. In the social psychology field, Muzafer Sherif (1936) provided a seminal contribution in the examination of the development of social norms. He studied in a laboratory, a high controlled environment, those challenging situations of uncertainty which daily characterize our life where we are asked to express our opinion or to take decisions. To build an ambiguous situation, Sherif relied upon a scarcely known optical illusion, the so-called auto-kinetic effect, which consists of perceiving a static light as in motion, in a completely dark environment. In a nutshell, the participants, unaware of the optical illusion, were asked to estimate the length of the movement of the light spot in a dark room. Participants had to express 100 evaluations both individually and in a group context (with people they had never seen before). There were 40 people in the group: one half of the group made the evaluations first individually and then in group and the other half made the assessments first in group and then alone. Sherif expected that a collective norm would emerge in the group session about the estimated length of the movement, and this norm would still be preferred by individuals compared to their personal evaluation. Regarding people assigned first to the individual session and then to the group session, Sherif predicted and found that people would abandon the individual norm in favor of the collective norm when asked to make their evaluation in the group session. As for the participants assigned first to the group session and then to the individual session, it emerged even more interestingly that the group evaluation was internalized by the people who continued to apply it even alone in the individual session. This social phenomenon, typical of situations where there is no majority agreement regarding a single answer considered correct, is defined normalization. This research is worth note because it shows mutatis mutandis how powerful the effect of a group and its emergent norms can be when it comes to opinions, values and attitudes. In everyday life, there are several situations where people placed in groups, because of mutual influence, can converge towards the creation of a group norm.

In a situation of uncertainty, such as the one just described and tested by Sherif, people make a reasonable choice: they model their behavior relying on the assessments of a group and adopting them as an anchor for their judgment. Although the group could be wrong and could not guarantee a certainty with respect to the quality of the choice, trusting the group has an adaptive value. But what behavior do people adopt when their group expresses a judgment that is undoubtedly wrong, a judgment that goes against the evidence? This is the question that Solomon Asch has tried to answer, "studying the social and personal conditions that induce the individual to resist or conform to group pressures when this group expresses an opinion contrary to perceptual evidence" (1951, 177). Asch adopted the same basic procedure in many experiments. It consisted of asking a single individual to perform a simple task within a group, that is, to identify which line, among three lines of different length, was equal to another line taken as a point of reference. The task was extremely simple, except for the fact that the group expressed in a compact and coherent way the wrong answer. The results showed that, while in the control group (i.e., in the group where there was no confederate of the experimenter), participants expressed few incorrect judgments, in the experimental groups the erroneous evaluations of the majority influenced about one third of the participants' opinions (32% of the overall answers). Although independence had far prevailed among the participants in Asch's experiments (68% of the responses), a large number of individuals had succumbed at least once in the face of a majority. Conformity (or compliance) to a majority, the phenomenon of adherence to a prevailing opinion or behavior, even when this is in contrast with one's way of thinking, is particularly relevant when we examine ethical behaviors in organization.

Compliance with group norms guarantees inclusion in the group, makes the group members feel good about their group membership, and it is a way to express loyalty and commitment (Cialdini & Trost, 1998). Pagliaro et al. (2011) showed that morality is crucial in group functioning and that group members comply with moral group norms because they expect to receive ingroup respect. If compliance with group norms is perceived as a sign of loyalty to the group, then deviance and dissent are often seen as a sign of disloyalty and disengagement (Jetten & Hornsey, 2014).

Deviance can present negative consequences for the sound functioning of the group or its very existence, and thus, the group elicits behaviors from its members aimed at reducing or eliminating it. Moreover, as Moore and Gino (2013) have argued, "repeated exposure to behavioral norms that are inconsistent with those of society at large [...] may socialize people to alter their understanding of what is ethical, causing broader moral norms to become irrelevant" (p. 57).

5.4.2   Ethical Leadership and Ethical Culture

Two social psychological theories apply to understand the key relevance of ethical leadership and ethical culture in organizations. According to Social Learning theory (Bandura, 1977), people learn norms and proper behaviors by observing and mimicking the behaviors of peers as well as other persons who are credible and trustworthy. The other relevant theoretical contribution to consider is the Social Identity theory. According to Henry Tajfel (1981), social identity is "that part of an individual's self-concept which derives from his knowledge of his membership of a social group (or groups) together with the value and emotional significance attached to that membership." (p. 255). A central notion of Social Identity theory is the adoption of the group's prototype as a point of reference in terms of behavior to adopt and in terms of norms to follow. When examining the leader-follower dynamics, then, the social identity approach considers the way in which the leader is able to represent core characteristics of the group as a whole, thus creating and maintaining shared identities (Hogg, 2001). For this reason, leadership is crucial in reducing corruption since leaders are prototypical members and as such are asked to define the values and appropriate behaviors to adopt in their organizations and accordingly promote those behaviors (Mishra & Schmidt, 2018). Ethical leadership can be meant as "the demonstration of normatively appropriate conduct through personal actions and interpersonal relationships, and the promotion of such conduct to followers through two-way communication, reinforcement, and decision making" (Brown et al., 2005, p. 120). Brown et al. (2005) distinguish the two following main and interdependent components of ethical leadership: (1) being a moral person; and (2) being a moral manager. The dimensions of ethical leadership include taking care of communications with employees and treating them fairly as well as fostering a climate of trust.

Research has shown that ethical leadership positively affects the ethical behavior of employees (Mayer et al., 2009). Ethical leaders are effective because they constitute a role model for integrity: defining the activities they desire to encourage and reward and the activities they discourage and punish, they outline and implement ethical standards not only for themselves but also for their subordinates (Brown et al., 2005). In each organization at different levels of the hierarchy, there are multiple leaders and consequently leaders at lower levels of the organization can first observe and then internalize the ethical values and standards of higher-level leaders. Research refers to this type of role modeling in the leadership as "cascading effects" of leadership (Bass et al., 1987) and it can be crucial in developing an ethical culture in that organization.

Ethical culture is "a subset of organizational culture and represents the interplay among the ethics-related formal (e.g., rules and policies, performance management systems) and informal (e.g., norms, language, rituals) organizational systems that influence employee ethical and unethical behavior" (Treviño et al., 2014, p. 641). Kaptein (1998, 2008) posits that the virtuousness of an organization depends on the extent to which the organizational culture stimulates employees to act ethically and prevents them from acting unethically. He identifies accordingly seven dimensions of an organization's ethical culture. The first is *clarity*, or the degree to which an organization defines its values, norms and ethical principles in a concrete and understandable way for workers. The risk of unethical conduct is significantly higher when employees are left to their own discretion and moral intuition and cannot rely upon a guiding organizational frame of reference. Moreover, the lack of clarity on the ethical norms to follow encourages employees' self-justification. Another central aspect concerns managerial *congruency* or the degree to which people who hold a role of responsibility in the organization apply to their behavior the ethical standards that they expect from other employees in their organization. As we already stated, leaders are fundamental behavioral models that can promote or discourage the importance of organizational ethics with their own behavior. In summary, a transgression is more likely to be reported to the manager of an organization if they have not committed that same transgression or are not somehow implicated in other transgressions. *Feasibility* refers to the degree to which there is sufficient time, resources and information available in an organization for workers to perform their work adequately. This is a central dimension of ethical culture, since if in an organization people have to carry out their task with scarce material and temporal resources, there are no chances of talking and discussing possible unethical behaviors in progress and of how to confront them. In addition, low levels of feasibility push workers to think that stopping unethical behaviors is not a priority of the organization since there are more important and urgent objectives to be achieved. The organizational dimension of *supportability* corresponds to the extent to which organizations provide support to the ethical conduct of employees fostering their identification with, and commitment to the normative expectations of the organization. Another dimension identified by Kaptein (1998) strongly connected with the previous one is the *discussability*, that is, the possibility in the organization of speaking and discussing ethical issues. When this dimension is scarce, we see a closed organizational culture where criticism is neither encouraged nor accepted. The fifth dimension is labelled *transparency* in the organization and it is defined as the degree to which employees' conduct and its consequences are visible to those individuals in the organization who can act upon it, such as colleagues, supervisor, subordinates. Transparency presents a horizontal and vertical component. The vertical component pertains to the extent to which leaders can observe unethical conduct and its consequences in employees (top–down) and vice versa (bottom–up). The horizontal component refers to the extent to which employees are able to observe unethical conduct and its consequences in their peers. The last dimension of the ethical culture is *sanctionability*, that is, the extent to which workers have confidence because the misconduct will be formally punished once it has been identified. This is also connected with the willingness to report misconduct. Indeed, to report a misconduct, it is essential that one has confidence that the incorrect behavior will be stopped and punished after the report.

The ethical culture of an organization can be also meant as the set of informal and unwritten rules of the organizational context that discourage unethical behavior on the one hand and promote ethical behavior on the other (Treviño & Weaver, 2003). Therefore, it presents a key relevance when members of an organization have to choose to blow or not blow the whistle, that is, to report misconduct that occurs within their group to other persons inside or outside the organization (Pacilli et al., 2020). Research has shown that the propensity to blow the whistle is higher in the organizations where informal norms that support the employee's choice to report are present (Sims & Keenan, 1999). Whistleblowing occurs more often in organizations that are perceived by employees as responsive to complaints (Miceli & Near, 1988) and where workers have the possibility of reporting alleged offenses to their managers and colleagues without fear of reprisals or sanctions (Bjørkel & Matthiesen, 2011). The perception of support by supervisors is indeed, positively associated with whistleblowing intentions (Mesmer-Magnus & Viswesvaran, 2005).

5.4.3 Workplace as a Moral Laboratory

As Isaac H. Smith and Maryam Kouchaki (2021) argue, "workplace can serve as a moral laboratory that allows individuals to engage in an ongoing process of ethical learning." (p. 2). According to the authors, the transformation of the workplace into a moral laboratory is possible only after having made three main mental shifts. The first one pertains to the recognition that people do not have a stable and immutable moral character at work. It is strategic to set aside the idea that people are inherently moral or immoral, and to embrace the awareness that individuals' choice to act in moral or immoral ways depends upon a complex interaction among psychological, social and contextual factors. This means that moral character development is a lifelong pursuit as well as that relevant effort and intensive work is needed for ethical learning. The second mental shift –which is associated with the first one—regards the fact that the workplace is not only a proper but the ideal setting in which to engage in ethical learning and moral character development. People spend a significant amount of their daily time at work, and often they face morally relevant situations in the workplace. To this purpose, it is crucial to recognize the specific moral domain at stake in each workplace and the importance of an ethical training tailored to the specific needs of that organization.

Janoff-Bulman et al. (2009) have shown that individuals differently perceive moral behavior according to behaviors supposed to be acted (i.e., proscriptive morality) and behaviors supposed not be acted (i.e., prescriptive morality) and that usually proscriptive morality is perceived as more mandatory than prescriptive morality. When we think about ethical challenges, we tend to think in terms of who needs to pay if something goes wrong, but ethics comes into play not only in case of damage. For this reason, the third mental shift proposed by Smith and Kouchaki (2021) regards the acknowledgment that focusing on ethics and morality at work is not just a matter of avoiding the bad, but also about pursuing the good.

Working towards the construction of an ethical organization is key not only because processes at macro level change and present better functioning but because research has shown that when an organization cultivates an ethical culture, employees present higher job satisfaction, higher levels of productivity and efficiency and last but not least higher levels of well-being (Promislo et al., 2012; Zhu et al., 2015).

5.5 Codes of Ethics as a Tool for Preventing Corruption

The strategy of fighting corruption by measures which may influence the behavior of agents, not only *ex post* but also *ex ante*, finds an important tool in the definition of codes of conduct or codes of ethics. Codes of ethics are lists of duties supported by controls and legal sanctions of disciplinary nature, although the violation of the duties they contain may also result in other types of liabilities, such as the criminal one.

These codes provide important guidelines for the expected and desirable behaviors of civil servants, including guaranteeing the right to good administration. At the same time, they are also communication tools, which illustrate, to employees and stakeholders, the self-image that the administration projects outside. An important role of codes is also to guide the entire organization in its relationship with users. If, when the administration uses its public power, laws and procedures guide the action impartially, when it relates to its services, the law cannot codify everything. Organizational tools are therefore essential to ensure integrity in relationships.

International organizations highly recommend the use of codes of ethics as a means of preventing corruption. The Recommendation of the Committee of Ministers of the European Counsel n. R(2000)10 heads towards this direction, and before that, the UN's International Code of Conduct for Public officials (1996) and the Recommendations of the OECD Council on Improving Ethical Conduct in the Public Service (1998). On an European level, since the first report analyzing corruption in the EU Member States adopted by the Commission (Annual Report to the EU Parliament and Council—COM 2014/38) in 2014, the need to adopt clear ethical standards and to foster the development of a culture of integrity in the various administrative organizations of the Member States has been stressed.

Since 2000, the European Commission has had its own Code of good administrative behavior for its staff. The following year, a code was also adopted for the European Parliament members of staff. These codes, as aforementioned, are inspired by the principles of the right to a good administration and also carry out the function of informing European citizens of their rights in their relations with the administration. It is precisely for the latter reason, however, that the codes of EU administrations are inspired by the principles of the quality of the service rendered by the administration, rather than by the integrity of behavior needed in order to fight illegality.

Almost all European countries have laws that contain principles that public employees must abide by, and that are inspired by values such as impartiality, loyalty, or integrity. In many cases, like in Italy and Spain, some principles are contained in the Constitution. In recent years, in most European countries, the law has also provided for the adoption of codes of conduct.

Some countries opt for a single code of conduct, which applies to the majority of public administrations; others, such as Estonia, prefer a decentralized approach, where each administration has more freedom to define the duties of their employees. Still others, such as Italy, Netherlands, Spain, have a mixed approach: they adopt a national code of conduct and refer to the individual administrations for the specification of the common code through dedicated regulations.

Different types of regulation of public employees' duties may be found. In France, for example, it is the general Statue of civil service which contains the duties of public employees, together with statues that separately deal with the branches of administration. In 2016, the French legislator, by approving Loi n° 2016–483 of the 20th April 2016 relating to *à la déontologie et aux droits et obligations des fonctionnaires*, updated the Statue of civil service with a number of new rules of conduct, with the aim of creating «*une fonction publique exemplaire*» (Lettre rectificative au projet de loi (n° 1278) relatif à la déontologie et aux droits et obligations des fonctionnaires, 2015).

France has some *chartes de déontologie* for business sectors which are considered at risk, but they mostly hold an informative function regarding expected behavior and do not serve as a basis for specific disciplinary liability.

Similarly to France, in Spain the duties of public employees are also part of the Statue of civil service, as defined with Ley 7/2007, bearing the *Estatuto Básico del Empleado Publico*. Within the latter legal framework, as reformed with *Real Decreto Legislativo 5/2015,* articles from 52 to 54 contain the norms which comprise the *Código del conducta.*

Portugal has a similar situation, where the rules of conduct of public employees are included in *the Estatuto Disciplinar dos Trabalhadores Que Exercem Funções Públicas*, adopted with law 58/2008.

Other types of code, of legislative nature, take the form of a single text bringing together the rules contained in various laws and regarding the duties of conduct of civil servants, as is the case, for example, of Germany. These types of codes are often followed by illustrative documents which help to better understand the rules of conduct to be followed. One example of these documents are the ones adopted by the Swedish agency (Statskontoret).

A different type of code is the one that is added to the laws by introducing rules of disciplinary nature, as in the cases of Italy, Poland and Denmark. These codes are used both to specify the contents of duties already identified by the laws in terms of necessary compliance with general principles, such as impartiality, and to prohibit, by providing for the application of disciplinary sanctions, behavior which cannot be considered as a violation of a specific legal norm, but are considered undesirable. Generally, however, these types of codes focus more on the expected rather than forbidden behavior, trying to outline the right attitude to hold in various situations.

Another different practice is that of codes, which do not contain rules whose violation is punished with sanctions, but are dedicated to illustrating the values that should inspire the actions of civil servants, such as the Civil Service code in the United Kingdom or the Code of conduct in the Public Sector adopted by the Danish Agency for Modernisation in 2017. These codes often follow norms which contain actual rules of conduct backed by sanctions. In the United Kingdom this latter function is performed by the Civil Service Management Code, which is adopted by a secondary source and has disciplinary application.

Finally, there are also those countries where there is no code of ethics, despite having several rules of conduct in the laws concerning civil servants. The various codes of ethics tend to have common principles, all falling into the same broad categories, namely impartiality, transparency, integrity, legality, loyalty, equal treatment, reliability, service and professionalism (OSCE-ODIHR and GRECO, Guidance for the Code of Conduct of Italy's Public Administration, for the event on "Codes of conduct for public administrations" organized in Rome on April 4, 2019).

However, there are some differences in the wording of the resulting duties, which may also have significant effects on the fight against corruption. For example, in countries where there are fewer corruption cases, the concept of loyalty is almost always interpreted with reference to the Constitution, to the norms and to the citizens. While in countries where corruption is more widespread, loyalty is owed, first and foremost, to hierarchical superiors and the government. Other differences may relate to the scope of the principles.

Better performance in fighting against corruption can be found, for example, in countries where principles such as transparency are interpreted more broadly and cover almost all areas of administration.

Normally, codes of conduct have a broad approach which, in addition to promoting standards of good administration, aims at avoiding incorrect behavior from several point of views concerning aspects such as the relationship with decision-makers in politics, hierarchical superiors, colleagues and citizens, or how to use the tools and resources available to perform one's own function. Within this scenario, however, one can also find some examples of codes aimed primarily at fighting corruption. One such case is Regulation on integrity, adopted by the German Federal Ministry of the Interior, Building and Community, which contains a Code of Conduct expressly dedicated to anti-corruption. In Austria too, in 2012, a Code of Conduct to Prevent Corruption was adopted and even in Sweden, a country where there is no real uniform code of ethics, among the documents drawn up to better explain the various laws governing the behavior of public officials, there is one dedicated to the culture of anti-corruption. An interesting case is the Italian one, where measures laid down in the Prevention of Corruption Plan are assisted by the same type of sanctions provided for the violation of the code. This way, behaviors included in the Plan gradually integrate, *de facto*, the code of conduct.

There are different ways in which all codes of ethics, even those with a more general approach, may contribute effectively to the fight against corruption. One of these is certainly the one relating to the regulation of conflicts of interest.

A conflict of interests is a situation where the personal interest (one's own or of a close person) of financial nature or relating to other benefits, of the civil servant, interferes with the public interest which he or she must look after by his or her actions.

In order to avoid conflict of interest or to prevent the cases in which it may occur, disclosure obligations are required, with regards to membership of associations or professional relationships with persons other than the administration, abstention duties and transparency measures.

Some codes dedicate a large number of rules to regulating conduct in the event of conflicts of interest and focus on the main cases in which conflicts may arise between the interests that the civil servant has to take care of in carrying out his administrative activity and his own interests or those of people close to him. Since conflict of interest is not easy to circumscribe, it is important for the code to contain examples referring to different areas of administration. In some cases, precisely for this purpose, the codes are accompanied by illustrative documents containing examples and guides, as in the case of the documents drawn up by the Swedish Agency for Public Management.

In this respect, United Kingdom also seems like a particularly interesting example, where the Government manages a website listing the different issues that a civil servant may encounter during their work and recommendations on how to behave. Other measures aimed at preventing conflicts of interest are also those concerning restrictions on the possibility of working for subjects other than the administrative authority that one belongs to, outside one's working hours.

Normally it is the law that indicates which activities are not allowed and which ones can be carried out. In addition to this, however, there is almost always the possibility for the administration to authorize, on request, the temporary performance by its own employees of other professional activities. In France, where the regulation of this aspect is very complex, in some cases it can also be arranged for the request to be passed on to an ethics committee.

Individual administrations and, within those administrations, their managers usually monitor compliance with the rules of conduct. Some countries, such as France and Romania, have deemed useful to establish an ethics committee within the institutions, to always be available for clarifications and advice. In other countries, such as Slovakia, Albania and Estonia, there are also national authorities that monitor compliance with the codes, they take care of their updating and training and deal with the most serious disciplinary violations.

In France and Italy, some updating and monitoring functions of the codes are carried out centrally by the authorities that also deal with anti-corruption. Sweden too has a special public agency (Swedish Agency for Public Management) which deals with good behavior of the civil servants, providing explanations, training and drawing up operational guidelines.

In Italy, since the contents of the Plan, as aforementioned, are integrated with the duties of the code and form a part of it, the Anti-Corruption officer ends up being called upon to supervise and monitor also the proper functioning of the rules of conduct, meaning, in particular, the preparation of appropriate training policies to promote knowledge and the supervision to ensure that any violations become apparent.

Although most European countries have rules on the behavior of public employees, the sensitivity with which behavior, deviant from the one expected and codified is pursued, varies.

Protective and category-based attitudes, indeed, often prevail in the culture of public administration, which discourage the reporting of behavior that is contrary to the standards set out in the codes.

In this context, training initiatives on public ethics and behavioral duties, which can develop a common culture of integrity, are very important.

5.6 The Role of Public Management in Fighting Corruption and Their Independence: Anti-corruption Measures, Recruitment, Career, and Performance

The reforms which have transformed the functioning and organization of public administrations in Europe over the last thirty years (Hammerschmid et al., 2016), and which go under the name of New Public Management, have given public managers a very important role and new powers also in the management of public personnel (Aguinis, 2013).

Several countries, such as Italy, have expanded the skills and decision-making capacity of public managers, also with a view to investing more in the impartiality of public administration. They have been entrusted with the power to decide on specific interests in order to take these types of decisions away from political bodies.

Public managers in all European countries have the task of managing the resources of the administration, ensuring the smooth running of the organization and the proper performance of activities and, as many studies have shown, an administration that performs its tasks well is more resistant to corruption.

Management powers also apply to public administration staff, which makes public managers important players in promoting anti-corruption measures among civil servants. Public managers are responsible for monitoring the conduct of the employees assigned to the office they manage, as well as monitoring for any disciplinary liability. However, before suppressing undesirable behavior, public managers must ensure that the duties of fairness, service and impartiality are promoted among the staff assigned to them: communicating ethical values and outlining the expected behavior is a very important aspect, especially in those grey areas of integrity that are not dealt with by legal regulations. Public managers play an essential role here, so much so, that some codes of conduct, such as the Italian one, stipulate that they should set an example to all employees.

Operatively speaking, it is the public managers who, in most cases, also have to manage organizational anti-corruption tools concerning staff, such as replacing an employee in conflict of interest with another in the management of an individual procedure, or rotating staff in positions most exposed to corruption risks.

Lastly, as mentioned above, public managers also exercise various public powers, either directly or by assisting the top management of administrations. In this role, they are themselves addressees of anti-corruption rules, such as those on conflicts of interest, incompatibility or transparency.

In view of the key role played by public managers today, important factors in the fight against corruption are their professional quality (Tanzi, 1998; Treisman, 2000), and their independence.

To ensure the good quality of public managers, a good selection process for recruitment is important. Indeed, politicization and the absence of meritocracy in the recruitment and career of civil servants foster corruption in public administration and damage the quality of services (Meyer-Sahling & Mikkelsen, 2016), so the selection of managers according to a meritocratic system is an important tool for the fight against corruption.

A manager who holds a position of responsibility because he or she has been selected on the basis of their skills and abilities is less likely to be influenced by political and economic interests and less inclined to take advantage of a situation of power for undue personal benefit. For this reason, it is important that people are carefully and impartially selected for leadership roles. A state examination is the prevailing recruitment method for public managers in Europe.

Before examining its characteristics, however, it should be pointed out that in many European countries there are senior positions in public administrations that are assigned to people chosen without a public selection procedure, through appointments made directly by the political leadership. Forms of guarantee can also be identified in this type of appointment. In the British case, for example, there is a Commissioner for Public Appointments, independent of the executive, who ensures that the processes are transparent and that shortlists of candidates are drawn up that are genuinely suited to the type of post and responsibility to be filled. In France, the list of names from which the Minister chooses the ministry's top leader, is proposed by the ministry's technical management itself. Another form of guarantee is the extreme limitation of the number of positions that politicians can fill directly through informal appointments, as is the case in the Netherlands, Denmark and Norway. In countries, such as Poland, where the selection of public managers, without a state exam, concerns not only the top management of ministries, but also some lower positions (Act of 30 December 2015 on Amendments of the Act on Civil Service and Other Act), the situation of an excessive number of managers appears unstable and subject to a relationship of trust that may break down, and this weakens the guarantees of integrity.

The way in which the selection of public managers in an administration is regulated is important to guarantee their professional quality and impartiality. Detailed regulation of public exam procedures, as in Italy and France, ensures greater uniformity and rigor in the conduct of the committees. A wider discretion of the commissions, on the other hand, may open up spaces for patronage choices. In Latvia, for example, there are no standards for the selection process, leaving a wide choice to the committees of which instruments to use, weakening the guarantee function of a competitive selection for management.

Another important guarantee factor is the technical nature of the selection. It is indeed important that politicians are as far as possible outside the selection process, even when the final appointment is their responsibility. In almost all countries, politicians are not allowed to be members of exam committees. Providing requirements for membership of the commission is also important to limit arbitrariness in the appointment of commission members by politicians. When these measures are weaker, the guarantees of merit in the choice of manager and therefore of his or her independence from politics are also reduced. A case of weak guarantees due to a strong involvement of politics is, for example, the case of Poland where the examination committee is appointed by the political leadership of the administration wishing to recruit managers and concludes its evaluation process with the definition of a list of suitable candidates, which is then transmitted to the same political leadership, which has the power to make the final choice of the candidate.

A third element of guarantee in the selection, is the presence of technical bodies to regulate and control the selection process, as in the case of Ireland, where the CPSA (Commission for Public Service Appointments) sets the rules and supervises the selection process, but also ensures that appointments are made on the basis of merit and that they result from a fair and transparent selection process.

A fourth aspect that favors the quality and impartiality of the selection process is the fact that it is carried out directly by technical bodies, which ensure distance from interests within the administration (political and career) and uniformity of procedures. In Ireland, again, the selection of senior management in the administration is carried out by the TLAC (Top Level Appointment Committee), made up of 9 members, 4 internal and 5 external to the public administration.

The function of guaranteeing the quality and integrity of management entrusted to selection is further strengthened by the provision of forms of access to the management role entrusted to national schools, which also provide training to consolidate the *esprit de corps* of managers and their sense of belonging to an authoritative and responsible category of public officers. One such example is the *Ecole Nationale d'Administration (ENA)*. ENA is an organ of the administrative system, under the Prime Minister's office, whose main task is to select suitable civil servants for advanced studies and provide them with professional training. Selection by the ENA involves one year of training and one year of professional training in three different administrations and in the private sector. In early 2021, the French President Emmanuel Macron announced the transformation of the school into *Institut du service public*. The institution will maintain its function of public managers' selection, even though the way in which they are recruited by administrations will change.

In Italy, recent reforms of access to management have strengthened the role of the National School of Administration in the training and selection of managers in the national administration. In the United Kingdom, too, there was a major reorganization of executive education during the 1990s. During the Blair government, indeed, the Civil Service College was transformed into the National School of Government and assumed a key role in executive education.

In the selection process of managers, it would also be useful and important to take into consideration their sensitivity to public ethics and their overall ethical competence (Merloni & Pirni, 2021). However, the only case in which public ethics orientation is expressly included among the competences to be assessed for candidates is that of the French ENA (Arrêté du 16 avril 2014).

In addition to quality, ensured by careful recruitment of public managers, attention should be paid to their independence, as another key element to ensure their role as actors in anti-corruption measures.

Impartial leadership independent of political and economic interests needs stability. In some countries, such as Italy and France, while managerial appointment are temporary, the manager's employment relationship acquired through public competition, is permanent. In other countries, such as Belgium or Portugal, the temporary nature of the assignment and membership of the management role coincide. In Belgium, appointments last six years and are only renewable in the event of positive performance evaluations and following a comparative selection process. In this case, independence is guaranteed more by the quality of the selection than by stability of the employment relationship. Selection procedures in Belgium are carried out by a public agency: *SELOR (Sélection et Organisation)* and the role of the political body only concerns the identification of top positions and only operates after the selection of a shortlist of suitable candidates by the agency. In Portugal, managerial appointments last three years and senior managerial appointments last five, and both are renewable once. Only for senior managers, the selection process is centralized and entrusted to a permanent commission, the *CReSAP (Comissão de Recrutamento e Selecção para a Administração Pública)*. In all other cases, the selection procedures are carried out by each administration respectively. The independence of managers in this case is also less protected due to the lack of a standard selection procedure entrusted to an external party.

Another important aspect to ensure the independence of public managers concerns the limits to the positions they may hold because of their background and the incompatibilities between managerial positions in public administration and other activities they perform outside working hours. In Italy, for example, Legislative Decree 34 of 2013 has provided for various rules about unfitness for office and incompatibilities, which should protect managerial decision-making from political and economic interests. In France, certain incompatibilities are provided for in the Criminal Code (*Articles 432–12 and 432–13 Code pénal*), which punishes the offence of *prise illégale d'intérêt* where there is an assumption of office in subjects under the control of the administration of origin. In Italy, France, Austria and Germany, there are also bans for a number of years (from less than one year in Austria to five years in Germany) to carry out activities in the private sector in areas relating to the previous administrative activity: the so-called *pantouflage* or "revolving doors" phenomenon. In Spain, this measure only applies to senior officials, while in the United Kingdom it is assessed according to seniority and the nature of the duties performed. In Norway, the guidelines for civil servants provide for a conflict of interest clause to be included in the employment contract, with sanctions for its breach. In other Member States, such as Denmark, Finland and Sweden, corruption prevention is mainly based on a strong culture of integrity and there are few formal rules and controls on these aspects.

Another aspect which is important to consider, again with a view to guaranteeing the independence of public managers, is that of performance assessment. In almost all European countries, over the last 30 years, systems have been introduced to assess managerial performance, which is linked to salary and career incentives and, in Belgium, Portugal and Italy, also to the renewal of managerial appointments. An exception is Poland, where, since 2016, the performance of public managers is no longer assessed.

The models adopted in Europe belong to two types: a highly standardized and centralized system, as in Great Britain, which has a uniform system for assessing the performance of all senior civil servants, Belgium or Portugal; or a decentralized and more flexible system, as in Germany and Spain.

Italy has moved from the latter model, which was present until 2009, to greater standardization of the evaluation mechanism, achieved through careful legal regulation.

In the evaluation of public managers, it is important to ensure the reliability of the process in order to avoid that limits to the politicization of appointments are thwarted by the possibility of politics intervening in their renewal or in their remuneration. As a rule, the evaluation is carried out by the senior manager, but several countries also provide for a second evaluator to ensure greater reliability of the process. This is the case, for example, of Belgium, France or Great Britain, where the second evaluator is the hierarchical superior of the first one. In Italy, on the other hand, the function of second evaluator is carried out by an internal body with independent characteristics. In Portugal, there is also an internal body, but it has only a supervisory function in the evaluation.

In some countries, such as Italy, the assessment of public managers who occupy top positions, and who therefore do not have a hierarchical superior, is carried out by an internal body, which acts as a second assessor for other managers. In Belgium, the assessment of senior managers is carried out by an external body.

In recent years, a common trend has emerged at European level to use performance appraisal not only to measure the work product within the administration, but also to assess the quality of the outcome and user satisfaction. This has led to greater control and transparency, also outside the administration, of the functioning of public offices, which has also helped to fight corruption.

References

Aguinis, H. (2013). *Performance management* (3rd ed.). Pearson/Prentice Hall.
Asch, S. E. (1951). Effects of group pressure upon the modification and distortion of judgment. In H. Guetzkow (Ed.), *Groups, leadership and men*. Carnegie Press.

Bandura, A. (1977). *Social learning theory*. General Learning Press.
Bass, B. M., Waldman, D. A., Avolio, B. J., & Bebb, M. (1987). Transformational leadership and the falling dominoes effect. *Group & Organization Studies, 12*, 73–87. https://doi.org/10.1177/105960118701200106
Bicchieri, C. (2005). *The grammar of society: The nature and dynamics of social norms*. Cambridge University Press.
Bjørkel, B., & Matthiesen, S. B. (2011). Preventing and dealing with retaliation against whistleblowers. In D. Lewis & W. Vandekerckhove (eds.), *Whistleblowing and democratic values* (pp. 127–149). Open Source eBook: The International Whistleblowing.
Brown, M. E., Treviño, L. K., & Harrison, D. A. (2005). Ethical leadership: A social learning perspective for construct development and testing. *Organizational Behavior and Human Decision Processes, 97*, 117–134. https://doi.org/10.1016/j.obhdp.2005.03.002
Carloni, E. (2017a). Fighting corruption through administrative measures. The Italian anti-corruption policy. *Italian Journal of Public Law, 9*(2), 261–209.
Carloni, E. (2017b). Italian anti-corruption and transparency policies. Trends and tools in combating administrative corruption. In A. Grasse, M. Grimm, & J. Labitzke (Eds.), *Italien zwischen Krise und Aufbruch* (pp. 365–386). Springer.
Cassese, S. (2009). *Il diritto alla buona amministrazione*. https://www.irpa.eu. Accessed 27 March 2011.
Cerrillo i Martìnez, A., & Ponce, J. (2017). *Preventing corruption and promoting good government and public integrity*. Bruylant.
Cialdini, R. B., & Trost, M. R. (1998). Social influence: Social norms, conformity, and compliance. In D. Gilbert, S. Fiske, & G. Lindzey (Eds.), *The handbook of social psychology* (pp. 151–192). McGraw-Hill.
Ellemers, N. (2017). *Morality and the regulation of social behavior: Groups as moral anchors*. Routledge.
Ellemers, N., & Van der Toorn, J. (2015). Groups as moral anchors. *Current Opinion in Psychology, 6*, 189–194. https://doi.org/10.1016/j.copsyc.2015.08.018
Fortsakis, T. (2005). Principles governing good administration. *Eur Public Law, 11*(2), 207–217.
Hammerschmid, B., Gerhard, F., et al. (2016). *Public administration reforms in Europe. The view from the top*. Edward Elgar Publishing.
Hogg, M. A. (2001). A social identity theory of leadership. *Personality and Social Psychology Review, 5*, 184–200. https://doi.org/10.1207/S15327957PSPR0503_1
Janoff-Bulman, R., Sheikh, S., & Hepp, S. (2009). Proscriptive versus prescriptive morality: Two faces of moral regulation. *Journal of Personality and Social Psychology, 96*, 521–537. https://doi.org/10.1037/a0013779
Jetten, J., & Hornsey, M. J. (2014). Deviance and dissent in groups. *Annual Review of Psychology, 65*, 461–485. https://doi.org/10.1146/annurev-psych-010213-115151
Ka'nska, K. (2004). Towards administrative human rights in the EU impact of the charter of fundamental rights. *European Law Journal, 10*, 296–326. https://doi.org/10.1111/j.1468-0386.2004.00218.x
Kaptein, M. (1998). *Ethics management: Auditing and developing the ethical content of organizations.* : Springer.
Kaptein, M. (2008). Developing and testing a measure for the ethical culture of organizations: The corporate ethical virtues model. *Journal of Organizational Behavior, 29*, 923–947. https://doi.org/10.1002/job.520
Kristjànsdòttir, M.V. (2013). Good administration as a fundamental right. *Icelandic Review of Politics & Administration, 9(1)*, 237–255. https://doi.org/10.13177/irpa.a.2013.9.1.12
Lettre rectificative au projet de loi (n° 1278) relatif à la déontologie et aux droits et obligations des fonctionnaires, Compte rendu du Conseil des ministres du 17 juin 2015. http://www.assemblee-nationale.fr/14/projets/pl2880.asp. Accessed 20 April 2021.

Mayer, D. M., Kuenzi, M., & Greenbaum, R. L. (2009). Making ethical climate a mainstream management topic: A review, critique, and prescription for the empirical research on ethical climate. In D. D. Cremer (Ed.), *Psychological perspectives on ethical behavior and decision making* (pp. 181–213). Information Age Publ.

Mendes, J. (2009). Good administration in EU law and the European Code of Good Administrative Behaviour, *EUI Working Paper Law*. https://cadmus.eui.eu/bitstream/handle/1814/12101.

Merloni, F., & Pirni, A. (2021). *Etica per le istituzioni. Un lessico*. Donzelli.

Mesmer-Magnus, J. R., & Viswesvaran, C. (2005). Whistleblowing in organizations: An examination of correlates of whistleblowing intentions, actions, and retaliation. *Journal of Business Ethics, 62*, 277–297. https://doi.org/10.1007/s10551-005-0849-1

Meyer-Sahling, J.-H., & Mikkelsen, K. S. (2016). Civil service laws, merit, politicization, and corruption: The perspective of public officials from five East European countries. *Public Administration, 94*, 1105–1123. https://doi.org/10.1111/padm.12276

Miceli, M. P., & Near, J. P. (1988). Individual and situational correlates of whistle-blowing. *Personnel Psychology, 41*, 267–281. https://doi.org/10.1111/j.1744-6570.1988.tb02385.x

Mishra, P., & Schmidt, G. B. (2018). How can leaders of multinational organizations be ethical by contributing to corporate social responsibility initiatives? Guidelines and pitfalls for leaders trying to do good. *Business Horizons, 61*, 833–843. https://doi.org/10.1016/j.bushor.2018.07.011

Moore, C., & Gino, F. (2013). Ethically adrift: How others pull our moral compass from true north, and how we can fix it. *Research in Organizational Behavior, 33*, 53–77. https://doi.org/10.1016/j.riob.2013.08.001

Nehl, H.-P. (2009). Good administration as a procedural right and/or general principle? In H. Hofmann & A. Türk (Eds.), *Legal challenges in EU administrative law* (pp. 322–351). Edward Elgar.

OSCE-ODIHR and GRECO, Guidance for the code of conduct of Italy's public administration, for the event on "Codes of conduct for public administrations" organized in Rome on April 4, 2019.

Pacilli, M. G., Sant, G., Giovannelli, I., Pagliaro, S., Sacchi, S., Brambilla, M., & Spaccatini, F. (2020). La denuncia delle condotte illecite in ambito organizzativo: Una rassegna sul fenomeno del whistleblowing. *Psicologia sociale, 15*, 369–401. https://doi.org/10.1482/98461

Pagliaro, S., Ellemers, N., & Barreto, M. (2011). Sharing moral values: Anticipated ingroup respect as a determinant of adherence to morality-based (but not competence-based) group norms. *Personality and Social Psychology Bulletin, 37*, 1117–1129. https://doi.org/10.1177/0146167211406906

Promislo, M. D., Giacalone, R. A., & Welch, J. (2012). Consequences of concern: Ethics, social responsibility, and well-being. *Business Ethics: A European Review, 21*(2), 209–219. https://doi.org/10.1111/j.1467-8608.2011.01648.x

Sherif, M. (1936). *The psychology of social norms*. Harper.

Sims, R. L., & Keenan, J. P. (1999). A cross-cultural comparison of managers' whistleblowing tendencies. *International Journal of Value-Based Management, 12*, 137–151.

Smith, I. H., & Kouchaki, M. (2021). Ethical learning: The workplace as a moral laboratory for character development. *Social Issues and Policy Review, 15*, 277–322. https://doi.org/10.1111/sipr.12073

Tajfel, H. (1981). *Human groups and social categories: Studies in social psychology*. Cambridge University Press.

Tanzi, V. (1998), Corruption around the world: Causes, consequences, scope, and cures. *IMF Working Papers* WP/98/63. : IMF.

Treisman, D. (2000). The causes of corruption: A cross-national study. *Journal of Public Economics, 76*(3), 399–458.

Treviño, L. K., & Weaver, G. R. (2003). *Managing ethics in business organizations: Social scientific perspective*. Stanford University Press.

Treviño, L. K., Den Nieuwenboer, N. A., & Kish-Gephart, J. J. (2014). (Un)ethical behavior in organizations. *Annual Review of Psychology, 65*, 635–660. https://doi.org/10.1146/annurev-psych-113011-143745

Wakefield, J. (2007). *The right to good administration*. Alphen aan den Rijn.

Zhu, W., He, H., Treviño, L. K., Chao, M. M., & Wang, W. (2015). Ethical leadership and follower voice and performance: The role of follower identifications and entity morality beliefs. *The Leadership Quarterly, 26*, 702–718. https://doi.org/10.1016/j.leaqua.2015.01.004

Chapter 6
Transparency, Digitalization and Corruption

Benedetto Ponti, Agustí Cerrillo-i-Martínez, and Fabrizio Di Mascio

6.1 Introduction

Administrative transparency, or the condition of an administration made visible and understandable in its processes, is a tool for preventing corruption under two profiles, each connected to the other. The first concerns transparency as a natural antidote to the condition of opacity, a concealment in which corrupt transactions occur: corrupt exchange is hidden, because it is concerned in concealing the deviated/illegal interest that it aims to satisfy and the associated distraction/waste of funds. Secondly, public monitoring ensured by transparency acts as a deterrent to such behavior. This essay is devoted to exploring the way by which transparency enabled by digitalization may prevent and detect corruption. The essay is structured as follows: the first paragraph explores the different paths to transparency enabled by digitalization; the second paragraph offers a special focus on means enabled by open data, big data and machine learning to detect and prevent corruption; the final paragraph analyzes those anticorruption tools in context, highlighting critical success factors and barriers.[1]

---

[1] Although the ideation of the essay is a collective work, the paragraphs 1 and 2 are to be attributed to B. Ponti, the paragraph 3 to A. Cerrillo-i-Martínez, and the paragraph 4 to F. di Mascio.

B. Ponti (✉)
Department of Political Science, University of Perugia, Perugia, Italy
e-mail: benedetto.ponti@unipg.it

A. Cerrillo-i-Martínez
Faculty of Law and Political Sciences, Universitat Oberta de Catalunya, Barcelona, Spain
e-mail: acerrillo@uoc.edu

F. Di Mascio
Interuniversity Department of Regional and Urban Studies and Planning, University of Turin, Turin, Italy
e-mail: fabrizio.dimascio@unito.it

© The Author(s), under exclusive license to Springer Nature Switzerland AG 2021   97
E. Carloni, M. Gnaldi (eds.), *Understanding and Fighting Corruption in Europe*,
https://doi.org/10.1007/978-3-030-82495-2_6

6.2   The Digital Paths to Transparency

The processes of digitalization, which we can describe for brevity as the application of information and communication technologies to the organization and functioning of public administrations and to the provision of public services, represent that element of innovation that—on a technological level—has made a decisive contribution to the transformation of transparency from a vague aspiration, or mere potentiality, into a concrete factor of reform and conformation of public powers. If transparency is a recognized guiding principle of constitutional importance, at international level (Bianchi, 2013), as "one of the basic values and principles governing public administration",[2] this depends first of all on the fact that the techniques of production and management of its raw material—information—have been affected by an epochal paradigm shift. If information is in itself an immaterial good, upon the invention of writing it has been conveyed, handed down and managed for millennia through material goods (stone, clay, parchment and then paper—first hand-written, later printed), and which has conditioned its potential and fields of applications. With the advent of information technology and digital communication networks, the immaterial nature of information has finally been reflected in the equally immaterial nature of the medium that enables its formation, preservation and transmission (bits). Among the many consequences, attention should be drawn to the subsequent radical change in terms of accessibility and re-elaboration, and which has made (insofar as of interest here) effectively feasible an availability and use of information produced by public authorities for transparency purposes.

If the connection that exists between the advent of ICTs and the establishment of transparency as an eminent principle in the organization and functioning of public authorities has peacefully been acquired, the trajectories (paths) along which the connection is articulated are less obvious and certainly multiple. A review of these trajectories is useful in order to take stock of the contribution that digitalization can offer in the fight against corruption. We should keep in mind that, while it is possible to identify specific times (over the last thirty years) in which these paths come to prominence, it does not mean that one has replaced a preceding one: rather it has been added, so that—concurrently—they coexist and provide a particularly rich and diversified landscape of digital paths of transparency.

6.2.1   Transparency as a Byproduct of Informatization

A first essential contribution of digitization to transparency is what we could define—in slightly paradoxical terms—as "involuntary", in that connected to those aspects of e-government through which the computerization (and, according to the

---

[2] Constitutional Court of South Africa, Brummer v. Minister for Social Development and Others, Judgement of 13 August 2009, Case CCT 25/09.

most recent terminology, the digitization) of operational processes, and of the sources/databases that feed them, have been carried out. These interventions, dating back to the late seventies, have acquired a significant impact (in terms of intensity and extension) since the early nineties of the last century, in conjunction with the deployment of administrative reforms inspired by New Public Management (NPM), and in support of the objectives of these reforms (Homburg, 2004). Computerization is seen as a useful means to review processes and simplify steps (even eliminating those deemed pointless), and also to import operational strategies borrowed from business organization; computerization enables the "measurement" of the time for procedures, and in so doing facilitates controls aimed at increasing operational efficiency (as well as reducing costs). In the philosophy of the NPM, computerization is therefore an instrument with which to make operational the managerial approach applied to public organization, with a view to efficiency. Within this horizon, transparency has a role above all in terms of *internal transparency*, at the service of performance evaluation (Homburg & Snellen, 2007). Even from the perspective of *external* transparency, the NPM approach uses information on the performance of services not in terms of accountability due to *the citizen*, but in that of competitive comparison (on the quality and costs rendered by the public sector) which has *the consumer* as a goal (Brüggemeier & Lenk, 2011).

Transparency is therefore not a specific goal of computerization and digitization of operational processes, but rather a side effect (because it facilitates the tracking and readability of operational processes), or a functional element in the implementation of specific public sector reform philosophies, especially NPM (Halachmi & Greiling, 2013; Homburg, 2004).

6.2.2 Transparency as an e-Government Service

With the advancement of internet (and the world wide web), ICTs are exploited (also) to directly pursue the objective of transparency. The web lends itself specifically as a useful infrastructure for the immediate, widespread and low-cost dissemination of information, thereby adeptly creating a service whose specific objective is availability of information for the benefit of public citizens. It is not incidental that this aptitude is reflected in the very definition of "egovernment": if the numerous (but largely coinciding) versions of the concept of egovernment revolve around the use of internet as a tool for "the delivery of online government services", in most definitions the provision of information is explained separately from other services,[3] to indicate both the centrality and importance in the economy of this phenomenon (Pardo, 2000, Fang, 2002). As proof, consider—for example—that in the tool for

---

[3] See the collection of definitions used in literature and in international relations "What is Electronic Government (e-Government)", in https://www.igi-global.com/dictionary/electronic-government-e-government/9385.

evaluating the quantity and quality of services provided online in the EU context (the *eGovernment Benchmark*)—one of the four dimensions measured is called "Transparency", and answers the following question: "Are public administrations providing clear, openly communicated information about how their services are delivered? Are they transparent about the responsibilities and performance of their public organizations?".[4]

The dissemination of information via the web by public administrations (Carloni, 2005), implemented mostly through the creation of institutional websites used as dissemination channels (within the single-direction mindset of the so-called Web 1.0) responds to a multiplicity of objectives. Public administrations provide information in order to illustrate the functioning of services (both online and offline), so as to facilitate their use by citizens. In this sense, we can speak of an instrumental transparency or transparency as a service. Furthermore, in line with what is recommended by the NPM strategy, the dissemination of information regarding the recorded performances by the services, aims to enable a transparency useful for an evaluation of those services, to encourage competition among them (again with a view to improving performance and lowering costs) and to increase users/consumers' power of choice. In both cases, we can speak of a market-oriented transparency. Finally, wider availability of information can still (potentially) enable an external control, in terms of verification of legality, impartiality and economy of choices made, activating a transparency in function of accountability.

The acquired centrality of the web network as a means of dissemination of information is interpreted in the literature with the affirmation of the so called "computer-mediated transparency" (Meijer, 2009; Grimmelikhuijsen & Welch, 2012), of which—as well as even too obvious potentialities—two possible risks (among others) are highlighted. Firstly, the transparency mediated by the web is able to guarantee dissemination only of some information: that which is evidently recorded and that is better lent to representation in quantitative terms. This leads to the risk that transparency conveys only a partial representation, a sort of *hyperreality* (Meijer, 2009), with consequent ineffectiveness of the accountability processes set in motion. Secondly, to the extent that it is the administrations themselves that determine what information to disseminate (for transparency purposes), a risk arises that a selection is carried out in order to highlight predominantly or only the aspects deemed most positive, with the result that—instead of widespread control—transparency ends up activating processes of legitimation (Grimmelikhuijsen, 2011), all the more so should the dissemination of data be accompanied by an ad hoc *narrative* (Piotrowski et al., 2019).

---

[4] See https://ec.europa.eu/digital-single-market/en/news/egovernment-benchmark-2020-egovernment-works-people.The other three top-level benchmarks are: User centricity; Cross-border mobility and Key enablers.

6.2.3   The Web as a Means of Dissemination of Information and the Embedding in the FOIA Laws

While the focus on transparency as a mechanism that—in the administrative realm—would contribute to the improvement of public services' performance, a tie to the democratic principle (Merloni, 2008) and constitutionalism (Meijer et al., 2018) places at the center of attention—in the political realm—the instrumentality of transparency in the activation of accountability. However, a relationship of this nature—in order to be effective—requires (among other things) that the entity asking for an accounting can have the information it deems useful and necessary (Halachmi & Greiling, 2013). The traditional solution to this end, has been to guarantee a right to know information, as determined particularly in FOIA laws. Now, there is no doubt that computerization and digitization have also been driving factors with respect to the exercise of the right to access information (the so-called reactive disclosure), insofar as they have enhanced the ability to manage public information assets. However, the advent of egovernment and its unprecedented potentiality in terms of information dissemination (so-called proactive disclosure) have added a new weapon in the arsenal of the right to know. Alongside the more traditional "right to have access, on request, to official documents held by public authorities",[5] which constitutes the center of gravity of the international FOIA standard, a model has been added with the purpose of fulfilling the right to know by imposing specific obligations on administrations to disseminate information via the web. Within this scheme, the disclosure of information through its dissemination constitutes a compulsory measure, and is explicitly aimed at creating the conditions for transparency and accountability.

The modalities experimented to impose forms of compulsory publication/dissemination have also been considerably diversified: from targeted measures related to specific public policies (we can think for example of the publication measures related to the granting of funds in the agricultural sector, in the EU), through to entire classes of data (preeminent the case of fiscal data related to revenues and expenditures); from the promotion of systematic policies of proactive dissemination of information,[6] through to the identification of detailed and uniform obligations imposed on all administrations (notable the cases of Spain and Italy). It must be pointed out that in certain cases this strategy has been embedded into the FOIA disciplines (UK,[7] Italy,[8]

---

[5] Art. 2 of the "Council of Europe Convention on Access to Official Documents", signed in Tromsø in 2009.

[6] Significant is the case "Memorandum on Transparency and Open Government" with which President Obama inaugurated his first term at the White House.

[7] Under the UK Freedom of Information Act, adopted in 2000 and came into force on 1 January 2005, the access to information from public sector organisation is guaranteed via the traditional channel of *reactive disclosure* (members of the public are entitled to *request information*), and via a complemetary channel of *proactive disclosure* (every public authority must adopt a *publication scheme* and to routinely publish information covered by the scheme via a websites).

[8] The Legislative decree n. 33/2013 introduced the obligation for all Italian public bodies to publish and keep up-to-date on their website a vast number of different information of public interest (more

Spain[9]), so that obligations for publication/dissemination for transparency purposes end up by integrating organically the protection of the right to know. Embedding into the FOIA disciplines signals that *affirmative disclosure* effectively constitutes the frontier of a new, further advanced FOIA standard (Pozen, 2017; Carloni & Pettinari, 2019), aligned and consistent with the technological paradigm characterized by the society of knowledge. A paradigm in which the fact-finding claim that feeds the instances of transparency (accountability and others related to it, including prevention of and the fight against corruption) is guaranteed also by the possibility to search for and employ directly and immediately information that administrations must make available through the web, so that—through this path—the ICTs, from an instrument for the transformation and improvement of public services (egovernment) are placed as a structural component of the right to know. In this sense, to the extent that transparency is not just an organizational principle, but also a legal right (a constitutional right to transparency, as recently affirmed by the Italian Constitutional Court[10]), meaning a legally protected claim on the part of the individual *uti cives*, its accomplishment assumes a specific, digital nature.

6.2.4 The Open Data Approach

In the dynamics of egoverment, the dissemination of information is configured in the same manner as a public service, and therefore that same information is considered the object of a service. This implies that transparency is understood (and expected) as an effect/consequence of the fruition of this service (the fruition of information as it is represented and distributed). However, information, for the reasons already summarily presented in the introduction, can be considered not only as the object of a service, but also as an asset, an asset with specific characteristics (an intangible asset, and therefore, by its nature, a non-rival good). These characteristics, if projected onto the assets of informations held by public bodies—seen as a collective good, both because they are owned by the public, and because they are collected for public purposes, and because they are formed through the investment of public

---

than two hundred and eighty contents): in the event of non-compliance that duty to publish is subject to a specific enforcement mechanism, which can be activated by anyone. An amendment introduced in 2016 then added the right to access information on request (reactive disclosure), while leaving the disclosure obligations substantially unchanged.

[9]La *Ley de transparencia* (Act of law n. 19/2013) aims to expand and reinforce the transparency of public activity, and is grounded on two complementary pillars: the right of access to information held by poblic bodies, and the *"publicidad activa"* (proactive disclosure), that is the duty for all the bodies affected by the law to publish all the relevant information, as listed in the second chapter of the law regulate and guarantee to expand and reinforce the transparency of public activity.

[10]Cfr. Italian Constitutional Court, ruling 20/2019. Interestingly, the Italian Constitutional Court has declared that the right to transparency integrates a constitutional right by clarifying that it has "equal importance" with respect to the right to privacy and to protection of personal data.

resources (Boyle, 2003; Burkert, 2004)—have conspired for the rapid affirmation of a different approach, aimed at emphasizing (and claiming) the potential of information as raw material, to be made available to all, free of charge and without limitations (representing the essential content of the notion of *open data*), so as to encourage the creation of further products and services. In this regard, it should be noted that while the EU framework on the re-use of public sector information is in many ways pioneering,[11] it should also be stressed that the regulatory model has approached with a degree of caution the *open* paradigm (in terms of formats, licenses and tariffs)[12] (Cerrillo-i-Martinez, 2012). *Open (government) data* constitute an essential piece of a more general (re)vision of the relationship between citizens and public administrations, namely the so called *Open Government*, which precisely starting from the sharing of information and its use, aims to promote transparency, participation and collaboration: "open data shifts the relationship between state and citizen from a monitorial to a collaborative one, centered around using information to solve problems together" (Noveck, 2017). Open government is a policy option that has rapidly become mainstream and politically transversal: the expansion of data.gov portals for the systematic publication of datasets is global, and is promoted by numerous international agreements and initiatives (from the Open Government Partnership-OGP to the Open Data Charter), as well as embraced by major financial institutions such as the World Bank, the International Monetary Fund, the OECD, etc. The emphasis placed on open data suggests to highlight the terms in which they are understood as vehicles and promoters of transparency.

6.2.4.1 The Availability of Open Data as Transparency in Itself

First of all, the very availability of datasets published as open data is considered an element of transparency, to the point that the two (open data and transparency) eventually and substantially are deemed to coincide. The rationale for this interpretation revolves around the idea that the public administration that—by default—shares information assets externally in open format is to be considered transparent (Magalhaes & Roseira, 2020; Jaeger & Bertot, 2010), so the attention is focused on the organizational modalities and the best suited procedures to make the provision of open data efficient, continuous and frictionless (Lourenço, 2015; Máchová & Lnénicka, 2017), and on the quality of that data (Eijk & Janssen, 2015; Vetrò et al., 2016). In this sense, for example, the principles of the *Open Data Charter* are concerned only with the access and release of data; or—again—it is sufficient to run through the "commitments" assumed by the various nations partner of OGP, to verify how data opening policies are an essential, if not the preponderant, part. This

---

[11] Directive 2003/98/EC of the European Parliament and of the Council of 17 November 2003 on the re-use of public sector information.

[12] Directive (EU) 2019/1024 of the European Parliament and of the Council of 20 June 2019 on open data and the re-use of public sector information.

is an interpretation that centers on the physiological resistance (passive and active) that a process of unconditioned sharing of information assets can encounter inside the public sector (Ruijer et al., 2020a), and therefore focuses on the (political and organizational) conditions and the solutions necessary to overcome them. In this respect, open data policy is understood as an ideal policy in itself—when it is successful—for increasing the transparency of administrations. The policies of openness are however also assessed with regard to the analysis of the impact produced: for example, opendatabarometer.org—in formulating "a global measure of how governments are publishing and using open data for accountability, innovation and social impact"—also takes into account the impact that open data are having on business, politics and civil society[13]; but it must be pointed out that the scope of impact considered is far broader and diversified than the accountability of public authorities alone, which, rather, constitutes a secondary aspect, compared to the effects produced on the market and the third sector (Magalhaes & Roseira, 2020). This, furthermore, contributes to a vision that tends to reduce the dimension of transparency to the wide availability of data in open format. A recent study also shows how, conversely, a very as a large part of the research on the topic of "open government" it focuses almost exclusively on transparency issues (Tai, 2021).

6.2.4.2 Data Reuse and Mediated Transparency

A more complex, but also more realistic, interpretation of the contribution forwarded by the open data approach to transparency in public administrations moves instead from the recognition that the availability of row data is only a prerequisite for the realization of transparency. In fact, it is necessary that the data made available are effectively put to good use, that some meaning is extracted, so as to enable an understanding of the phenomena that are under investigation/control, and that only through this understanding comes the transparency (the condition of whoever observes a phenomenon from the outside and is in a position not only to "see" but also to understand what is happening inside). In this regard, as well as the availability of data, equally essential factors are the context in which the data are made available (Ruijer et al., 2020b), the stakeholder interests (Cerrillo-i-Martínez, 2013) and above all, the *mediators* role, meaning that diversified typology of actors (journalists, universities, research centers, civil society groups, businesses, ONG, etc) who have access to the open data and use them in order to 'create' transparency. And it is exactly the activity of reuse (variously encompassing: re-elaboration, mash-up, business intelligence, visualization, but also big data analysis and machine learning) that constitutes the moment in which a meaning can be attributed to the data with the result that such an activity (reuse) becomes central in the dynamics of transparency (Matheus & Janssen, 2020; Ponti, 2012, 2019).

---

[13] Cfr. https://opendatabarometer.org/barometer/

While in transparency 'as an egovernment service' it is the administration that gives meaning to the information, selecting or processing it in order to distribute information products ready to be enjoyed by end users, in the case of open data such activity takes place outside the administration, and it is subject to a series of further conditions and premises, ranging from the nature of the activity in which the reuse takes place (business or non-profit activities), to its relative degree of stability, to the circumstances that transparency is its explicit purpose, or only a possible side effect (Ponti, 2012).

Depending on the type of integration with the FOIA/Affirmative Disclosure regulations, the open data approach may vary from a mere policy option, to the subject of a legally protected feature of the right to know, so that this constitutes a possible but not a necessary element of the regime of the right to access public information. EU Directive 2019/1024 pushes in this direction and in some national disciplines (see Italy, for example) the two regimes tend to overlap.

Also the open data approach is impacted by the importance assumed by big data analytics and machine learning. Two effects, among others, should be underlined. From the moment in which open data feed into the algorithms of the so-called black box society (Pasquale, 2015), we are witnessing the paradox in which an instrument *available to all* and with the purpose of implementing *transparency* is attracted inside a dynamic characterized by the *opacity* of the algorithms based on which data acquire meaning and by their *patented regime*. Furthermore, from the moment that the added value of machine learning analytics consists precisely in the ability to allow unexpected correlations to emerge, the process of transparency construction takes uncharted paths, and potentially disruptive, compared to more traditional and recognized paths of meaning (Ananny & Crawford, 2018). This could further amplify an effect already inherent in the open data approach: that of enabling a plurality of transparencies, co-present and in competition with each other. Under these terms. Accountability may end up being the result of a competition to win attention to a specific transparency outcome as opposed to others.

6.2.5 The Mixed Impact of Digital Transparency, But for Corruption

Transparency is sanctioned and pursued by legal systems by reason of a series of promises, intended to unfold on the levels of political and administrative realms (Meijer et al., 2018), and to produce some expected outcomes: effects on citizens (legitimacy, participation, trust in government, satisfaction), and effects on government (accountability, corruption, performance, decision-making process, financial management, collaboration between governments) (Cucciniello et al., 2017). However, the effective ability of transparency, and in particular that of digital-enabled transparency, to produce positive results in terms of accountability, trust (Etzioni, 2010; Bovens, 2003) and legitimacy (Grimmelikhuijsen, 2012) has been questioned.

A recent review of the scientific literature on transparency (Cucciniello et al., 2017) aimed to verify whether the data emerging from the empirical research confirm or refute this skepticism: indeed, the analysis of the investigated literature does not provide unequivocal indications supporting the thesis that positively links transparency to accountability, trust and legitimacy, but rather "mixed" indications, some of which contradict this thesis. But concerning the expected outcome in terms of reduction of/fight against corruption, the empirical tests analyzed provide wholly unequivocal indications, thereby confirming the contribution of digital-enabled transparency in terms of contrasting corruptive phenomena (in the same sense, see also Brusca et al., 2018).

6.3 Open Data, Big Data and Machine Learning as Tools to Detect and Prevent Corruption

6.3.1 Open Data and Public Collaboration in the Fight Against Corruption

The goal of open government is to strengthen the relationship between the general public and the authorities through transparency, participation and public collaboration by means of the intensive use of electronic media and the fostering of public innovation (Cerrillo i Martínez, 2017).

Open government is transparent and participative. Through transparency and participation, open government seeks to boost authorities' accountability and thereby improve public oversight of their activities (Corojan & Campos, 2011), ultimately bolstering democratic principles (Villoria Mendieta, 2010).

All this helps to strengthen public integrity and prevent corruption (Cerrillo i Martínez, 2017). As noted in the September 2011 Open Government Declaration, signed by 54 countries as part of the Open Government Partnership, the signatories accept "responsibility for seizing this moment to strengthen our commitments to promote transparency, fight corruption, empower citizens, and harness the power of new technologies to make government more effective and accountable".[14]

Open government fosters open public data to permit public participation and collaboration in the fight against corruption by means of the reuse of public information, amongst other tools.

---

[14] Available at https://www.opengovpartnership.org/process/joining-ogp/open-government-declaration (last consulted: January 2021).

6.3.1.1   Open Public Data and Its Impact on the Fight Against Corruption

Transparency is one tool for preventing corruption. As the famous saying by Supreme Court Justice Louis D. Brandeis goes, "sunlight is said to the best disinfectant". Indeed, any policy for preventing corruption and improving integrity must be based on public transparency (Haute Autorité pour la transparence de la vie publique, 2016).

Beyond any public transparency policies previously analysed, this section seeks to highlight how the public can also contribute to the prevention of corruption via the reuse of public information. To be able to do this, governments need to open up their data. It is not enough to merely make public data available via transparency portals: what is required is that these data be open, in other words that they be made available to the public in formats that foster their reuse and under technical and legal conditions that permit such reuse. As stated in Directive (EU) 2019/1024 of the European Parliament and of the Council of 20 June 2019 on open data and the re-use of public sector information, open data are "data in an open format that can be freely used, re-used and shared by anyone for any purpose", i.e. those "made available to the public without any restriction that impedes the re-use of documents".

The opening up of public data helps prevent and aids in the fight against corruption. As the G20 and the OECD note, "Open government data (OGD) is public sector information (PSI) that has evolved to adapt to the digital world and to the needs of national open data ecosystems" (G20 and OECD, 2017: 17). In particular, the G20 Anti-Corruption Open Data Principles suggest that data be open by default; timely and comprehensive; accessible and usable; for improved governance and citizen engagement; for inclusive development and innovation; and comparable and interoperable.[15]

These days, it is common for government authorities to make open data available on specifically-created web portals to facilitate their findability and reuse.

6.3.1.2   Public Collaboration in the Fight Against Corruption: Collaborative Transparency

Open data allows for public collaboration in the analysis and oversight of public activities through the reuse of public data via electronic means and its subsequent dissemination in easily understandable formats by the public on the Internet or social media networks (Granickas, 2014).

Public collaboration in public transparency gives rise to what is known as collaborative transparency, which is transparency channelled by the public via the

---

[15] Accessible at: http://www.g20.utoronto.ca/2015/G20-Anti-Corruption-Open-Data-Principles.pdf (last consulted: January 2021).

reuse of public information. Collaborative transparency forms a vital part of any anti-corruption strategy (Beke and Blomeyer & Sanz, 2015: 31; Web Foundation, 2018).

Open data allows the public to collaborate in the analysis of public data through its reuse, which can be useful in monitoring the activities of governments and identifying irregularities and cases of corruption. As Kaufmann notes, this turns the members of the public into thousands of auditors (Kaufmann, 2002: 19).

There are already numerous public initiatives channelling collaboration in the prevention of and the fight against corruption (OECD, 2017; Open Contracting, 2018).

Collaboration might consist in disseminating information in formats that are easily understandable to the public, so that it may oversee or monitor the activities of the government. This is the case, for example, of the *¿Quién paga la obra?* (Who pays for the works?) project promoted by Spain's Civio foundation, which uses public procurement data to provide simple, graphics-based information on Spain's leading public works contractors.

Collaboration can also consist in the analysis of open data, permitting the monitoring of the activities of governmental authorities and seeking patterns and relationships between the data and, on this basis, to be able to identify possible irregularities, conflicts of interest or cases of corruption. A number of initiatives are already working in this direction, including the Red Flags project, which aims to enhance the transparency of public procurement processes in Hungary and support the fight against corruption using an interactive tool that allows the monitoring of procurement processes on the basis of data published in the Tenders Electronic Daily (TED) and identifies the risk of fraud in the different procurement stages through a special algorithm.[16]

6.3.1.3 The Limits of Open Data and Collaborative Transparency in the Prevention of and Fight Against Corruption

Despite that positive impact that both open data and collaborative transparency can have in the prevention of and fight against corruption, transparency may on occasion be limited and its effects lessened in this field.

Governments may limit transparency when it might harm other public or private interests whose protection the legal system regards as a priority. So it is that most laws governing access to public information state that governments may deny access to such information when it may affect issues such as public safety; the prevention, investigation and prosecution of criminal activities; disciplinary investigations; inspection, control and supervision by public authorities; commercial and other economic interests; the deliberations within or between public authorities concerning the examination of a matter or privacy and other legitimate private interests like personal data protection.

---

[16] Accessible at https://www.redflags.eu/ (last consulted: January 2021).

However, transparency may also be limited because governments do not fulfil their transparency obligations, in a wish to prevent information from becoming known by the public, because the information is incomplete or because it cannot be found, is incorrect or excessively complex. Another limitation can come when a governmental authority releases too much information, leading to confusion or disinformation.

In practice, one can often see how, despite open data's potential in the fight against corruption, it has achieved relatively little real-life impact (Vrushi & Hodess, 2017).

6.3.2   Big Data and the Use of Artificial Intelligence in the Fight Against Corruption

6.3.2.1   Big Data and the Fight Against Corruption

Governments' activities give rise to increasing amounts of data. At the same time, they gather more data on the public and businesses.

When these data are collected in large volumes, are extremely varied (e.g. structured in the form of spreadsheets or relational databases rather than text, images or video) and produced at great velocity (the "three Vs", Kwon et al., 2014), we are dealing with what is technically known as "big data".

As noted by Dávid-Barrett and Fazekas, the greater availability of data on government activities together with advances in computing capacity have made it increasingly easy to collect and analyse such data (Dávid-Barrett & Fazekas, 2019).

Big data permits the carrying out of predictive analysis to understand the patterns arising from existing data, discover relationships between them that are not identifiable without automation and extrapolate them into the future to prevent risks or anticipate measures to combat them. Big data is key to evidence-based policy.

From the standpoint of the fight against corruption, data mining and the analysis of big data can be used to identify irregularities, conflicts of interest or cases of corruption (OECD, 2009: 38). Indeed, the use of computer hardware and software facilitates the monitoring, oversight and control of the activities of governments and the officials and workers in them to allow conflicts of interest and cases of corruption to be detected (Sturges, 2004: 7; Bertot et al., 2010: 265).

For example, this is the goal of the Arachne program, developed by the European Commission. Arachne is a fraud risk-scoring tool to identify those projects, contracts, contractors and beneficiaries of public aid with a greater risk of the commission of irregularities. Arachne alerts the fund's managing authority of the most risky cases based on a set or automatically defined indicators of the risk of fraud or quality assurance of European funds. To do this, it uses different databases and information systems that permit the analysis of all risky operations and contracts, the seeking of links between beneficiaries and contractors, the analysis of potential conflicts of interest and the examination of the structure of groups of companies.[17]

6.3.2.2   The Use of Artificial Intelligence in the Fight Against Corruption

Artificial intelligence (AI) is destined to transform the workings of government. AI can be a useful technology in the prevention of and fight against corruption. In particular, it can be used for data analysis; for example, by processing natural language, algorithms can analyse the content of a public procurement contract or conversations between a public official and a contractor to detect conflicts of interest. It can also be used to automate decision-making (for example, using an aid-granting algorithm to minimise the risks of corruption) or to prepare behavioural profiles and patterns that allow for the identification of the risks of corruption, irregular conduct or people or companies likely to have committed irregularities. An example of this last one is the analysis of the data that can be generated by differing procurement contract types or profiles of bidders that can more easily commit irregularities.

To this end, analysing large volumes of data with AI can help identify patterns or profiles that would otherwise be difficult to find based on the study of a single administrative procedure or tender process. At the same time, it cuts down on the resources required to carry out these tasks, which can imply considerable savings. The use of AI in the fight against corruption can lead those committing irregularities to change their behaviour and comply with the rules (Cotino Hueso, 2021).

Some governments have therefore begun to use AI for data analysis and the detection of irregularities and cases of corruption. Nevertheless, as noted by Capdeferro Villagrasa (2019), "at the present time, smart anticorruption systems are limited, functionally, to act as guidance when prioritising, as the case may be, the inspection work of the relevant body in cases of alleged corruption or irregularity with the framework of government actions, and their algorithms have been programmed manually, undergoing no autonomous change whatsoever during the system's workings".

This has been seen in the early warning system of the Generalitat Valenciana, the Valencian regional government. This system is based on analysis of the data created by the public authorities themselves to identify irregular situations (Puncel Chornet, 2019). The aggregated and interconnected processing of the data created by such authorities via complex algorithms may facilitate the detection and discovery of behaviour, conduct and situations concealing conflicts of interest and cases of corruption.[18] As stated by Law 22/2018, of 6 November, of the Generalitat

---

[17]Information obtained from: https://ec.europa.eu/social/BlobServlet?docId=14836&langId=en and https://ec.europa.eu/social/main.jsp?catId=325&intPageId=3587&langId=en (last consulted: January 2021).

[18]Whatever the case, we should note that, at the time of writing, the project is still at an early stage and does not yet include AI in its operations (Cotino Hueso, 2021).

Valenciana, on the Services Inspectorate General and the warning system for the prevention of malpractice in the government administration and its associated public sector, "the warning system shall be put into practice by means of a set of tools whose interaction permits the detection of possible irregularities and administrative malpractice, on a preventative basis, based on the analysis of the information obtained and the evaluation of risks factors that may potentially give rise thereto" (Article 17). In particular, the logic and computerised data processing system for preventing irregularities comprises, amongst other elements, "the data analysis mechanisms that, via risk indicators defined for each of the different fields of administrative management upon which the system acts, permit the detection of irregular situations that are the possible object of investigation" (Article 20). To this end, it contemplates the design of a system of indicators with the goal of detecting the presence of possible irregularities or malpractice, in each of the management fields, which shall be periodically updated to guarantee the highest possible level of specificity, by means of the application of the information and conclusions arising from the implementation of the system itself (Article 27).

6.3.2.3   Legal Problems with the Use of Artificial Intelligence in the Fight Against Corruption

The use of artificial intelligence can make the prevention of and fight against corruption more effective. It can also make the fight against corruption more efficient by reducing the human resources required to analyse data or investigate irregularities. Furthermore, it can prevent bias and, in general, any problems that may arise from human involvement in the fight against corruption.

Nevertheless, the use of AI in the prevention of and fight against corruption may involve some risks (Cerrillo i Martínez, 2019). To deal with the risks listed below, human oversight of the working of the algorithms may be of use, as may the adoption of codes of conduct that contemplate the governing principles of algorithm design, or, lastly, the fostering of procedures to guarantee the reliability of the design and the adoption of corruption-fighting algorithms.

Opacity in the Fight Against Corruption

Algorithms are black boxes (Pasquale, 2015). Indeed, opacity is the norm in government use of artificial intelligence (De Laat, 2017; Burrell, 2016: 1). The opacity of algorithms may have different causes that prevent the public from knowing which algorithms are used by the government, how they operate and how decisions are automatically adopted via algorithms and what they are based on.

All this is a consequence of the complexity of the algorithms themselves. We should not ignore the fact that understanding how an automatic learning-based algorithm works is *almost* impossible and, in any case, highly expensive (Coglianese & Lehr, 2017: 1206). Opacity is also the result of the application of the limits of transparency and, in particular, that regarding the protection of intellectual property. Additionally, as noted in a number of studies, opacity arises from the difficulty in the government providing access to all the information on algorithms requested or not responding to requests to access it (Brauneis & Goodman, 2017: 22; Fink, 2017). Lastly, opacity may be due to the difficulty in understanding the information on an algorithm or its workings (Burrell, 2016). In the case of the use of algorithms used in the fight against corruption, opacity may also aim to keep subjects from understanding algorithm-based decisions, which would allow them to avoid their application, that is, allow those potentially responsible for irregularities or cases of corruption to become able to circumvent the use of the algorithms (De Laat, 2017; Lepri et al., 2018: 10).

To prevent opacity in the algorithms used in the fight against corruption, governments must adopt the measures necessary to guarantee that the public can know which algorithms are used in this fight, how they work and which data are used, providing information on the algorithms to provide accountability on their existence and so that the public may monitor their workings. Additionally, governments could promote the use of programming languages and procedures that facilitate analysis of the algorithms used to prevent and fight corruption (Kroll et al., 2017, 643).

The opacity of algorithms has already been the subject of a number of legal rulings, which have recognised the need to guarantee algorithms' transparency.

In this regard, we could mention the judgement of Italy's Council of State, number 8472, of 8 April 2019, which concludes that "everybody has the right to be aware of the existence of an automated decision-making process that affects them and, in this case, receive significant information on the logic employed" (Carloni, 2020). We should also refer to the judgement of the Hague District Court of 5 February 2020 (ECLI:NL: RBDHA: 2020: 865), with regard to an algorithm used to detect social security fraud (SyRI), which concludes that "the SyRI legislation is insufficiently transparent and verifiable to conclude that the interference with the right to respect for private life which the use of SyRI may entail is necessary, proportional and proportionate in relation to the aims the legislation pursues" (6.86) and that "without insight into the risk indicators and the risk model, or at least without further legal safeguards to compensate for this lack of insight, the SyRI legislation provides insufficient points of reference for the conclusion that by using SyRI the interference with the right to respect for private life is always proportionate and therefore necessary" (6.95). Whatever the case, we cannot ignore the fact that things have not always been this way, as can be seen in the State v. Loomis judgement of the Wisconsin Supreme Court of 13 July 2016 where Loomis challenged the use of the algorithm COMPAS at his sentencing because the could not "review how the factors are weighed and how risk scores are determined, the accuracy of the COMPAS assessment cannot be verified". However, the Wisconsin Supreme Court took a middle road stating that Loomis could "at least review and challenge the resulting risk scores set forth in the report attached to the PSI" (52) and that "to the extent that Loomis's risk assessment is based upon his answers to questions and publicly available data about his criminal history, Loomis had the opportunity to verify that the questions and answers listed on the COMPAS report were accurate" (55).

The Lack of Grounds for the Decisions Adopted in the Fight Against Corruption

The inclusion of AI in the prevention of and fight against corruption could revolutionise the way in which decisions are made, even sidelining human involvement. Governments can take automated decisions in the fight against corruption using algorithms, for example, on which companies to investigate, which contractors must be required to comply with an integrity programme or which persons are at risk of a conflict of interest.

Nevertheless, in such cases, governments may find it difficult or impossible to explain the grounds of a decision due to the complexity of establishing how a particular algorithm has worked to be able to have taken or proposed said decision or what data it has taken into account and the relative importance attached to them in the decision-making process. So, the use of algorithms may have a negative impact upon data subjects' rights in inspection or penalty proceedings.

Given this risk, there is—as we have already noted—a need to guarantee human oversight. In this regard, France's Constitutional Council, in its decision of 27 December 2019 (Decision no. 2019–796 DC) on the system for selecting tax authority inspection targets, states "no criminal, tax or customs proceedings may be initiated without an individual assessment of the person's situation by the administration, which cannot then be based exclusively on the results of an automated processing" (legal basis 90).

Discrimination in the Fight Against Corruption

The use of algorithms in the fight against corruption can give rise to bias and hence to discrimination (Lehr & Ohm, 2017). An automated corruption risk warning system could provide more frequent risk alerts for companies based in a particular country or businesspersons of a certain ethnicity without there being any objective, reasonable justification for differentiating the treatment given to the different data subjects.

Discrimination can be caused by the algorithms themselves or by the data used by the former (Barocas & Selbst, 2016). Bias in algorithms may be caused, voluntarily or not, by their designers. However, bias can also be because of poor-quality, out-of-date or badly structured data, or data arising from patterns that conceal pre-existing inequalities or discrimination.

To deal with this issue, governments can promote a range of measures to encourage the participation of data subjects in the decisions taken with the use of algorithms, create expert working parties to analyse the development of the algorithms (Lepri et al., 2018, 8) or perform risk analyses (Mantelero, 2018).

Infringement of Data Protection and Privacy Rights in the Fight Against
Corruption

The use of algorithms in the fight against corruption may negatively impact fundamental rights such as data protection and privacy (Crawford & Schultz, 2014; Citron
& Pasquale, 2014).

The fact is that the algorithms used to detect cases of corruption will frequently
analyse personal data or may infer personal data based on the analysis of other data.
With regard to this issue, France's Constitutional Council has analysed which data
can be used and, in particular, whether automated systems can also process data
obtained from social media networks. In any case, it will be necessary ensure the
compatibility of the purpose of the processing with the purpose for which the
personal data were initially collected (Article 6 GDPR). Additionally, the rights of
the data subjects must be guaranteed, particularly the right to be informed of the
purposes of the processing for which the personal data are intended and the legal
basis for the processing or, if applicable, the existence of automated decision-making
(Articles 13 and 14 GDPR).

When the fight against corruption is based upon the formulation of profiles or on
the automated taking of decisions involving the processing of personal data, it needs
to be borne in mind that the GDPR acknowledges the right of data subjects not to be
subject to a decision based solely on automated processing that produces legal
effects concerning them or similarly significantly affects them, unless one of the
contemplated grounds occurs. Should this be the case, it shall be necessary for the
data controller to adopt the contemplated measures to safeguard the rights, freedoms
and legitimate interests of the data subject, including at least the right to obtain
human intervention on the part of the controller, to express their point of view and to
contest the decision (Article 22) (Casey et al., 2019).

6.4   Digitalization and Anticorruption Policies in Context: Critical Success Factors and Barriers

Information and communications technology (ICT) tools have been widely perceived to offer new effective means for the prevention, detection and prosecution
of corruption (Bertot et al., 2010). Numerous studies have posited that e-government
can support control of corruption by reducing information asymmetries, limiting
public officials' discretion, reducing intermediaries and red tape, and increasing the
certainty and celerity of sanctions (Grönlund et al., 2010; Adam & Fazekas, 2020).
ICT also facilitates the information flow between government and citizens, across
government institutions, and among citizens. Potentially, this fosters transparency,
accountability and citizen participation (Kossow, 2020).

The literature contains many studies that address questions as to what extent ICT
aids the fight against corruption on a macro level (Andersen, 2009). The next section

reviews those studies that looked at the impact of ICT on a global or regional scale of corruption. With the exception of a few cases (Basyal et al., 2018), the empirical findings of this strand of large-N analyses underpin a statistical relationship between different measures of e-government adoption and reduced corruption (Gans-Morse et al., 2018). Although these quantitative analyses reveal a positive anticorruption impact of e-government, what is presented is largely decontextualized. Cross-country studies could be considered useful for providing a broad comparison among a large number of countries, but they seldomly explain the mechanisms of the effects of digitalization (Khan et al., 2021).

In particular, quantitative studies seek to link control of corruption with variables that derive from some form of global rankings. The latter focus on the level of nation-states that are considered as monolithic entities, whereas it is widely acknowledged that corruption risks vary across policy sectors (Heywood, 2017). In-depth investigation of specific experiences is, thus, crucial in gaining an understanding of anticorruption in different contexts and generating relevant policy implications. However, the link between e-government and corruption reduction has rarely been thoroughly investigated beyond *ad hoc* case studies (Cho & Choi, 2004; Kim et al., 2009; Sheryazdanova & Butterfield, 2017). To help researchers and policymakers better anticipate the opportunities and challenges presented in adopting different digitalization initiatives that target anticorruption, a more nuanced understanding is needed (Wu et al., 2020).

More specifically, ICT for anti-corruption should not be understood as a single approach, since different tools, and different modes of technology adoption, create different dynamics. Whether or not a particular tool can bring anti-corruption benefits will depend on the design of a specific implementation, the incentives driving its adoption, and the wider context in which it is applied (Davies & Fumega, 2014). As a first step, it is crucial to theorize corruption and its drivers in order to properly understand under what conditions the use of a specific ICT tool can enhance the effects of anti-corruption measures. Accordingly, theories about the nature of corruption are reviewed in the second section. These theories can help diagnose the underlying problems behind corruption with a view to design context-specific solutions. Based on this analysis, the third section outlines recommendations on how to use ICT within a broader anticorruption agenda. ICT alone cannot lead the fight against corruption, but technologies can be a crucial and powerful addition to a broader anti-corruption policy—provided they are implemented within a supporting framework and in a fitting context (Kossow & Dykes, 2018). The final section ends with a consideration on what implications can be drawn from established ICT solutions and applied to emerging technologies like artificial intelligence and blockchain.

6.4.1 Review of the Literature on Digitalization as a Tool for Anticorruption

The large majority of empirical investigations use quantitative approaches to analyse cross-country data with regard to the impact of ICT on corruption. Shim and Eom (2008) highlighted that e-government has a positive impact on reducing perceived corruption, as do the traditional anti-corruption factors (bureaucratic professionalism, bureaucratic quality, and law enforcement). In a later paper, Shim and Eom (2009) found that that ICT is an effective tool for reducing corruption; social capital also has positive effects on anti-corruption, but various dimensions of social capital may have different impacts; and the relationship between social capital and ICT is inconclusive. Choi (2014) argued that all three dimensions of e-government (telecommunication infrastructure, online participation and online services) have a statistically significant influence on the control of corruption. Elbahnasawy (2014) revealed that e-government is a powerful tool in reducing corruption—via telecommunication infrastructure and the scope and quality of online services—which is strengthened by greater internet adoption.

Many studies explored mediating and moderating factors that affect the relationship between e-government and corruption. Kim (2014) found that e-government could be an effective tool to curb corruption in government in spite of the fact that the rule of law is the most powerful predictor of anti-corruption. Furthermore, digital government is more effective when it is strengthened with high quality public bureaucracies. Analyzing a longitudinal dataset of 80 countries, Zhao and Xu (2015) suggested that e-government readiness can be effective in reducing perceived corruption. It can be more effective when combined with measures to enhance government effectiveness and rule of law.

Charoensukmongkol and Moqbel (2014) found a U-shaped relationship between ICT investment and corruption. Although the increase in ICT investment provides technology infrastructures that can effectively monitor and control corruption, more investment itself can also provide an opportunity for corruption to occur. Bhattacherjee and Shrivastava (2018) emphasized that ICT laws moderate the effect of ICT use on corruption, suggesting that ICT investments may have limited effect on corruption, unless complemented with appropriate ICT laws. Nam (2018) found that e-government service maturity contributes to controlling corruption, but this effect is weakened by national culture.

Panel data analysis conducted by Park & Kim (2020) revealed that e-government as a whole significantly reduces corruption, while the effects of open government as one type of e-government are unclear. However, the rule of law moderates the relationship between open government and corruption. Žuffová (2020) highlighted that the effects of open government on corruption are conditional upon the quality of media and internet freedom. Moreover, other factors, such as free and fair elections, independent and accountable judiciary, or economic development, are far more critical for tackling corruption than increasing access to information.

6.4.2 Theories Behind Digitalization for Anticorruption

Most theories about the nature of corruption look at it as an expression of the principal-agent problem (Di Mascio & Piattoni, 2020). This conceptualisation looks at citizens as the principal and government officials, political leaders, and bureaucrats alike, as agents acting on their behalf. As agents have political discretion and often a monopoly over the distribution of resources, there is potential for corruption. Consequently, strategies to fight corruption in the sense of the principal-agent problem commonly focus on decreasing discretionary power of government officials and establishing better oversight and accountability.

According to a recent strand of research, the solutions to the 'principal-agent' issue consider corruption as a problem of individual deviance from the system, implicitly assuming that corruption can be tackled if control instruments affect individual agents' motivations to engage in corrupt behavior. Persson et al., 2013 underline that this assumption is flawed in those contexts where corruption is systemic, meaning that corruption is widely perceived as the norm, and those principals monitoring the agents are themselves corruptible if they cannot trust that others will resist corruption. The roots of this insight are attributed to collective action problems that require a more complex approach. Strategies to fight corruption as a collective action problem draw on a more comprehensive approach that focuses on fostering anti-corruption norms and building coalitions against corruption.

Based on these two approaches, ICT for anticorruption can be represented differently. Corruption that shows characteristics of a principal-agent problem can be addressed through better oversight. In the context of the principal-agent approach, ICT tools serve the fight against corruption by enhancing access to public information, monitoring officials' activities, digitalising public services. Most of these tools have their roots in e-government projects, originating within the public sector as part of public management reforms that are primarily driven by the intent to raise efficiency in public service delivery (Bussell, 2012). ICT tools are applied in the internal operations of the public sector to integrate workflows, enable open information transfers, decrease waiting times. The digitalisation of public services automates administrative tasks and reduces direct contact points between citizens and public officials, therefore removing corruption opportunities induced by traditional paper-based systems. However, it is worth noticing that improvements through the application of ICT are only incremental and that routine tasks are much more amenable to improvement than exceptional or highly discretionary tasks, which are much more dependent on the quality of existing institutions (Adam & Fazekas, 2020).

The digitalization of public services has the added advantage of making government operations more accessible and intelligible to citizens, opening up new opportunities for transparency, where government activities are made public to citizens which facilitates vertical accountability. However, the effect of ICT tools on transparency hinges upon a variety of contextual factors connected to the quality of data and the avenues to use data-driven insights. It should not be taken for granted that the disclosure of data automatically equates to better oversight; for this to be the case, data needs to be released in structured, analysable formats and, ideally, presented in ways that make it intelligible and accessible to the general public. This makes governance areas that are measurable and attributable to the efforts of specific government officials much more amenable to improve with the use of ICT for ensuring better oversight. Furthermore, transparency can bring about improvements in governance only if it is complemented by institutional arrangements that channel public discontent with malfeasance exposed by disclosure such as participatory mechanisms that lower the costs of political engagement and reliable inter-institutional oversight mechanisms providing an avenue by which to utilize information to issue sanctions (Bauhr & Grimes, 2014).

With regard to the approach that tackles corruption as a collective action problem, a majority of ICT anti-corruption tools were developed by civil society groups and were later adopted by governments or replicated in new settings. These tools aim to mobilise citizens against corruption through various means (Kossow & Kukutschka, 2017). In particular, crowdsourcing platforms can foster civil mobilisation against corruption as they invite citizens to provide input on incidences of corruption, often in the form of sharing personal experiences of petty corruption. These platforms can help identify specific trends as to where and how corruption happens. The data gathered can raise public awareness on the pervasiveness of corruption and government authorities can follow up on this information to focus anticorruption measures on those areas that are more prone to corruption. However, the value of crowdsourcing platforms depends on user participation that can be influenced by a number of factors like the ease of use of the platform, skills and abilities of the citizenry, and follow-up action (Zinnbauer, 2015).

ICT-enabled whistleblowing is another tool that supports collective action of public employees who report on cases of corruption with sufficient detail to enable follow-up with legal action. The protection of whistleblowers' identities, confidential advice embedded within the internal reporting system, appropriate follow-up action, and publicity for the platform are crucial to their success (De Graaf, 2019; Taylor, 2018). So far the potential of both crowdsourcing and whistleblowing systems has mainly been approached from a technology-centered perspective, ranging from issues of anonymity guarantee to information validation. In contrast, limited attention has been paid to logics of collective action that interact with technological features to condition the success of digitalization efforts.

The shift from a perception of systemic corruption to a mobilizing message of achievable change can be triggered only if reporting platforms are embedded within broader communication strategy that guides toward action options, showcases positive examples, and sustains follow-ups. This strategy should also consider that digital activism is situational, meaning that it is particularly consistent with the organizational structure of the collective actors in which individual agency is embedded. As revealed by research on grassroot campaigns against corruption, activists' engagement with digital tools requires a collective effort to recombine and contextualize individuals' acts, voices, and claims that would otherwise remain dispersed digital traces with low political potential (Mattoni, 2017).

6.4.3   Policy Recommendations on Digitalization for Anticorruption

In reviewing the field of anticorruption we find that, while some progress has been made, there is little actual focus on the "missing middle": the interventions themselves and how they can be made to work better. In analyzing these interventions, it has been argued that anticorruption projects mostly fail because of excessive "design-reality gaps"; that is, too great a mismatch between the expectations built into their design as compared to on-the-ground realities in the context of their implementation (Heeks & Mathisen, 2012). Placing ICT for anticorruption within an empirically-grounded perspective is the main policy recommendation that can be advanced in this section. This implies taking into account the many barriers that hinder the implementation of digital tools by virtue of a fine-grained assessment of local contexts (Adam & Fazekas, 2020; Kossow & Dykes, 2018).

Firstly, digitalization of a government can only have an impact if citizens know about the existence and the functioning of ICT tools. For this reason, an effective strategy for publicising digital anti-corruption tools needs to be part of any potential project (Porumbescu et al., 2020). This strategy should consider the presence or absence of intermediaries as partners with complementary skills and deep roots in and capabilities for reaching out to particular communities. The power of amplification (through media campaigns) and translation (by skilled intermediaries) can make it more likely that certain ICTs will reach a large number of people and have an impact.

Secondly, capacity building should be part of any project implementing ICT for anticorruption. This means that the implementation of ICT against corruption should always take potential users of digital tools into account and provide capacity building as needed to support the success of civil society mobilization. ICT for anticorruption should also address capacity gap within the public sector that ranges from shortcomings in the technical and organizational support for digital transformation, to the lack of staff with adequate digital skills complemented by the legacy of fragmented datasets. These gaps often reflect a much larger difficulty such as the lack of top-level leadership and professional management. This implies that greater involvement of senior public managers in the implementation process is an essential prerequisite for success of any anticorruption effort (Dràpalovà & Di Mascio, 2020).

Thirdly, most of ICT tools require a specific legal framework in order to be effective. Project designers, policymakers, and stakeholders should work together to prepare implementation simultaneously with the legislation process. Amended legislation is expected to provide a fair balance between preventing corruption on the one hand and data protection on the other. It should also include guarantees for a free press and for the right to freedom of information. It is worth highlighting that new legislation that is meant to tackle corruption can instead create cynicism if there are no institutions to enforce accountability. This is particularly applicable to tools that promise greater transparency and are aimed at mobilising citizens.

Finally, the crucial role for enforcement bodies in the implementation of digital tools should not be understood as a replacement of political commitment that is needed for funding ICT for anticorruption within a coherent and comprehensive performance management framework. The latter provides factors like measurability, that is distinguishing specific areas of action and matching them with specific outcomes; performance milestones to track progress; and goal clarity that provides a clear direction to the entire government. Effective management of ICT for anticorruption therefore requires setting up responsibilities and capacities at the centre of government that are much needed to promote a shared vision across the public sector and towards the citizens (Di Mascio, 2019).

6.4.4 Conclusive Remarks

Most of the anti-corruption strategies in the last years have been driven by the promotion of specific digital tools, generally overestimating the power of technologies to enhance oversight or encourage civic mobilization for integrity. This also holds true for emerging technologies like artificial intelligence and blockchains. Many hope that the autonomous learning abilities of artificial intelligence can contribute to data-driven efforts to detect corruption (Lima & Delen, 2020). By leveraging a shared and distributed database of ledgers, blockchain eliminates the need for intermediaries, cutting red-tape and reducing discretionality (Kossow & Dykes, 2018). However, difficulties associated with data quality and trust are not acknowledged as thoroughly as needed by those accounts that praise the uses of artificial intelligence and blockchain for anticorruption efforts.

Drawing on a review of the literature focusing on ICT in anticorruption, this chapter has highlighted that the fight against corruption may well often be done most successfully by embracing more indirect reform paths that address broader goals like more efficient public services (Verdenicci & Hough, 2015). ICT anti-corruption tools should also be developed with a local focus and keep specific corruption problems in mind since their power to curb corruption varies by the type of service and activity in local contexts (Marquette & Peiffer, 2018). This chapter has also put forward a set of policy recommendations for project managers when designing digital tools for anticorruption.

Firstly, top-down mandates should be combined with clear benefits and opportunities for use of tools in specific contexts. In other words, any ICT project should start with the problem, not with the technology, drawing on stakeholder engagement practices that are much needed to assess the users' demands and capacities. A favourable public governance area to target with ICT should be characterised by a demand for information and motivation from citizens to use digital tools complemented with connectivity and a certain level of ICT proficiency which remain an issue in less-developed contexts.

Secondly, technical barriers related to legacy and interoperability, but also to the resistance and lack of know-how to share data as well as the low quality of the data, should be taken into proper account. The lack of data skills is obviously a key barrier but it is not limited to the absence of a sufficient number of data scientists and ICT project managers within the public sector. It refers to the more general problem of data literacy among civil servants, and notably policymakers.

Thirdly, digitalization is a long-term process, implying that expectations need to be managed correctly. Hype should be avoided and any digital transformation effort should be underpinned by a clear understanding of the steps to take in the short and medium-term to reach intermediate goals that encourage system-wide engagement. Finally, it is important that the role of digitalization in anticorruption is firmly aligned with other areas of work in the field of public management reform to ensure that a collection of disparate ICT projects turns into a coherent framework. Any ICT tool can do little to meaningfully fight corruption when it is considered in isolation without taking into account government effectiveness that enhances the impact of digitalization.

References

Adam, I., & Fazekas, M. (2020). *Are emerging technologies helping win the fight against corruption? A review of the state of evidence*. Government Transparency Institute. http://www.govtransparency.eu/index.php/2020/04/20/are-emerging-technologies-helping-win-the-fight-against-corruption-a-review-of-the-state-of-evidence/

Ananny, M., & Crawford, K. (2018). Seeing without knowing: Limitations of the transparency ideal and its application to algorithmic accountability. *New Media & Society, 20*, 973–989. https://doi.org/10.1177/1461444816676645

Andersen, T. B. (2009). E-Government as an anti-corruption strategy. *Information Economics and Policy, 21*(3), 201–210.

Barocas, S., & Selbst, A. D. (2016). Big data's disparate impact. *California Law Review, 104*, 671–732.

Basyal, D. K., Poudyal, N., & Seo, J. (2018). Does e-government reduce corruption? Evidence from a heterogeneous panel data model. *Transforming Government: People Process Policy, 12*(2), 134–154.

Bauhr, M., & Grimes, M. (2014). Indignation or resignation: The implications of transparency for societal accountability. *Governance, 27*(2), 291–320.

Beke, M. B., & Blomeyer & Sanz. (2015). *'Towards a European strategy to reduce corruption by enhancing the use of open data*. National Research Spain.

Bertot, J. C., Jaeger, P. T., & Grimes, J. M. (2010). Using ICTs to create a culture of transparency: E-government and social media as openness and anti-corruption tools for societies. *Government Information Quarterly, 27*(3), 264–271. https://doi.org/10.1016/j.giq.2010.03.001

Bhattacherjee, A., & Shrivastava, U. (2018). The effects of ICT use and ICT Laws on corruption: A general deterrence theory perspective. *Government Information Quarterly, 35*(4), 703–712.

Bianchi, A. (2013). On power and illusion: The concept of transparency in international law. In A. Bianchi & A. Peters (Eds.), *Transparency in international law* (pp. 1–20). Cambridge University Press.

Bovens, M. A. P. (2003). *De digitale republiek: Democratie en rechtsstaat in de informatiemaatschappij (The digital republic: Democracy and the rule of law in the information society)*. Amsterdam University Press.

Boyle, J. (2003). The second enclosure movement and the construction of the public domain. *Law and Contemporary Problems, 66*(1), 33–74.

Brauneis, R., & Goodman, E. P. (2017). Algorithmic transparency for the smart city. *Yale Journal of Law & Technology, 20*, 104–176.

Brüggemeier, M., & Lenk, K. (2011). *Bürokratieabbau im Verwaltungsvollzug (Downsizingbureaucracy in administrative processes)*. Sigma.

Brusca, I., Manes Rossi, F., & Aversano, N. (2018). Accountability and transparency to fight against corruption: An international comparative analysis. *Journal of Comparative Policy Analysis: Research and Practice, 20*, 486–504. https://doi.org/10.1080/13876988.2017. 1393951

Burkert, H. (2004). The mechanics of public sector information. In G. Aichholzer & H. Burkert (Eds.), *Public sector information in the digital age: Between markets, public management and citizens' rights* (pp. 3–19). Edward Elgar.

Burrell, J. (2016). How the machine 'thinks': Understanding opacity in machine learning algorithms. *Big Data & Society, 3*(1). https://doi.org/10.1177/2053951715622512

Bussell, J. (2012). *Corruption and reform in India: Public services in the digital age*. Cambridge University Press.

Capdeferro Villagrasa, Ó. (2019). Las herramientas inteligentes anticorrupción: Entre la aventura tecnológica y el orden jurídico. *Revista General de Derecho Administrativo, 50*.

Carloni, E. (2005). Nuove prospettive della trasparenza amministrativa: Dall'accesso ai documenti alla disponibilità delle informazioni. *Diritto pubblico, 2*, 573–600.

Carloni, E. (2020). IA, algoritmos y Administración pública en Italia. *Revista Internet, Derecho y Política, 30*, 1–12.

Carloni, E., & Pettinari, G. (2019). Obblighi di pubblicazione e affirmative disclosure. La trasparenza oltre la libertà di informazione. In G. Gardini & M. Magri (Eds.), *Il FOIA italiano: vincitori e vinti. Un bilancio a tre anni dall'introduzione* (pp. 181–213). Maggioli.

Casey, B., Farhangi, A., & Vogl, R. (2019). Rethinking explainable machines: The GDPR's 'Right to explanation' debate and the rise of algorithmic audits in enterprise. *Berkeley Technology Law Journal, 34*.

Cerrillo i Martínez, A. (2017). *Contratación Abierta*. Generalitat de Catalunya.

Cerrillo i Martínez, A. (2019). El impacto de la inteligencia artificial en el Derecho administrativo ¿Nuevos conceptos para nuevas realidades técnicas? *Revista General de Derecho Administrativo, 50*.

Cerrillo-i-Martinez, A. (2012). The reuse of public sector information in Europe and its impact on transparency. *European Law Journal, 18*, 770–792. https://doi.org/10.1111/eulj.12003

Cerrillo-i-Martínez, A. (2013). Fundamental interest and open data for re-use. *International Journal of Law and Information Technology, 20*(3), 203–222. https://doi.org/10.1093/ijlit/eas014

Charoensukmongkol, P., & Moqbel, M. (2014). Does investment in ICT curb or create more corruption? A cross-country analysis. *Public Organization Review, 14*(1), 51–63.

Cho, Y. H., & Choi, B. D. (2004). E-government to combat corruption: The case of Seoul Metropolitan Government. *International Journal of Public Administration, 27*(10), 719–735.

Choi, J. W. (2014). E-government and corruption: A cross-country survey. *World Political Science, 10*(2), 217–236.

Citron, D. K., & Pasquale, F. (2014). The scored society: Due process for automated predictions. *Washington Law Review, 89*, 1–33.

Coglianese, C., & Lehr, D. (2017). Regulating by Robot: Administrative decision making in the machine-learning era. *The Georgetown Law Journal, 105*, 1147–1223.

Corojan, A., & Campos, E. (2011). Gobierno abierto: Alcance e implicaciones. *Documentos de trabajo. Fundación ideas*, 03/2011.

Cotino Hueso, L. (2021). De la transparencia 1.0 a la 4.0. Poniendo a las «máquinas» a rastrear todos los datos de la administración, y más allá. In C. Ramió Matas (Ed.), *Repensando la administración digital y la innovación pública* Madrid: Instituto Nacional de Administración Pública.

Crawford, K., & Schultz, J. (2014). Big data and due process: Toward a framework to redress predictive privacy harms. *Boston College Law Review, 55*, 93–128.

Cucciniello, M., Porumbescu, G. A., & Grimmelikhuijsen, S. (2017). 25 Years of transparency research: Evidence and future directions. *Public Administration Review, 77*, 32–44. https://doi.org/10.1111/puar.12685

Dávid-Barrett, E., & Fazekas, M. (2019). Grand corruption and government change: an analysis of partisan favoritism in public procurement. *European Journal on Criminal Policy and Research.* https://doi.org/10.1007/s10610-019-09416-4.

Davies, T., & Fumega, S. (2014). *Mixed incentives: Adopting ICT innovations for transparency, accountability, and anti-corruption.* U4 Anti-Corruption Resource Centre. https://www.cmi.no/publications/5172-mixed-incentives

De Graaf, G. (2019). What works: The role of confidential integrity advisors and effective whistleblowing. *International Public Management Journal, 22*(2), 213–231.

De Laat, P. B. (2017). Algorithmic decision-making based on machine learning from big data: Can transparency restore accountability? *Philosophy & Technology*, 1–17. https://doi.org/10.1007/s13347-017-0293-z.

Di Mascio, F. (2019). The role of transparency in anticorruption reform: Learning from experience. In E. Carloni (Ed.), *Preventing corruption through administrative measures* (pp. 323–333). Morlacchi.

Di Mascio, F., & Piattoni, S. (2020). Corruption control in the developed world. *Politics and Governance, 8*(2), 72–77.

Dràpalovà, E., & Di Mascio, F. (2020). Islands of good government: Explaining successful corruption control in two Spanish cities. *Politics and Governance, 8*(2), 128–139.

Eijk, A. Z., & Janssen, M. (2015). Participation and data quality in open data use: Open data infrastructures evaluated. Resource document. *Proceedings of the 15th European conference on e-Government.* http://resolver.tudelft.nl/uuid:c3e2530d-eaa2-409b-a700-b7107db7e159. Accessed 13 March 2021.

Elbahnasawy, N. G. (2014). E-government, internet adoption, and corruption: An empirical investigation. *World Development, 57*, 114–126.

Etzioni, A. (2010). Is transparency the best disinfectant? *Journal of Political Philosophy, 18*, 389–404. https://doi.org/10.1111/j.1467-9760.2010.00366.x

Fang, Z. (2002). E-government in digital era: Concept, practice, and development. *International Journal of the Computer, the Internet and Management, 10*(2), 1–22.

Fink, K. (2017). Opening the government's black boxes: Freedom of information and algorithmic accountability. *Information, Communication & Society*, 1–19.

G20, & OECD. (2017). *Compendium of good practices on the use of open data for Anti-corruption: Towards data-driven public sector integrity and civic auditing.*

Gans-Morse, J., Borges, J. M., Makarin, A., Mannah-Blankson, T., Nickow, A., & Zhang, D. (2018). Reducing bureaucratic corruption: Interdisciplinary perspectives on what works. *World Development, 105*, 171–188.

Granickas, K. (2014). Open Data as a Tool to Fight Corruption. *European Public Sector Information Platform Topic Report*, 2014/04.

Grimmelikhuijsen, S. G. (2011). Being transparent or spinning the message?: An experiment into the effects of varying message content on trust in government. *Information Polity, 16*, 35–50. https://doi.org/10.3233/IP20110222

Grimmelikhuijsen, S. G. (2012). A good man but a bad wizard. About the limits and future of transparency of democratic governments. *Information Polity, 17*(3/4), 293–302.

Grimmelikhuijsen, S. G., & Welch, E. W. (2012). Developing and testing a theoretical framework for computer-mediated transparency of local governments. *Public Administration Review, 72*, 562–571. https://doi.org/10.1111/j.1540-6210.2011.02532.x

Grönlund, A., Heacock, R., Sasaki, D., Hellström, J., & Al-Saqaf, W. (2010). *Increasing transparency and fighting corruption through ICT: Empowering people and communities.* SPIDER ICT4D Series No. 3. https://upgraid.files.wordpress.com/2010/11/ict4d_corruption.pdf

Halachmi, A., & Greiling, D. (2013). Transparency, E-government, and accountability. *Public Performance & Management Review, 36*(4), 562–584. https://doi.org/10.2753/PMR1530-9576360404

Haute Autorité pour la transparence de la vie publique. (2016). *Open data & intégrité publique. Les technologies numériques au service d'une démocratie exemplaire.* Available from http://www.hatvp.fr/wordpress/wp-content/uploads/2016/12/Open-data-integrite-publique.pdf.

Heeks, R., & Mathisen, H. (2012). Understanding success and failure of anti-corruption initiatives. *Crime Law & Social Change, 58,* 533–549.

Heywood, P. M. (2017). Rethinking corruption: Hocus-pocus, locus and focus. *The Slavonic and East European Review, 95*(1), 21–48.

Homburg, V. (2004). E-government and NPM: A perfect marriage? In M. Janssen, H. Sol, R. W. Wagenaar (Ed.). *ICEC '04: Proceedings of the 6th international conference on Electronic commerce* (pp. 547–555). https://doi.org/10.1145/1052220.1052289.

Homburg, V., & Snellen, I. (2007). Will ICTs finally reinvent government? – The mutual shaping of institutions and ICTs. In C. Pollitt, S. van Thiel, & V. Homburg (Eds.), *New public management in Europe* (pp. 135–148). Palgrave Macmillan.

Jaeger, P. T., & Bertot, J. C. (2010). Transparency and technological change: Ensuring equal and sustained public access to government information. *Government Information Quarterly, 27*(4), 371–376. https://doi.org/10.1016/j.giq.2010.05.003

Kaufmann, D. (2002, 11–12 April). *Transparency, Incentives and Prevention (TIP) for corruption control and good governance empierical findings, practical lessons, and strategies for action based on internacional experience.* Paper presented at the Qinghua University-Carnegie Conference on Economic Reform and Good Governance: Fighting Corruption in Transition Economies, Beijing.

Khan, A., Krishnan, S., & Dhir, A. (2021). Electronic government and corruption: Systematic literature review, framework, and agenda for future research. *Technological Forecasting and Social Change, 167,* 120737.

Kim, C. K. (2014). Anticorruption initiatives and e-government: A cross-national study. *Public Organization Review, 14*(3), 385–396.

Kim, S., Kim, H. J., & Lee, H. (2009). An institutional analysis of an e-government system for anti-corruption: The case of OPEN. *Government Information Quarterly, 26*(1), 42–50.

Kossow, N. (2020). Digital anti-corruption: Hopes and challenges. In A. Mungiu-Pippidi & P. Heywood (Eds.), *A research agenda for studies on corruption* (pp. 146–157). Edward Elgar.

Kossow, N., & Dykes, V. (2018). *Embracing Digitalisation: How to use ICT to strengthen anti-corruption.* Deutsche Gesellschaft für Internationale Zusammerarbeit – GIZ. https://research.mysociety.org/publications/embracing-digitisation

Kossow, N., & Kukutschka, R. M. B. (2017). Civil society and online connectivity: Controlling corruption on the net? *Crime Law & Social Change, 68*(4), 459–476.

Kroll, J. A., Barocas, S., Felten, E. W., Reidenberg, J. R., Robinson, D. G., & Yu, H. (2017). Accountable algorithms. *University of Pennsylvania Law Review, 165,* 633–705.

Kwon, O., Lee, N., & Shin, B. (2014). Data quality management, data usage experience and acquisition intention of big data analytics. *International Journal of Information Management, 34*(3), 387–394.

Lehr, D., & Ohm, P. (2017). Playing with the data: What legal scholars should learn about machine learning. *University of California Davies Law Review, 51,* 653–716.

Lepri, B., Oliver, N., Letouzé, E., Pentland, A., & Vinck, P. (2018). Fair, transparent, and accountable algorithmic decision-making processes. *Philosophy & Technology, 31*(3), 611–627. https://doi.org/10.1007/s13347-017-0279-x

Lima, M. S. M., & Delen, D. (2020). Predicting and explaining corruption across countries: A machine learning approach. *Government Information Quarterly, 37*(1), 101407.

Lourenço, R. P. (2015). An analysis of open government portals: A perspective of transparency for accountability. *Government Information Quarterly, 32*, 323–332. https://doi.org/10.1007/978-3-642-40358-3_6

Máchová, R., & Lnénicka, M. (2017). Evaluating the quality of open data portals on the national level. *Journal of Theoretical and Applied Electronic Commerce Research, 12*, 21–41. https://doi.org/10.4067/S0718-18762017000100003

Magalhaes, G., & Roseira, C. (2020). Open government data and the private sector: An empirical view on business models and value creation. *Government Information Quarterly*. https://doi.org/10.1016/j.giq.2017.08.004.

Mantelero, A. (2018). AI and Big Data: A blueprint for a human rights, social and ethical impact assessment. *Computer Law & Security Review, 34*(4), 754–772. https://doi.org/10.1016/j.clsr.2018.05.017

Marquette, H., & Peiffer, C. (2018). Grappling with the "real politics" of systemic corruption: Theoretical debates versus "real-world" functions. *Governance, 31*(3), 499–514.

Matheus, R., & Janssen, M. (2020). A systematic literature study to unravel transparency enabled by open government data: The window theory. *Public Performance & Management Review, 43*, 503–534. https://doi.org/10.1080/15309576.2019.1691025

Mattoni, A. (2017). From data extraction to data leaking: Data-activism in Italian and Spanish anti-corruption campaigns. *Partecipazione & Conflitto, 10*(3), 723–746.

Meijer, A. (2009). Understanding modern transparency. *International Review of Administrative Sciences, 75*, 255–269. https://doi.org/10.1177/0020852309104175

Meijer, A., Hart, P., & Worthy, B. (2018). Assessing government transparency: An interpretive framework. *Administration & Society, 50*, 501–526. https://doi.org/10.3233/IP20110222

Merloni, F. (2008). Trasparenza delle istituzioni e principio democratico. In F. Merloni (Ed.), *La trasparenza amministrativa* (pp. 3–28). Giuffrè.

Nam, T. (2018). Examining the anti-corruption effect of e-government and the moderating effect of national culture: A cross-country study. *Government Information Quarterly, 35*(2), 273–282.

Noveck, B. S. (2017). Rights-based and tech-driven: Open data, freedom of information, and the future of government transparency. *Yale Hum. Rts. & Dev. L.J., 19*(1), 1–45.

OECD. (2009). *OECD principles for integrity in public procurement*. OECD.

OECD. (2017). *'Compendium of good practices on the publication and reuse of open data for Anti-corruption across G20 countries: Towards data-driven public sector integrity and civic auditing'*. Paris: Organisation for Economic Co-operation and Development. Available from https://www.oecd.org/gov/digital-government/g20-oecd-compendium.pdf.

Open Contracting. (2018). 'Open up guide: Using open data to combat corruption'. Available from https://open-data-charter.gitbook.io/open-up-guide-using-open-data-to-combat-corruption/.

Pardo, T.A. (2000). Realizing the promise of digital government: It's more than building a web site. *Information Impact*. https://www.ctg.albany.edu/media/pubs/pdfs/realizing_the_promise.pdf. Accessed 13 March 2021.

Park, C. H., & Kim, K. (2020). E-government as an anti-corruption tool: panel data analysis across countries. *International Review of Administrative Sciences, 86*(4), 691–707.

Pasquale, F. (2015). *The black box society: The secret algorithms that control money and information*. Harvard University Press.

Persson, A., Rothstein, B., & Teorell, J. (2013). Why anticorruption reforms fail – Systemic corruption as a collective action problem. *Governance, 26*(3), 449–471.

Piotrowski, S., Grimmelikhuijsen, S., & Deat, F. (2019). Numbers over narratives? How government message strategies affect citizens' attitudes. *Public Performance & Management Review, 42*, 1005–1028. https://doi.org/10.1080/15309576.2017.1400992

Ponti, B. (2012). Open data and transparenct: A paradigm shift. *Informatica e Diritto*, (1–2), 305–320 (2011). https://papers.ssrn.com/sol3/papers.cfm?abstract_id=2087397. Accessed 13 March 2021.

Ponti, B. (2019). La mediazione informativa nel regime giuridico della trasparenza: spunti ricostruttivi. *Diritto dell'informazione e dell'informatica, 2*, 383–421.

Porumbescu, G., Cucciniello, M., & Gil-Garcia, J. R. (2020). Accounting for citizens when explaining open government effectiveness. *Government Information Quarterly, 37*(2), 101451.

Pozen, D. E. (2017). Freedom of information beyond the freedom of information act. *U. Pa. L. Rev., 165*(5), 1097–1158.

Puncel Chornet, A. (2019). Inteligencia artificial para la transparencia pública: El Sistema de Alertas Tempranas (SALER) de la Generalitat Valenciana. *Boletín económico de ICE, Información Comercial Española, 3116*, 41–61.

Ruijer, E., Détienne, F., Baker, M., Groff, J., & Meijer, A. J. (2020a). The politics of open government data: Understanding organizational responses to pressure for more transparency. *The American Review of Public Administration, 50*, 260–274. https://doi.org/10.1177/0275074019888065

Ruijer, E., Grimmelikhuijsen, S., van den Berg, J., & Meijer, A. (2020b). Open data work: Understanding open data usage from a practice lens. *International Review of Administrative Sciences, 86*, 3–19. https://doi.org/10.1177/0020852317753068

Sheryazdanova, G., & Butterfield, J. (2017). E-government as an anti-corruption strategy in Kazakhstan. *Journal of Information Technology & Politics, 14*(1), 83–94.

Shim, D. C., & Eom, T. H. (2008). E-Government and anti-corruption: Empirical analysis of international data. *International Journal of Public Administration, 31*(3), 298–316.

Shim, D. C., & Eom, T. H. (2009). Anticorruption effects of information communication and technology (ICT) and social capital. *International Review of Administrative Sciences, 75*(1), 99–116.

Sturges, P. (2004). Corruption, transparency and a role for ICT? *International Journal of Information Ethics, 2*(11). http://www.i-r-i-e.net/inhalt/002/ijie_002_25_sturges.pdf.

Tai, K.-T. (2021). Open government research over a decade: A systematic review. *Government Information Quarterly.* https://doi.org/10.1016/j.giq.2021.101566.

Taylor, J. (2018). Internal whistleblowing in the public service: A matter of trust. *Public Administration Review, 78*(5), 717–726.

Verdenicci, S., & Hough, D. (2015). People power and anti-corruption: Demystifying citizen-centred approaches. *Crime Law & Social Change, 64*(1), 23–35.

Vetrò, A., Canova, L., Torchiano, M., Orozco Minotas, C., Iemma, R., & Morando, F. (2016). Open data quality measurement framework: Definition and application to Open Government Data. *Government Information Quarterly, 33*, 325–337. https://doi.org/10.1016/j.giq.2016.02.001

Villoria Mendieta, M. (2010). La democratización de la administración pública: marco teórico. In J. Ruiz-Huerta, & M. Villoria Mendieta (Eds.), *Gobernanza democrática y fiscalidad* Madrid: Tecnos.

Vrushi, J., & Hodess, R. (2017). *Connecting the dots: Building the case for open data to fight corruption.* Transparency International.

Web Foundation. (2018). *Barómetro de los Datos Abiertos – Edición de los Líderes.* World Wide Web Foundation.

Wu, A. M., Yan, Y., & Vyas, L. (2020). Public sector innovation, e-government, and anticorruption in China and India: Insights from civil servants. *Australian Journal of Public Administration, 79*(3), 370–385.

Zhao, X., & Xu, H. D. (2015). E-Government and corruption: A longitudinal analysis of countries. *International Journal of Public Administration, 38*(6), 410–421.

Zinnbauer, D. (2015). Crowdsourced corruption reporting: What petrified forests, street music, bath towels, and the taxman can tell us about the prospects for its future. *Policy & Internet, 7*(1), 1–24.

Žuffová, M. (2020). Do FOI laws and open government data deliver as anti-corruption policies? Evidence from a cross-country study. *Government Information Quarterly, 37*(3), 101480.

Chapter 7
Public Procurement and Corruption: Perspectives, Rules, Experiences

Enrico Carloni, Paolo Polinori, and Daniele David

7.1 Introduction

Corruption is one of the major economic and political problems, although to different extents, affecting countries worldwide. Generally speaking, corruption leads to mistrust in institutions, and impacts negatively on a number of fronts including notably, increased long-term costs, a reduction in competitivity, the discouragement of foreign investment, and increased income inequality.

The problem of corruption is quite distinct in the area of public procurement.

The OECD, for example, has highlighted, on the basis of judicial data, the specific criticality of public contracts: it is precisely in this area that approximately two thirds of cases of international corruption are found (Brybery report 2015); while based on estimates, the overall consistency of the "cost" of corruption in public contracts ranges between 10% and 30% in the OECD member countries (OECD, 2016). According to European Commission, corruption increases the costs of public procurement among 20% and 25%, and in some cases up to 50% (European Commission, 2014).

This, moreover, in a context of extraordinary economic importance, and no less strategic given that contracts are increasingly entrusted with the implementation of public objectives and policies, including environmental ones. From the point of view

E. Carloni (✉)
Department of Political Science, University of Perugia, Perugia, Italy
e-mail: enrico.carloni@unipg.it

P. Polinori
Department of Economics, University of Perugia, Perugia, Italy
e-mail: paolo.polinori@unipg.it

D. David
PHD University of Perugia, Comune of Villasimius, Villasimius, Italy
e-mail: daniele.david@comune.villasimius.ca.it

© The Author(s), under exclusive license to Springer Nature Switzerland AG 2021
E. Carloni, M. Gnaldi (eds.), *Understanding and Fighting Corruption in Europe*,
https://doi.org/10.1007/978-3-030-82495-2_7

of the "market", this is estimated, again by the OECD, at approximately 13% of GDP and 29% of total expenditure by public administrations. A field that is all the more important in the context of the Covid-19 health crisis and public investments planned for the recovery following the related economic crisis.

The reason for the connection between corruption and public procurement is also the most obvious: "corruption tends to concentrate wherever there is more money to spend" (Mattarella, 2015, p. 337), and where this expenditure is not constrained but left to the choices of the administration. Hence the widespread recognition that "la contratación es el ámbito de la gestión pública más vulnerable a la corrupción" (Martinez Fernandez, 2017, p. 435).

Alongside the perception of a high level of risk and the recognition of the overall value of the sector, there is the acquired awareness of the negative effects deriving from corruption in the field of public contracts: damage not only to public finances (due to the higher cost of the work burdened by the "price" of corruption), but no less so damage to the candidacy and competitivity of enterprises, for the quality of the works and services, and therefore ultimately, the resultant jeopardizing of rights.

Since this is an issue that strictly affects the functioning of one specific market, that of public contracts, and the implications of which are relevant for the whole development of economic systems, its treatment requires the inclusion of an economic perspective, and the economics of regulation, with an analysis of the evolution of the rules that, in the European reality, have tried and continue to try to determine a careful balance between efficiency, competititiveness and anti-corruption in public procurement.

7.2 Procurement and Corruption: An Economic Perspective

For almost a decade now there has been a significant international focus on corruption as a threat to economic and human development. Several multilateral organizations, like the UN, the World Bank, the WTO and OECD and several national authorities, aims at fighting the problem. So far, however, the strategies to transform the alleged practices of a state administration from corrupt to honest and clean have initially failed in most cases. There are several ways to explain this persistence of corruption, consequently new appropriate analysis is required focusing on corruption transmission channels and the needs of adequate data set. Indeed, any good strategy to fight corruption: first, requires adequate information, second its musts be continually monitored/evaluated in order to adapt it to every possible change. This is of crucial importance given that an inadequate level of information often only allows to conduct aggregate analysis according to which it is not possible to adequately analyze the corruption phenomena and this limitation had produced contradictory empirical results in the past.

From economic point of view two main questions exist. First, how to understand the relationship between corruption and economic efficiency. Second, how to identify the channels through which corruption can alter the mechanisms of resource allocation both at aggregate and disaggregate level: it is with regard to this second question that, as we shall see, the need for a regulation of public procurement arises.

7.2.1 The Relationship Between Corruption and Economic Efficiency

In the literature mixed results exist on the corruption effects both from empirical and theoretical point of views according to the *Grease vs. Sand the wheels hypotheses* which suppose a possible U-shaped relationship between corruption and economic efficiency.

Sand the wheels This approach underlines the negative effects of the corruption on economic activities. Particularly, investments and economic growth (see among others, Mo, 2001; De Vaal & Ebben, 2011; Gründler & Potrafke, 2019) should be negatively affected. In detail, investments are negatively affected by corruption that impose a negative weight on economic growth (Méon & Sekkat, 2005). By the corruption the efficiency of public investment, being diverted towards unproductive sectors (Mauro, 1995).

Another central issue refers to the financial markets (see among others, Zhang, 2012; Ahmed, 2020). In this context, Ng (2006) find that: "corruption is associated with higher firm's borrowing cost, lower stock valuation, and worse corporate governance". Furthermore, corruption affects the accountability of institutions (Hunt, 2005; Hunt & Laszlo, 2005) limiting the economic growth (Méon & Sekkat, 2005). Focusing on European countries Amarandei (2013) confirms that a negative and significant relation between corruption and FDI exist (Wei, 2000; Lambsdorff, 2003). By using the Corruption Perception Index arise that reforms of public administration in order to reduce all the forms of corruption and bribery are urgently required to change the investors perception.

Corruption might negatively affect the productivity of capital stocks in several ways such as: X-inefficiency, rent seeking behavior, distorted public decision, circumvented of the control mechanism for the contract quality level. Particularly, Lambsdorff (2003) finds that corruption significantly reduce the productivity. The most significant channel for the corruption activity are: bureaucratic quality of the public administration even if also civil liberty and government stability are determinant with their quality.

By reducing the costs of environmental protection, technological change is crucial for promoting green growth. The adoption of new technology strongly depends on the willingness to accept of the citizens (Bigerna et al., 2017) but also corruption plays a central role. Italian provinces experiences show that rent seeking and corruption may be an issue for clean technologies. Using a difference-in-difference regression strategy across Italian provinces, Gennaioli and Tavoni (2011) find evidence of greater criminal activity in provinces with high wind energy potential after the passage of policies favorable to the wind energy sector. They also find evidence that greater corruption leads to faster expansion of wind energy.

Finally, when the political and institutional contexts appear uncertain, corruption may be seen as an insurance against risks, although it is an illegal agreement very difficult to secure. Thus, the uncertainty due to corrupt acts may just add to that caused by political instability enhancing its negative effect on the efficiency of the economic system (Lambsdorff, 2003).

Grease the wheels According to some scholars, corruption may positively affect economic systems. These authors leaving aside any moralistic judgments, argue that corruption may positively affect the productivity of an economic system because it counterbalances the inefficiency of the governance, overcoming relevant barriers to economic development such as bureaucratic inefficiency.

This hypothesis suggests that corruption may exert positive effects on economic development, leaving aside any moralistic judgments on it. The line of reasoning is that corruption may be able to solve the problem of bureaucratic inefficiency and bad public policies, these being barriers to economic development. This hypothesis, even if going back to 50 years, still has its relevance today. Corruption represents an efficient way to decrease the time wasted dealing with bureaucrats (Leff, 1964; Leys, 1965; Lui, 1985), In addition, corruption seems to be able to offset the inefficiency of regulations or bad public policies. For example, foreign private investors may select economic environments where it is possible to acquire a certain degree of stability through bribery and corruption is less detrimental in countries where bureaucracy is slow and cumbersome and therefore more prone to be greased.

In 2010 Halkos and Tzeremes found a U-shaped relationship between corruption and economic efficiency, suggesting that an increase in corruption beyond a certain level can impact positively on economic performance.

These results mainly rely on aggregated data at country level and several authors have highlighted the need to undertake more fine-grained investigations of the relationship between corruption and the different dimensions of performance.

Svensson (2005 p. 40) highlights that: *"The link between the macro literature on how institutions provide a more-or-less fertile breeding ground for corruption and the micro literature on how much corruption actually occurs in specific contexts is weak. As more forms of corruption and techniques to quantify them at the micro level are developed, it should be possible to reduce this mismatch between macro and micro evidence on corruption."*

Accordingly with this perspective Dal Bó and Rossi (2007) p. 941) state that: *"Work examining consequences at the micro level should be important because it will help pin down the ways in which corruption damages the economic perfor-mance of nations."*

For instance, the same authors (Dal Bó & Rossi, 2007) studying the market of electricity distribution in Latin America countries find that when the level of 'environmental' corruption is high, firms tend to be more inefficient in terms of labor use.

Abrate et al. (2015) show that 'environmental' corruption significantly increases inefficiency when looking at solid waste collection activities in Italian municipalities. It is important to notice that, in this perspective some studies rely on country-level measures of corruption that being subjective indices may suffer of potential distortions. In order to avoid this criticism, in other works scholars use objective measure of 'environmental' corruption also using micro-level data. Yan and Oum (2014) show that airport productivity in the U.S. is negatively affected by the corruption rate at state level. Abrate et al. (2015) find that both 'environmental' corruptions, measured by the number of criminal charges against the public institutions as well as by the Golden and Picci index[1] (Golden & Picci, 2005), and a low degree accountability of public operators negatively affect the cost efficiency of the solid waste collection and disposal activity in Italy. Even if, several articles on corruption give the impression that the real world is populated by two types of corruptors it is important to underline the overall negative effect of the corruption. Indeed, although the first type refers to idea that corruption is an obstacle to development (sanders), while the second one refers to the idea that corruption can (in some cases) foster development (greasers). Summing up, it is important to put forward that both hypotheses state that corruption negatively affect economic performance when the institutional framework is efficient. They differ only in the case of inefficient institutional framework suggesting negative (sand) versus positive (grease) effects of corruption on efficiency. We take a critical look at this position underling that the evidences supporting the 'greasing the wheels hypotheses are very weak. Empirical results have shown that even if corruption may have little average effect on the growth rate of GDP per capita, it is a likely source of unsustainable development. This critical position is enhanced by the empirical evidences that arise focusing on the public procurement procedures. In this context imprecise and qualitative information, such as enhancement plans, quality and performance, must be considered in order to avoid that for every tender, the award deliberation may become a time-consuming and expensive process. Especially, if both prices and technical aspects are to be take into account and if the number of bidders is relatively very large the selection of the winning proposal could be a highly complex process especially in absence of information. Indeed, given that decisions must be based on a strict and unambiguous ranking of the available offers, the largest possible level of information to ensure objectivity is required in the awarding method. In details, the efficiency in public procurement depends on determinants such as: quality of institutions, uncertainty, opportunistic behavior, incompleteness of the contract, lack of coordination, excessive bureaucracy. Accordingly, public procurement requires more attention in term of economic analysis in order to prevent corruption

---

[1]This indicator account for the difference between the amount of physically existing public infrastructure -roads, schools, hospitals, etc.- and the amount of money cumulatively allocated by government to create this public works.

phenomena. For example, it is possible to measure the efficient management of public works focusing on two main dimensions (Guccio et al., 2012):

(i) the output/outcome of the work (e.g., the quality of the work, its capability of satisfying the objectives and the needs for which it has been carried out, etc.);
(ii) the process of the execution of the contract, which is instrumental to the realization of the output/outcome.

Since the first empirical papers studying the effects of corruption, its measurement has represented a serious problem, leading to different approaches.

Different measures of corruption have been suggested in the literature: subjective as well objective indexes have been used. For example, subjective indexes are based on the collection of the results of several cross-country surveys of citizens and experts being asked to state their corruption perceptions while main objective indexes that refer to economic aspects could be prices of inputs procured by the public sector or the gap between the number of physically existing public infrastructures and the financial resources cumulatively allocated by government to build them. Among objective indexes which refer to criminal-justice the number of crimes against the public administrations is one of the more used.

7.2.2 Public Procurement: A Possible Transmission Channel

Public procurement hugely contributes to a state's economy delivering the required inputs to the public administration at appropriate cost and quality. Unfortunately, it often fails to fulfill expectation and objectives. Cost and time overrun, suboptimal performance and project failures determine a general dissatisfaction. Corruption determining misuse of public office for private gain, produce distorted prices and inflated procurement costs. As consequence first, businesses could be placed in a disadvantageous position and second a "tax" is added to the cost of providing public services, third, the public sector's ability to provide adequate levels of public goods to facilitate private sector development might be heavily jeopardized (Olken, 2007).

Consequently, it would be relevant to study the pattern of public procurement corruption in multiple organizations from the perspectives of different countries. For examples, Italian economists found that the cost of several major public construction projects fell dramatically after the anticorruption investigations in the early nineties. This is a crucial issue given that when aggregated to a macro-economic level non-optimal choice of contractors can have a great negative effect on the economy.

According to the OECD (2016 p. 6): *"Public procurement is one of the government activities most vulnerable to corruption. In addition to the volume of transactions and the financial interests at stake, corruption risks are exacerbated by the complexity of the process, the close interaction between public officials and businesses, and the multitude of stakeholders."*

Indeed, several reports and scientific papers have highlighted that public procurement is a critical area for corruption given that this criticism represents a paramount

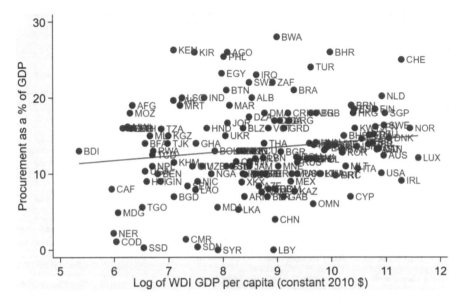

Fig. 7.1 Public procurement expenditure as % of GDP. *Sources:* World Bank (2020)

area for the economy worldwide. According to the World Bank (2020) 12% of global GDP is spent following procurement regulation without substantial differences among countries. Indeed, across low-, middle- and high-income countries goods and services are procured, on average, with a percentage that's range between 12 and 14% (Fig. 7.1). European and emerging countries, among others, are characterized by a higher share of public procurement reflecting a larger engagement by the government in providing goods, services and works. On the contrary, weak states that exhibit a lower ability to deliver goods and services are less able to implement general procurement procedures.

Focusing on the EU, the efforts to monitor, measure, and fight the corruption are due to the importance of public procurement that is in the EU economy 15% of the EU GDP. In the recent past, the issue of corruption in public procurement has attracted the attention of both academicians and policy makers worldwide even if also in the past several scholars had addressed this topic. Myrdal (1968) and Kurer (1993) show that bureaucrats may slow down the provision of public goods to make subjects offering bribes to speed up the procedures. In the case of new license assignment, Rose-Ackerman (1997) reports that corrupt behavior may lower the probability that the winner is the most efficient competitor.

An extensive literature deals with the performance of procurement as well as with the effects of corruption on procurement. The performance of public contracts is usually affected by the features of procurement procedures such as (Bajari & Tadelis, 2001):

(i)   the selection of the private contractor (whether it is competitive or not);
(ii) the specification of the contract (whether it is fixed price of cost plus);
(iii) the enforcement of the contract.

Furthermore, the efficiency of public contracts is also negatively affected by corruption opportunities, which are widespread in procurement activities (Estache & Trujillo, 2009). In particular, the risk of corruption can occur on the various phases of the public procurement cycle, generating different problems:

(i)   when the demand is assessed;
(ii) when the process design and the bid documents are prepared;
(iii) when the contractor is selected and the contract awarded;
(iv) when the contract is implemented;
(v)   when final accounts are certified;
(vi) furthermore, corruption may be a relevant variable for the decision to adopt first price sealed bid auction instead of average bid auctions in the awarding of public work contracts.

In details, literature on this topic reports a negative relationship between infrastructures provision and corruption mainly looking at the procedures for the contractor selection and at the specification of the contract (Benitez et al., 2010). Bandiera et al. (2009) detect corruption in public procurement procedures looking at the prices paid for goods and services provided by the public sector. Guccio et al. (2012) report that high levels of corruption, as measured by Golden and Picci (2005) indicator, are associated to higher adaptation costs. In the analysis of the relationship between PP and corruption several scholars distinguish between the corruption called "active waste" and inefficiency in managing purchases called "passive waste" showing that the weight of passive waste is four times stronger than the one of active waste. More recently, Mashal (2011) terms corruption as the abuse of public offices in pursuit of private gains. This implies that corruption hinders public procurement in achieving development goals such as reducing poverty, providing health and infrastructure at large (Eyaa & Oluka, 2011). The misuse of public offices for private gain is rampant in developing countries like Tanzania frustrates all efforts rendered towards the achievement of development goals through public procurement (Chekol & Tehulu, 2014). According to Amemba et al. (2013) public procurement is an imperative function of the government as it significantly impacts on the economy and societal needs. Further it is also advocating that procurement is central to the government service delivery system, and promotes aims which are arguably secondary to the primary aim of procurement such as using procurement to promote social, industrial or environmental policies. Hence public procurement is the bedrock of national development when managed for public gain. Decarolis (2014) shows no statistically significant effect of measures of Italian public administrations corruption. In details, potentially relevant variables for the decision to switch to First Price Auction, such as:

  (i) competitiveness of the Average Bid Auction;
 (ii) measures of Public Administration corruption;
(iii) political orientation.

    are shown not to be statistically significant. Finocchiaro Castro et al. (2014) investigate the relationship between the efficiency in the execution of public works contracts and the level of corruption at the provincial level in Italy. They find that greater corruption in the area where the infrastructure is localized is significantly associated with lower efficiency in the execution of the public contract. Similar results have fund by Gennaioli and Tavoni (2011): "in the wind sector. In a context of weak institutions windier provinces (Avellino, Benevento, Campobasso, Cosenza, Foggia, Potenza, Sassari, Trapani) are more likely to experience corruption, especially after the introduction of a more favorable policy regime." The introduction of a favorable market-based regime of public incentives has spurred the criminal association activity especially in high-wind provinces increasing the number of wind energy projects in a given province with the extent of corruption. Renewable sector has showed that well designed policies can also have an adverse impact in heavily regulated environments with poorly functioning socio-political institutions.

    All these experiences underline that space exist for a deeper and more accurate regulation process.

7.3   Demand for Regulation and Corruption in the Public Procurement Context

The demand for regulation is mainly connected with two features of the group beneficiaries, the size of the group and whether the main stakes of the group are involved in the regulation process. According to Dal Bó (2006, pp. 204–5) excessive group size could hamper successful organization of the beneficiary group, while large stakes could mobilize group members and give them an incentive do demand regulation.

    Demand for regulation perspective suggests that groups with strong interests or large membership could be dangerous for regulators. Regulator, have to avoid and/or resist group pressures in order to choose and decide on behalf of the public interest. Indeed, empirical evidences suggest lobbyist continue to invest more and more funding in lobbying over time hinting that it is profitable irrespective of the fact that this behavior allow or not to capture the regulators (Falaschetti, 2008).

    The increasing of the lobby activity has a dangerous consequence in the public administration in economic term too. Interest groups might manipulate the organization of the contracting process in public procurement given that different interest groups might argue in favor and against to certain contracting process design only according to their own "personal interest".

Even if, centralized contracting structures have been historically favored to avoid allocative inefficiency due to these manipulation activities, recently contract delegation in public procurement projects has become more and more frequent over time (Theilen, 2008). In this context the regulation of lobbying could be regarded as a way to enforce the anti-corruption activity. Indeed, the diversion of public action from public interest, through the capture of the public decision-makers due to the action of the partial organized interests, is clearly attributable within the corruption.

Analyzing several public procurement procedures in Tuscany Vannucci (2011) underlines the sedimentation of "bad practices" jointly with abuse of powers that acting according to different internal regulation mechanisms. In the case of the occasional corruption the number of economic agents involved is finite and the typical behavior is the "eat and run" while if these bad practices are structural the higher number of actors adopt behavior leaded by the reiteration of the practices. Reiteration allows to build durable and stable relationships among these economic agents producing cohesion and selective reliability among them.

In details, among corrupt and corruptors, and therefore among all the insiders, is shared the "common knowledge" required in order to adopt the patterns of behavior that is absolutely necessary to build collusive arrangements and to distort the outcome of tenders (Vannucci, 2011).

Differences exist among these bad practices also according to the context in which they are applied. In "Mafia Capitale" one of the most interesting element is the strong linkage between intimidatory practices and corruptive practices. Corruptors have hugely used both these type of actions in a symbiotic way increasing the efficiency of each other's in a perverse learning by doing process. The result of this process has been the introduction of the illicit rules of the corruptors to a large proportion of public procurement (Martone, 2016) by the capacity of intimidation exercised on potential competitors, intimidation obtained in a highly omertose context also due to tacit collusion practices existing in the local public administration and in the local political environment.

From the economic point of view, the large corruptive market that regulated the public expenditure in Rome municipality, is the answer to the demand for regulation supplied by the mafia method in absence of a legal system able to provide the right answers.

The case of "Mafia Capitale" had highlighted how the "mafia organization" was not the main problem. A crucial role was been played by the pervasiveness of the corruptive circuits, to which the "mafiosi" can usefully adhere, without however being an essential component of them (Martone, 2016). These corruptive circuits are the results of both the stratification overtime of the bad practices and the lack of the technical knowledge among politicians and administrators. Technical knowledge understood as the ability to get information and develop strategies and the ability to assess feasibility and the outcome of the all-potential public choices. Without these skills and in the absence of the good practices both at the administrative and political level will be increasingly disregarded the general principle of regulation for which the public interest should have primacy over private and business interests.

7.4   Public Procurement as Part of Anti-corruption Strategy

The notion is widely and generally accepted that public procurement is particularly exposed to the risk of corruption, and that the matter requires careful regulation to contain these risks. To this end, numerous international bodies have encouraged the development and refinement of strategies of countering and containment in the area of public contracts: among others, the OECD, which has recommended a wide-ranging approach—not strictly limited to aspects of contractor selection proce-dures—to contain risks to integrity and the occurence of episodes of corruption (OECD, 2015).

Moreover, the theme is well-addressed in the often-cited UNCAC Convention which identifies public procurement as an area that requires special care. Here the attention however is above all given to the definition of standards capable of ensuring correct measures in tender procedures and consequently the identification of the private "supplier" (UNODC, 2013; Racca et al., 2016).

The construction of "appropriate systems of procurement, based on transparency, competition and objective criteria in decision-making, that are effective, inter alia, in preventing corruption" is the objective to which the various legal systems must aim, providing in particular: adequate information about the tenders, giving potential tenderers sufficient time to prepare and present their bids; prior definition and publication of the conditions for participation, including selection criteria; the adoption of predetermined and objective criteria for the choice of contractors; an effective appeals system to guarantee the application of the procedures thus defined; guarantees of the absence of conflicts of interest on the part of public personnel involved in the procedure.

The approach urged by the OECD combines the attention to the moment of the tender with attention to other aspects, pointing out that "integrity risks exist through-out the public procurement process", which necessitates "a holistic approach for risk mitigation and corruption prevention". The OECD recommendations on public procurement lead in this direction and identify a series of mutually-supportive prin-ciples with a view to direct or indirect prevention of corruption and the strengthening of good administration and accountability. These principles, further in this docu-ment, include the integrity of officials, transparency, stakeholder participation, accessibility, e-procurement, supervision and control (OECD, 2016).

Comparing supranational indications, two different strategies emerge. They are not mutually exclusive but have received different attention over time, particularly in the European experience: on one hand, the idea of the containment of corruption that passes above all (and essentially) through the definition of "good rules" aimed at discipline in public tendering (Shooner, 2002; Racca & Yukins, 2014), while on the other, that which sees in public contracts an area in which to concentrate in a targeted manner, with particular attention and strength, all the measures that in general terms are aimed at preventing corruption (the approach oriented to manage a risk, here particularly high; the definition of rules of conduct, more stringent; greater transpar-ency, etc.). In sum, it can be said on the one side the theme of anti-corruption emerges within the framework of public procurement rules; on the other, the theme of public procurement emerges within the framework of anti-corruption rules. In any case, the two approaches outline convergent paths as attention to the theme of corruption prevention increases (Cantone & Carloni, 2018).

7.5   The Discipline of Public Contracts and Corruption

If we look at the issue from the point of view of the discipline of public procurement, we can immediately see that a series of different needs are placed on its regulation: limitations on public spending, guarantees of quality in the works carried out and the services purchased by administrations, integrity and containment of the risks of corruption, protection of competition. These are needs that traditionally tend to find a common response in the provisions of an open tender, that allows the selection of the best offer on all fronts (see for example Racca & Yukins, 2014; Cerrillo, 2018).

The need to safeguard such an important stage is sometimes covered by specific hypotheses, such as the disruption of "bid-rigging", which primarily concerns collusion between economic operators (who agree, for example, on the tenders to submit, thus "defrauding" the administration; see OECD, 2012). This is not only to be found under criminal disciplines in the individual European legal systems but also under provisions in the European Commission (Communication 2021/C 91/01). It is however, above all in the discipline of the procedural rules of the tenders that the attention of the national systems and more recently of the European one is focused, where an organic and detailed framework of rules has been defined progressively through a series of directives among which those of 2014 stand out.

With regard to the regulation of public contracts, it is useful to introduce certain elements in order to understand its objectives and characteristics, which are partly linked to what has been seen in dealing with the economic perspective. As far as the objectives are concerned, the discipline that regulates the relationship between public administrations and economic operators has, as mentioned, a number of aims: the containment of public spending, the search for an optimal solution in terms of price and quality, the guarantee of competition and the market, the guarantee of impartiality and integrity of public contractors. In addition to these, increasingly evident in Europe with the so-called "fourth generation" directives (those of 2014), the discipline seeks to ensure other common aims of general interest, such as ecological transition, social inclusion, safeguarding the role of small and medium-sized enterprises and local economies (Lichère et al., 2014).

An important consideration is the fact that public contracting normally develops in a number of stages. We can return to what has been said concerning economic profiles but the question arises in broader terms. Put simply, the question concerns the moments that precede the tender (where needs are defined and the premises of the tender are laid), the planning stage (and, where necessary, design of operations), the tendering stage (with the formulation of bids by competing operators and the selection of the winning contractor/s), the post-tendering stage of contract execution (that is central above all in the area of public works, where numerous problems and possible real-time modifications to the work may arise) (Racca, 2019). Traditionally, the attention of the legislator (both national and European) has been focused, as mentioned, on the stage of the public tender, which they have tried to regulate with great detail and attention to avoid competition being "unfair", not least by the dynamics of corruption. More recently, but still relatively weakly, attention has been dedicated in Europe to the stages that come before and come after the tendering, and no less, to the very organization of the structures and the offices responsible for handling public contracts.

With regard to the discipline of European origin, that is open to all member countries of the EU and is projected towards those nations that aspire to entry into the Union, this is defined, as stated, by a series of directives, which are firstly established with a view to promoting the opening up of a strategic sector for the development of the internal market, that of public procurement. Hence an approach that tends to favour recourse to the public tender, with a discipline inspired by the principles of openness, transparency and non-discrimination in access to public contracts, but also to promote the greatest possible participation by competitors. In essence, we find ourselves faced with an approach that, among the various possible aims of regulating public contracts, tends to favor competition. This is reflected in a number of mechanisms, putting in particular, European legislation in tension with the solutions, often more rigid and "excluding", fixed in the framework of a national legislation oriented towards maximizing other needs (such as that of integrity, deflecting, for example, possible participation by 'unqualified' operators or that "unscreened" operators may join during implementation of the contract, as can happen, allowing ampler subcontraction) (Macchia, 2017; Rinaldi, 2019). Beyond this, noticeable in the structure of the directives, is a "pragmatic" approach (of native English and Northern European systems), oriented towards dialogue with operators, mutual trust between contracting authorities and economic operators, public-private partnership, and flexibility which often contrasts the more rigid and binding rules aimed at protecting administrations from the risks of corruption, which characterized the regulatory system in Southern European countries, whose regulations were often characterized by a lack of confidence in the ability of contracting authorities to relate to the economic operators: exemplary in this is Italy, where the containment of the danger of corruption has been translated, especially after the scandals of the nineties of the last century known as "Tangentopoli", into a system of meticulous rules, aimed at limiting the scope for discretion in tendering procedures (normally favoring the use of open tenders and awarding based on the lowest price) and to "separate", until the opening of the bid envelopes, the administration from the potential contractors (Merloni & Vandelli, 2010; Vannucci, 2011).

It is an approach however that has shown its limits, so much so that in the Italian experience it has not appeared capable of containing the dangers of corruption: in particular, the idea that the "discretion-corruption" equation is wrong has been consolidated, because it is precisely in the context of apparently binding procedures that important episodes of corruption have occurred. Effectively, if the tendering stage is scrupulously regulated, risks may appear before (with, for example, the definition of a 'made-to-measure tender"), or after (in the stage of execution, for example generously allowing "changes" to the contract) A particularly rigid system can result easily exposed to the risk of stalling and contention, raising possible derogations as solutions that allow the original terms and rules to be bypassed.

In overall terms, it can be said that the discipline of public procurement is not, however, by itself capable of preventing corruption: too light a regulation exposes to risks, which, moreover, depend very much on the context in which administrations but then again, too detailed and excessive regulation can also foster a loss of effectiveness in administrative action, even a loss of integrity.

The contradictions inevitably present in regulatory mechanisms mean that it is primarily on the transparency mechanisms that the attention, and also the confidence, of many commentators. Already in the same European Directive 24/2014 it is highlighted that "transparency of decision-making in procurement procedures is essential for ensuring sound procedures, including efficiently fighting corruption" (recital 126). A transparency that is understood as due documentation of the different moments and stages, such as preferential use of electronic communication solutions (the use of which can "simplify the publication of contracts and increase the efficiency and transparency of procurement processes", as affirmed in recital 52). The directive dedicates particular attention to the principle, which is elaborated in a dedicated section (Title II, Section II), where numerous transparency obligations are provided for both in the form of general publication of documents (for example, notices) and in the form of the right of access and information for participants (Racca & Yukins, 2014; Racca, 2019).

7.6   The Regulation of Anti-corruption and Public Procurement: Notes Starting from the Italian Case

This inadequacy of the discipline of public procurement alone is well highlighted in United Nations literature, and as mentioned, that of the OECD. A "holistic" approach therefore appears necessary. This entails a change in approach, centered on the administration and its way of being before even the specific "tender", as well as attention to all stages of the procurement process.

Hence an approach that tends to result in a strengthening of the measures for the prevention of corruption when the administration operates as "client" in tenders. Attention to the rules of conduct and integrity of the personnel in charge of the various stages and, in particular, those involving the public tender, specific duties of abstention, obligations to declare and verify the absence of situations of conflict of interest of public personnel, post-employment limits, find in the area of public procurement specific opportunities to be strengthened.

The case that sets out most evidently the theme of incorporation and integration of public procurement with that of anti-corruption is in Italy, where, with a reform in 2014 the Anti-Corruption Authority has been entrusted with all the competences in the field of supervision and regulation of public contracts previously entrusted to a separate independent authority. This "fusion" of anti-corruption and public procurement has been criticized by part of the doctrine (Torricelli, 2018; Delsignore & Ramajoli, 2019) mainly because it is seen as an expression of a "criminalization" of the sector, but also because it is capable of producing an "imbalance" (in favor of legality) of the equilibrum that must characterize a system of public procurement that must remain oriented at the same time towards efficiency, competition and transparency (Di Donato, 2020). From this "fusion" however a particularly enriched experience has emerged and that has led to the development of innovative solutions and an organic approach to the theme of guaranteeing integrity in the area of public contracts (Cantone & Carloni, 2018).

Without presuming here to examine all aspects, within the framework of the Italian legal system we now find special, stronger rules for transparency (such as a right of access for competitors, but above all as obligations of transparency through the dissemination of information on the administrations' websites) and for integrity (with specific obligations provided for under the code of conduct for contractual employees, with specific rules of non-transferability and incompatibility, post-employment and revolving door limitations) (Cantone & Carloni, 2018; Merloni, 2019; Cantone, 2020). The Anti-Corruption Authority has furthermore adopted sets of guidelines to prevent conflicts of interest by personnel who handle public contracts and in particular those who hold responsiblity for the procedures (ANAC, 2019). As the OECD points out, the provision of specific rules aimed at ensuring the absence of conflicts of interest in procurement procedures is, on the other hand, common to most OECD countries (OECD, 2016).

Furthermore, in the prevention of corruption approach as "risk management", the area of public contracts is seen as a high risk area and allows for careful attention to the adoption of measures for the risk management, of vigilance, and the training of the personnel involved in the sector. Despite differences in the various experiences, this approach is recurrent in the European scenario, where many countries have introduced specific rules of conduct for procurement officials, often also with guidelines or training activities to assist them in the management of the more complex and frequent situations that could jeopardize their integrity. The importance of training is particularly marked in the Anti-Corruption Strategy of the Austrian Federal Procurement Agency, and France also stands out with a good practice for the specialized training offered to public procurement officials (OECD, 2016) Competence in the subject really does appear key in order to best ensure efficiency and transparency in the processes of procurement in public administrations.

In this perspective, a central element in the Italian approach has been above all to define the standard of quality of the awarding administrations, this also in order to overcome an eccessive fragmentation of supply: in substance it should not be possible to award contracts above a low threshold of expenditure for administrations lacking adequate expertise. This, with a view to defining centers of competence which other administrations can consult and which the Anti-Corruption Authority can efficiently monitor. This aspect however, expected to in place as of 2016 has never been completely actualised consequently severely weakening the whole approach (Rinaldi, 2019; Corradino, 2020).

Though criticized, the Anti-Corruption Authority (ANAC) becomes the qualifying element at the center of a specific model of action in the public procurement sector and represents an undoubted change in trend compared to the previous structure of anti-corruption legislation: Italian legislature seems to have understood that the rules for the execution of public tenders, which condition their outcome, must have as their sole objective that of selecting the best possible offer and, therefore, lead to an efficient choice capable of safeguarding the market equilibrum. It is outside these tender rules that it is necessary to create an environmental context that innoculates the procedures from corruption and that guarantees integrity, beginning with the growth of competence of the contracting administrations.

The integration of anti-corruption and public procurement competencies enables ANAC to take an assimilated approach on both fronts. A significant example is the ability to develop corruption and anomaly indicators from the data it has at its disposal as a supervisory authority (see Chap. 3).

And it is thanks to integration in view to prevention that in the Italian experience it has been possible to develop innovative modes of control over correctness and legality, that become formidable strategies of efficiency in public contracting matters: this, in particular, through the working of a model of control-in-itinere, called "collaborative vigilance", which has been taken as a reference at an international level and has proved to be both efficient (reducing disputes and ensuring the correct relationship between budgeted and incurred expenses) and effective (ensuring the completion of works within timeframes that are sometimes particularly tight, as was the case with Expo Milan 2015). In substance, according to this mechanism, the ANAC works alongside the administrations, verifying step-by-step the main documents and ensuring the correctness, legality and timelines of the procedures. Moreover, the publication of the investigative activities on specific cases carried out by ANAC also allows other contracting authorities to acquire greater competence in the matter of public procurement, also in a logic of deflation of litigation, with the direct consequence that the decisions adopted by the Authority become parameters for self-judgement of activities by individual contracting administrations, alongside the jurisprudential activity carried out by the judicial authorities (Cantone & Carloni, 2018; Cantone, 2020).

It is a mechanism that merits further examination, with reference to an important case that also provides the occasion to look at the functionality of the corruption-prevention system and public procurement in operative and concrete terms—that of the post-seismic riconstruction in central Italy.

7.7 Disaster and Prevention of Corruption: The Case of the 2016 Earthquake in Central Italy

A case study can be interesting and useful to gather the issues that clearly arise in the area of public contracts in situations of emergency, and the peculiarities of the approach developed in Italy at a crossroads between anti-corruption and procurement.

On 24 August 2016, a seismic shock with a magnitude of 6.0, its epicenter at Accumoli, in the province of Rieti and one of magnitude 5.4 with the epicenter at Amatrice (Rieti) set off a period of exceptional seismic activity lasting eighteen months and covering an area of almost 8000 square kilometers across four regions (Lazio, Umbria, Marche and Abruzzo) and affecting approximately 600,000 people.

The seismic crater of 2016, meaning the group of municipalities recognized by law among those most affected, corresponds to one of the areas of the Italian territory with the highest seismic hazard and includes about 140 municipalities, mainly mountainous and characterized by scattered settlement systems, a particularly depressed economic sector and a fragile demographic: of the 140 affected municipalities 130 had less than 10,000 residents and 56 less than 1000. Of the approximately 600,000 residents of the crater, 25% were over 65 years old, while only 12% were less than 14 years old. From an economic and productive point of view, 97.1% of the surface of the most affected municipalities is characterized by scattered productive and residential settlements, with an average population density of 72.9 inhabitants/km^2, well below the national average of 200.6 inhabitants/km^2. It is evident, therefore, that in territories where the public and private real estate assets have been largely destroyed, including peaks that have exceeded 85%, the management and administration of reconstruction processes has required an immense effort, both in terms of planning and implementation: it was a fact well-known that the seismic crater of Central Italy would be among the largest construction sites in Europe with all the consequences, in terms of risk management that this entailed.

Reconstruction processes following a disaster imply the management of numerous risks (Calossi et al., 2012), some strictly linked to the construction stages, others latent, connected to opportunistic behaviors of maladministration up to more marked behaviors of criminal nature with criminal relevance, which can be occur because of the large sums of money that are placed in the territories through necessarily diversified procedures.

The Italian model adopted following the decree-law n. 189/2016, has been largely anchored to the principle of integration between the ordinary rules of public procurement and necessarily derogatory provisions (Spuntarelli, 2017). This choice, even with respect to the models of post-calamity reconstruction adopted in Italy over the years (Imperiale & Vanclay, 2019), although repeatedly criticized by external observers, who associate this decision with the sluggishness of the process, is derived from a number of observations.

The first of these related to the fact that the criminal phenomena that have affected other territories afflicted by previous natural disasters, needed conscious and prudent management in order not to generate, on the basis of urgency and necessity, developments that instead of ensuring competition would misguide it, further weakening competent professionals and small operators.

The second, directly connected to the first one, saw in the construction of the model of control an exponential logic designed to adapt the model of action and consequently of control, to the various levels of administrative action and to the various stages, in the knowledge that the reconstruction, if on one hand consists of meeting the needs surfacing in the aftermath of a calamitous event, on the other—or at least potentially—can become a means to relaunch the economy of the area.

Consequently, public action has also required and requires an appropriate control mechanism, not only of the chain of acts but also of the system of allocations, a control which, far from wishing to cancel the administrative discretion inherent in public action, must however allow the victims of such events to have knowledge of the propriety, not only formal but in substance, of administrative acts.

The system of controls and prevention of corruption has seen the collaboration and coordination of various figures that respond to the endogenous and exogenous risks to the reconstructive process, summarily presented below:

- Commissioner Extraordinary for the Earthquake under the Presidency of the Council of Ministers;
- Sub-Commissioners for Reconstruction/Presidents of the Regions involved
- the Anti-Corruption Authority with the task of controlling tenders in the area of public reconstruction;
- Ministry of the Interior mission structure
- Local Prefectures through the management of white lists of operators.

The control model is implemented around two "poles" or hubs that are not opposed but contiguous: at one end, the need to build protocols and effective procedures of action, at the apex of which is the Commissioner Extraordinary; at the other, the role of ANAC aimed at preventing corruption and maladministration, in a logic of "collaborative vigilance" (Cantone & Carloni, 2018).

The preventive-collaborative dimension of this form of vigilance is evident in the framework described above and is the qualifying element of the entire control system: this system is aimed at a preventive qualitative control of the legitimacy of the tender procedures carried out by the various administrations involved, starting from the stage of the call for tenders or the letter of invitation Secondly, it is carried out through collaboration with the Authority implemented through the various protocols of agreement with the contracting administrations involved.

The success of the model depends on an ability to actualize a sort of integrated and concomitant control on the progress of the various administrative steps, so as to intervene effectively as soon as a criticality emerges and, concurrently, initiate both a corrective and formative path, without delaying scheduling and without crushing the actions of the public entity.

The ratio of the model therefore, to the base of the system of control, appears obvious: it intends to put into effect a "form of preventive vigilance (. . .), with a view to reduce dispute or litigation, preordained to promote dialogue (...) with the purpose of stimulating (...) spontaneous adaptation".

Up to 31 December 2019 the Anti-Corruption Authority, through the Special Operational Unit, which is the office that deals directly with such controls, had analyzed and processed 256 tender procedures and had provided approximately 531 opinions in total relating to the post-earthquake reconstruction processes. Respectively, out of the total number of administrative procedures in which ANAC has been directly involved in collaborative supervision activities since 2014, they account for approximately 36% of the administrative tender procedures verified and 35% of opinions rendered demonstrating how, in practice, the public reconstruction sector has been the subject of particular attention in recent years by the Authority, with a decisive economic impact, as the supervision concerned tender procedures with a total value of almost 72 million euros (2016–19).

The territory of the "seismic crater", object of the reconstruction processes, is then confronted with some elements that characterize it and that affect both the lawmaking and the activity of the support structures, making complex the operative management of the whole control process.

The first aspect concerns the need to protect to the same degree, and in the same timeframe, individual interests/needs and collective interests/needs that are not always aligned and that, for this reason, require a commitment to the identification of solutions that can satisfy both.

The second aspect concerns the need to pursue, at the same time, objectives that are potentially opposing and heterogeneous and that, for this reason, require specific operational and control strategies at their disposal, strategies often subject to changes over time: for example it is on one hand, necessary to actualize reconstruction operations as swiftly as possible but, on the other hand, in order to safeguard the future safety of the population, adopt decisive further investigation on safety before moving forward with improved and appropriately anti-seismic building reconstruction; furthermore, if proceeding rapidly is evident required, it is necessary to guarantee that activities are carried out in a context of legality and transparency that does not allow criminal infiltration or other forms of corruption.

A third aspect to consider is that the good functioning of such a model is linked to the ability to contain "non-virtuous" (but not necessarily criminally relevant) behaviors, "accompanying" the growth of the administrations, with a supervisory action intended as guidance and support to operators in the sector, oriented towards the physiological rather than pathological aspects of the system. In this respect, a "model" of prevention of corruption has emerged from the elaboration without immediate or predefined answers, of possible solutions, expedients, and innovations, from a collaboration between the Anti-Corruption Authority and the administrations. Moreover, the experience of the management of the model of controls in the stages of reconstruction shows how necessary it is in the processes of transformation of public action, that the norms are vectors of changes, also cultural, and that only figures and fully legitimized at institutional level can carry out this transformation.

From the recognition of the role and functions of the Italian Anti-Corruption Authority, in a well-defined operational sphere, as well as the modalities of its operation and the spill-over effects of its activities, it is possible to appreciate the original vision opened up by the corruption prevention strategy, at a multi-level and multi-purpose perspective.

The analysis in certain respects briefly conducted on the role that ANAC plays in this model helps to understand how it has become, in daily practice, the point of reference for knowledge in matters that contribute to outlining a strategy to combat the phenomenon of corruption and to improve the decision-making processes and actions of public administration, above all in the public procurement sector. n a relatively short period of time, ANAC has been able to construct parameters for verifying the recurrence of behaviors that may be indicators/signs/indicators of maladministration, of behaviors that are prodromes of corruption. This is mainly due to the fact that ANAC has been built, and according to the context in which it has operated, to be at the center of a network of collection, processing, management and exchange of information, data and documents, all instrumental to the exercise of its powers of prevention of illegality and corruption, but also serving the action of criminal repression and judicial investigation of administrative illegality. And it is precisely the collaborative approach it uses that proves capable of enhancing its cognitive activity.

References

Abrate, G., Erbetta, F., Fraquelli, G., & Vannoni, D. (2015). The cost of corruption in the Italian solid waste industry. *Industrial and Corporate Change, 24*(2), 439–465.

Ahmed, W. M. (2020). Corruption and equity market performance: International comparative evidence. *Pacific-Basin Finance Journal, 60*, 101282.

Amarandei, C. M. (2013). Corruption and foreign direct investment. Evidence from Central and Eastern European States. *CES Working Papers, 5*(3), 311–322.

Amemba, C. S., Nyaboke, P. G., Osoro, A., & Mburu, N. (2013). Challenges affecting public procurement performance process in Kenya. *International Journal of Research in Management, 3*(4), 41–55.

ANAC – Autorità nazionale anticorruzione. (2019). Linee Guida n. 15 recanti «Individuazione e gestione dei conflitti di interesse nelle procedure di affidamento di contratti pubblici». : ANAC.

Bajari, P., & Tadelis, S. (2001). Incentives vs. transaction costs: A theory of procurement contracts. *RAND Journal of Economics, 32*(3), 387–407.

Bandiera, O., Prat, A., & Valletti, T. (2009). Active and passive waste in government spending: Evidence from a policy experiment. *American Economic Review, 99*(4), 1278–1308.

Benitez, D., Estache, A., & Søreide, T. (2010). *Dealing with politics for money and power in infrastructure.* Washington, DC.

Bigerna, S., Bollino, C. A., Micheli, S., & Polinori, P. (2017). A new unified approach to evaluate economic acceptance towards main green technologies using the meta-analysis. *Journal of Cleaner Production, 167*, 1251–1262.

Calossi, E., Sberna, S., & Vannucci, A. (2012). Disasters and corruption, corruption as disaster. In A. de Guttry et al. (Eds.), *International disaster response law.* Asser Press – Springer.

Cantone, R. (2020). *Il sistema della prevenzione della corruzione.* Giappichelli.

Cantone, R., & Carloni, E. (2018). *Corruzione e anticorruzione. Dieci lezioni.* Feltrinelli.

Castro, M. F., Guccio, C., & Rizzo, I. (2014). An assessment of the waste effects of corruption on infrastructure provision. *International Tax and Public Finance, 21*(4), 813–843.

Cerrillo, M. A. (2018). *El principio de integridad en la contratación pública. Mecanismos para la prevención de los conflictos de intereses y la lucha contra la corrupción.* Aranzadi-Thomson-Reuters.

Chekol, G. A., & Tehulu, T. A. (2014). Public procurement reform in Ethiopia: Factors leading to effective public procurement implementation. The Case of Amhara Region. *European Journal of Business and Management, 6*(23), 153–158.

Corradino, M. (2020). *L'Italia immobile.* Chiarelettere.

Dal Bó, E. (2006). Regulatory capture: A review. *Oxford Review of Economic Policy, 22*(2), 203–225.

Dal Bó, E., & Rossi, M. A. (2007). Corruption and inefficiency: Theory and evidence from electric utilities. *Journal of Public Economics, 91*(5–6), 939–962.

De Vaal, A., & Ebben, W. (2011). Institutions and the relation between corruption and economic growth. *Review of Development Economics, 15*(1), 108–123.

Decarolis, F. (2014). Awarding price, contract performance, and bids screening: Evidence from procurement auctions. *American Economic Journal: Applied Economics, 6*(1), 108–132.

Delsignore, M., & Ramajoli, M. (2019). La prevenzione della corruzione e l'illusione di un'amministrazione senza macchia. *Rivista trimestrale di diritto pubblico, 1*, 61–75.

Di Donato, L. (2020). Gli appalti pubblici tra istanze di semplificazione e normativa anticorruzione. Alla ricerca di un equilibrio tra legalità ed efficienza. *Quaderni di Ricerca Giuridica*, 89/2020. Roma: Banca d'Italia.

Estache, A., & Trujillo, L. (2009). Corruption and infrastructure services: An overview. *Utilities Policy, 17*(2), 153–155.

European Commission. (2014). *Report from the commission to the council and the European Parliament: EU anti-corruption report, document COM(2014)38.* European Commission.

Eyaa, S., & Oluka, P. N. (2011). Explaining non-compliance in public procurement in Uganda. *International Journal of Business and Social Science,* 2(art. 11).

Falaschetti, D. (2008). Can lobbying prevent anticompetitive outcomes? Evidence on consumer monopsony in telecommunications. *Journal of Competition Law and Economics, 4*(4), 1065–1096.

Gennaioli, C., & Tavoni, M. (2011). Clean or "dirty" energy: Evidence on a renewable energy resource curse. *SSRN Working Papers.*

Golden, M. A., & Picci, L. (2005). Proposal for a new measure of corruption, illustrated with Italian data. *Economics and Politics, 17*(1), 37–75.

Gründler, K., & Potrafke, N. (2019). Corruption and economic growth: New empirical evidence. *European Journal of Political Economy, 60*, 101810.

Guccio, C., Pignataro, G., & Rizzo, I. (2012). Determinants of adaptation costs in procurement: An empirical estimation on Italian public works contracts. *Applied Economics, 44*(15), 1891–1909.

Halkos, G. E., & Tzeremes, N. G. (2010). Corruption and economic efficiency: Panel data evidence. *Global Economic Review, 39*(4), 441–454.

Hunt, J. (2005). Why are some public officials more corrupt than others? *National Bureau of Economic Research* (No. w11595).

Hunt, J., & Laszlo, S. (2005). Bribery: Who Pays, who Refuses, what are the Payoffs? *National Bureau of Economic Research* (No. w11635).

Imperiale A. J., & Vanclay F. (2019). Command-and-control, emergency powers, and the failure to observe United Nations disaster management principles following the 2009 L'Aquila earthquake. *International Journal of Disaster Risk Reduction*, 36/2019.

Kurer, O. (1993). Clientelism, corruption, and the allocation of resources. *Public Choice, 77*(2), 259–273.

Lambsdorff, J. G. (2003). How corruption affects productivity. *Kyklos, 56*(4), 457–474.

Leff, N. H. (1964). Economic development through bureaucratic corruption. *American Behavioral Scientist, 8*(3), 8–14.

Leys, C. (1965). What is the problem about corruption? *The Journal of Modern African Studies, 3* (2), 215–230.

Lichère, F., Caranta, R., & Treumer, S. (Eds.). (2014). *Modernising public procurement: The new directive*. Diof Publishing.

Lui, F. T. (1985). An equilibrium queuing model of bribery. *Journal of Political Economy, 93*(4), 760–781.

Macchia, M. (2017). La qualificazione delle stazioni appaltanti. *Giornale di diritto amministrativo, 1*, 50–59.

Martinez Fernandez, J. M. (2017). Corrupcion en la contratacion publica. In A. Betancor (Ed.), *Corrupcion, corrosion del estato de derecho*. Cizur Menor.

Martone, V. (2016). Mafia Capitale: Corruzione e Regolazione Mafiosa nel «Mondo di Mezzo». *Meridian, 87*, 21–39.

Mashal, A. M. (2011). Corruption and resource allocation distortion for "ESCWA" countries. *International Journal of Economics and Management Sciences, 1*(4), 71–83.

Mattarella, B. G. (2015). Disciplina dei contratti pubblici e prevenzione della corruzione. *Atti del 61° Convegno di studi amministrativi, Varenna, 2015*. Milano: Giuffré, 337–353.

Mauro, P. (1995). Corruption and growth. *The Quarterly Journal of Economics, 110*(3), 681–712.

Méon, P. G., & Sekkat, K. (2005). Does corruption grease or sand the wheels of growth? *Public Choice, 122*(1–2), 69–97.

Merloni, F. (2019). *Corruption and public administration. The Italian case in a comparative perspective*. Routledge.

Merloni, F., & Vandelli, L. (Eds.). (2010). *La corruzione amministrativa*. Passigli.

Mo, P. H. (2001). Corruption and economic growth. *Journal of Comparative Economics, 29*(1), 66–79.

Myrdal, G. (1968). *Asian Drama: An inquiry into the poverty of nations* (Vol. II). Pantheon.

Ng, D. (2006). The impact of corruption on financial markets. *Managerial Finance, 32*(10), 822–836.

OECD. (2012). *Recommendation on fighting bid rigging in public procurement*. OECD.

OECD. (2015). *Public procurement recommendation*. OECD.

OECD. (2016). *Preventing corruption in public procurement*. OECD Publishing.

Olken, B. A. (2007). Monitoring corruption: Evidence from a field experiment in Indonesia. *Journal of Political Economy, 115*(2), 200–249.

Racca, G. M. (2019). Public procurement: Legal standards in the EU. In E. Carloni (Ed.), *Preventing corruption through administrative measures* (pp. 95–104). Perugia.

Racca, G. M., Cavallo, P. R., & Albano, G. L. (2016). Public contracts and international public policy against corruption. In M. Audit & S. W. Schill (Eds.), *Transnational law of public contracts* (pp. 845–860). Bruylant.

Racca, G. M., & Yukins, C. R. (2014). Introduction. Steps for integrity in public contracts. In G. M. Racca & C. R. Yukins (Eds.), *Integrity and efficiency in sustainable public contracts*. Bruylant.

Rinaldi, P. G. (2019). Transparency and anti-bribery measures in the Italian public procurement system. In E. Carloni (Ed.), *Preventing corruption through administrative measures* (pp. 105–117). Morlacchi.

Rose-Ackerman, S. (1997). The political economy of corruption. *Corruption and the Global Economy, 31*(60), 54.

Shooner, S. L. (2002). Desiderata: Objectives for a system of government contract law. *Public Procurement Law Review*, 107–123.

Spuntarelli S. (2017). Normatività ed efficienza del sistema delle ordinanze adottato in occasione della sequenza sismica di Amatrice, Norcia e Visso. *Costituzionalismo.it, 3*, 1–38.

Svensson, J. (2005). Eight questions about corruption. *Journal of Economic Perspectives, 19*(3), 19–42.

Theilen, B. (2008). Lobbying and contract delegation in public procurement. *The BE Journal of Economic Analysis & Policy*, 8(1), (art. 38).

Torricelli, S. (2018). Disciplina degli appalti pubblici e strumenti di lotta alla "corruzione". *Diritto pubblico, 3*, 953–977.

UNODC – United Nations Office on Drugs and Crime. (2013). *Guidebook on anti-corruption in Public procurement and the management of public finances*. United Nations.

Vannucci, A. (2011). Il lato oscuro della discrezionalità. Appalti, rendite e corruzione. In G. D. Comporti (Ed.), *Le gare pubbliche: il futuro di un modello* (pp. 291–305). Editoriale Scientifica.

Wei, S. J. (2000). How taxing is corruption on international investors? *Review of Economics and Statistics, 82*(1), 1–11.

World Bank. (2020). *How large is public procurement?* World Bank Blogs (Bosio, E. & Djankov, S.) https://blogs.worldbank.org/developmenttalk/how-large-public-procurement

Yan, J., & Oum, T. H. (2014). The effect of government corruption on the efficiency of US commercial Airports. *Journal of Urban Economics, 80*, 119–132.

Zhang, A. (2012). An examination of the effects of corruption on financial market volatility. *Journal of Emerging Market Finance, 11*(3), 301–322.